Chinese Character Stories
for Adult Beginners

Origin and Evolution of the Characters Used in

Yong Ho's

Beginner's Chinese
and
Intermediate Chinese

Clopper Almon

This book is NOT a study guide for NOR a summary of NOR an analysis of the book by Yong Ho.

Acknowledgement

My choice of Chinese characters to be explained is based on Yong Ho's text, *Beginner's Chinese, 2nd Edition.* (Hippocrene Books, Inc, New York, 2010) and his *Intermediate Chinese, 2nd Edition.* (Hippocrene Books, Inc, New York, 2013) Dialogues from these books have been used with knowledge and consent of their author, who, however is not responsible for any opinions or errors in the present text.

Unless otherwise specified, illustrations of early versions of characters are from the website www.chineseetymology.org, created by Richard Horace Sears. Without this website, creation of this book would have been impossible for its author. Revisions to this edition have made much use of the ever-improving websites of Wiktionary and especially the French Wiktionnaire.

Revised January 2021

Contents

Beginner's Chinese

Intermediate Chinese

The process of learning a language is more important than the results.

– Yong Ho (何勇)

Introduction

Yong Ho's maxim quoted above is especially important for English speakers learning Chinese. Fifty or sixty hours spent working through the ten lessons of Yong Ho's *Beginner's Chinese* will not make you proficient in Chinese. That would require over a year of diligent, full-time work. But those few hours will suffice to become acquainted with the Chinese folk soul in a way you can never do without studying the language, for the soul of a people lives in its language. In the case of Chinese, a unique and very special part of the language is formed by the characters with which it is written. Though it can be written perfectly well in the Latin alphabet using the pinyin system, that is seldom done, for the characters – the product of over three millennia of evolution by the people of China – are somehow quintessentially Chinese. The Chinese love their characters, delight in reading them, and make an art of writing them. The foreigner, the "out country man" as the Chinese say, who is learning Chinese to understand China must give particular attention to learning the basics of the characters *and how they evolved*. That is what this book is about. Though you may never learn enough characters to read Chinese fluently, it is the process of learning that is most important.

An adult who wants to study Chinese can now find a wide choice of texts and materials but none better than Yong Ho's book *Beginner's Chinese*, second edition and its sequel, *Intermediate Chinese*, second e+ +dition. I have studied or at least looked at a number of introductory texts, but these two always inspire a sense of gratitude to its author for the clarity with which he explains grammar, usage and Chinese culture. Yet, despite all their virtues, neither these two books nor any other introductory text of my acquaintance help you to really understand the characters with all their delights and problems. That is where this book comes in.

The delights are many; the problems only two, but they are huge, namely (1) how to remember characters you have learned (2) how to find a Chinese character in a glossary or dictionary . These are, indeed, the MAIN problems for adult foreigners in learning to read Chinese.

The traditional solution to the first problem, remembering characters, is drill, drill, drill: write every character fifty times and be shamed – and maybe get your knuckles rapped – if you ever forget it or write it wrong. Learning about 500 characters a year in this way is a major part of children's education for eight years. Then they then know at least the form and pronunciation of most characters they encounter. Those who have learned the characters in this traditional way may have difficulty believing that there may be other ways, both more efficient and more interesting.

If you have the retentive brain of a six-year-old and eight years to devote mainly to learning Chinese characters, the traditional method will work for you. If you don't, this book may help. *For originally every character somehow made sense to someone.* Wouldn't it be helpful – and indeed exciting – to be able to +see in the modern characters the ideas and images that lived long ago in the minds of their creators? In fact, that is possible for many – even most – of them, but the ancient forms have so evolved that their origins are usually by no means obvious. Often scribes did not grasp the idea back of the character they were imitating and produced versions which lost that idea. Sometimes these versions caught on, so the story of many a modern character is not a linear, rational development, but a winding tale fraught with misperception. Nevertheless, I have found the study of their evolution not only fascinating but also often helpful for remembering them. Sometimes, however, so much has been lost that one feels sad, as if in the presence of a once beautiful structure that has been demolished. And occasionally the etymology is so complex that it won't help you remember the character. But mostly you'll be glad to be better acquainted with these stories.

Of course, you should also write each character several times and make yourself some flash cards to drill recognition. But today recognition and knowing the pinyin pronunciation is far more important than writing the character precisely correctly – even for writing. For writing is nearly all done on a computer; you type pinyin, and the computer shows you various possible ways to write with characters your pinyin text. You need to *recognize* the correct way and select it. The computer will take care of the fine points of writing the characters. I have heard young Chinese adults – who are all fluent in pinyin – lamenting that they are forgetting the writing skills they once laboriously learned.

Not surprisingly, the most complete sources on the evolution of the characters are in Chinese and not accessible to the beginner, while the several pleasant accounts in English are highly incomplete. They present mostly characters that have easy and colorful stories, not the the ones the beginning student is encountering. Digging out and understanding an etymology can be time-consuming, and beginning students are often short on time. Therefore, the first aim of this *Study Companion* is to present quickly understandable etymologies of most of the basic characters in each lesson of *Beginner's Chinese*. Each new character should become a friend whose life story you know, not an opponent whose grim face you must remember. The etymologies offered are, as nearly as I can tell, historically accurate. They are not fanciful pictures drawn around the modern character. That said, I have not hesitated to include some "folk etymologies" that are not historically accurate but help in remembering the characters; but these folk etymologies are marked as such.

I wanted to discuss characters in the order in which they are encountered in an elementary textbook because the beginning adult learner needs help with the characters in the textbook, not some that happen to have easy or vivid etymologies. I looked at a number of textbooks to follow but picked the one by Yong Ho because I found it outstanding for clarity, interest and usefulness. Most modern elementary textbooks include much the same set characters, so if you are in a class using a different text, you can still find here many of the characters in your book. The decision to explain characters in the order in which they occur in a textbook means that we have to discuss some convoluted stories right from the beginning. The first character you meet is almost certain to be 你, the *ni* of *ni hao (hello),* and its etymology is as complicated and uncertain as they get.

The second major problem is finding a character in a dictionary. In *The Quick Guide to Chinese Characters,* Jean Léonard and I offer an effective solution to this problem. I use the *Quick Guide* a lot, and usually find the character I'm looking for in about 20 seconds. So the second purpose of this *Character Study Companion* is to introduce gradually the system for character finding, known as the *radicode system,* used in *The Quick Guide.* As you learn the characters, you will learn the 100 *radicals* used in the radicode system and also get practice in stroke encoding, the other half of the radicode system. By the middle of the book, you should be quite proficient in both and have a valuable tool for pursuing your study and use of Chinese. Knowing the radicode system is also very helpful in *remembering* the meaning of about 89 percent of the characters. For the system uses English names for 100 character components (called radicals) that indicate in a very general way what the character is about – is it a tree, or a bird, or a fish, or a flower? Does it relate to one of the five elements, fire, air, water, earth or metal? Does it relate to speech or to travel or to eating? And so on. In the radicode system, the names of these easily recognized meaningful character components are combined with a number instantly deduced from the strokes of the character to form a code that is then easily looked up in the *Quick Guide*. (If the character does not have one of the 100 meaningful radicals occupying one whole side, it is assigned the catchall category *aa*, unless it is split vertically in which case it is *ab*.) In recent years, it has become possible to look up characters with a cell phone. The time required is about the same as using the *Quick Guide*, but the process does not help you remember the meaning of the character.

You may well be wondering, How big a job is it to learn enough Chinese characters to read with some fluency? Professor Jun Da compiled a collection of documents from the Internet containing millions and millions of characters and then counted the number of occurrences of each character. He found that the 50 most frequent characters account for 31% of the text. That sounds encouraging. At the end of this book, you will know about 800 characters. If they were precisely the most frequent 800, you would recognize about 4 out of 5 characters you encounter in typical text. Not until you reach 3000 characters will you recognize 99 out of 100. Learning 400 characters is about what you can accomplish in a 3 semester-hour course. So to reach the 3000 character level you need about eight semesters of Chinese – a big investment, but not impossible. Even when you know 3000 characters you will still need to look up about 10 characters per page of typical text, so you will definitely need *The Quick Guide* for a long time.

Yong Ho's book gives the text only in the simplified characters used in mainland China and only in close proximity to their pronunciation spelled out phonetically in *pinyin* with Latin letters. The modern traditional forms are used in Hong Kong, Taiwan, Singapore and by overseas Chinese communities around the world. To offer practice in reading characters with no *pinyin* anywhere near, I have, at the end of each chapter, reproduced the conversation in three ways: (1) in simplified characters, (2) in modern traditional characters, and (3) in a font (HYZhuanShuF.ttf) that shows the characters as they looked at the time of the *Shuowen* dictionary made in about the year 100 AD. Reading the conversations in all three versions is a good review of what has been learned in the chapter.[1] The *Shuowen* font is, of course, just for fun, but it often reminds us of what was explained in the chapter. Moreover, while it gives the Shuowen form of the character if the character was in the Shuowen, it also gives a Shuowen-like form for characters created since the Shuowen was written. (The conversion from simplified to traditional was done mechanically and may be wrong where several traditional were merged into one simplified.) Any advantage of the simplified characters over the traditional ones lay largely in the speed of writing by hand. With most writing being done by computer, this advantage is largely disappearing.

I should be clear that my own knowledge of Chinese is very limited and hardly extends much beyond Yong Ho's text. I wrote this book as much for myself as for others. If you have corrections or improvements to offer, please send them to me at calmon@umd.edu.

---

1   When it comes to fonts, the simplified and the traditional versions of a character, if they are different, count as separate, unrelated characters. If you want to use the HYZhuanShuF.ttf font, you need to be aware that it provides Shuowen versions **only** for the simplified version of a character. Thus 马 and 馬 are the simplified and traditional versions of one and the same character as far as meaning is concerned. If you show 吗 in the HYZhuanShuF font you get the desired 𢒉 , but if you show 馬 in that font you get just 馬 .

In this introduction, we will explain how the radicode system works and then give some general background on the evolution of the characters.

The Radicode System in Brief

After studying a number of ways finding characters, I devised a new way I have called the *radicode method,* a hybrid of the traditional radical system and the revolutionary stroke encoding system of Li Jinkai and Li Yimin. It is easily learned as you are learning your first several hundred characters. Then you can look up an unknown or forgotten character in *The Quick Guide to Chinese Characters* about as quickly as you can look up an English word in a dictionary. In *The Quick Guide*, you will find the character in both the simplified and traditional forms, its pinyin pronunciation, an indication of its frequency, its meaning, and words and expressions beginning with the character included in the vocabulary for the intermediate level of the Chinese state examination of proficiency in Chinese, the Hanyu Shuiping Kaoshi or HSK. If you need more information about a character, you can, knowing the pinyin pronunciation, look it up in a dictionary or enter it into a computer and search on-line sources such as www.nciku.net.

First let's learn about stroke encoding. Each lesson in *Beginner's Chinese* has a table near the end showing how to write some of the characters used in the lesson as a sequence of *strokes.* A stroke code is a number with from one to six digits which is easily made up just by looking at the character and assigning digits from 0 to 7 to some of its strokes. Making it up requires that you have some familiarity with writing characters so that you can recognize what is all one stroke and what is several. You will soon acquire that familiarity. But making up the stroke code does **not** require that you know the "correct" *calligraphic* stroke *order* which is illustrated in the tables in *Beginner's Chinese..*

In a simple character – one with only one component – the strokes are taken in *geometric* order regardless of the calligraphic order. What is the geometric order? In comparing two points, A and B, in the square occupied by the character, Point A precedes Point B (or is first) if A is higher than B or if they are at the same height but A is to the left of B. In comparing two strokes, the one whose starting point is first is the first stroke. If they start at the same point, the one whose end point is first is the first stroke. In practice, if one stroke begins well to the left of another and at about the same height, the left stroke is taken first.

The code numbers assigned to each stroke are determined from the following table.

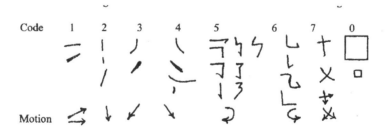

In deciding whether a stroke is a 5 or 6, the curvature at the end of the stroke is determining; a 5 stroke is moving clockwise while a 6 stroke is moving counter-clockwise.

8

Every student of characters learns to wave his index finger in the directions of the first four strokes while reciting " Yi, er, san, si," ("one, two, three, four") so remembering these numbers is very easy. For 5 and 6, note that if the numerals 5 and 6 were coded as if they were Chinese characters, they would be a 5 and 6, respectively. A 7 is a cross of a 1 and 2 or of a 3 and 4 calligraphic strokes; the numeral 7 is often written with a cross on its stem. A 口 , which is a combination of a 2, 5, and 1 calligraphic strokes, looks like a 0. So you have already learned the only part of the stroke coding system you have to memorize!

In some cases, the 5 and 6 strokes are, like the 7 and the 0, a combination of calligraphic strokes. There are rules for deciding when that happens, but they can wait.

Since you will be learning an order of writing strokes, the calligraphic order, it may seem strange not to use this order in coding. The main reason for not doing so is that the calligraphic order gives identical codes to many characters. Also, there is less than perfect agreement on the order of strokes in some characters. Finally, as a beginner, you may not guess the calligraphic order correctly, but you can *see* the geometric order.

Here are three characters with the individual stroke codes marked and the order given beneath each.

Here are more simple characters for practice. Never mind that you do not yet know the meaning of the characters. Here we code all the strokes, but that is only rarely necessary for identification.

丁 15   三 111   出 26262   大 314   卫 521   为 4354
木 734   末 7134   足 0231   止 2211   上 211   目 011
天 1314 田 07   月 3511   王 171   女 613   革 67201
老 73163 不 1324   心 4644 兴 443134 更 13014 面 130221
五 1251 甬 542571 生 3711   文 417

The original book on stroke codes, *The Stroke Encoding of Dictionary Consultation* by Li Jinkai and Li Yimin (Beijing, Foreign Language Press, 1985) used only stroke codes in classifying characters. However, many characters – about 89 percent of those in common use – have one of about 100 standard components called *radicals* in English. There is often some connection between the object pictured in the radical and the meaning of the character. (Formerly, there was more connection, as we shall see, because the meaning of the character has changed but not its radical.) These radicals become truly the student's best friend in learning characters, and we shall give them English names. If a character has one of these radical friends occupying one whole side – the whole left side or the whole right side or the whole top or the whole bottom – we will let that radical claim the character. And if there are two competing claims, the left is stronger than the right and the top stronger than the bottom, so we immediately know which is the *dominant* radical. If there is no radical occupying a whole side, but there is on in the upper left corner, it claims the character. About 89 percent of the 7000 common characters in the *Quick Guide* have a dominant radical. Their radicode is made up of the name of the dominant radical plus the first few digits of the stroke code of what remains after removal of the radical. Often it is enough to encode one or two strokes and seldom necessary to go past three to get very close to the character in the *Quick Guide*. We will learn the names of the radicals gradually as we encounter them; you can find complete tables in the introduction to *The Quick Guide* and on its back cover.

But what about the other 11 percent of characters? If one of them is clearly divided into a left part and a right part, we give it the artificial radical of *ab*. If it is not so divided, it gets the artificial radical of *aa*. About 2/3 of the 11 percent are *aa*. For the aa and ab characters, we stroke code the entire character because there is no radical to remove. In these characters, we often need to apply the *component rule*: if three strokes have been encoded from one component of the character and other components remain, we shift to the next component. For example, in the character 節 bamboo 5615 the first three strokes coded are from component in the lower left corner, but then – although two strokes remain in that component – the next stroke is from the next component, the one in the lower right corner. Usually it is clear what "component" and "next" mean, but to be sure we are consistent, these terms are carefully defined in the introduction to *The Quick Guide*.

As we work through the characters in the first several lessons, you will quickly get the hang of radicodes and find them and the *Quick Guide* a big help in finding the sound and meaning of new or forgotten characters.

Types of Characters

We will soon meet five of the traditional six[2] types of characters, namely:

1. Pictograms

These were originally an easily recognizable picture of something. In some cases, the subject of the picture is still fairly recognizable – like 馬, a horse with flying mane, four feet and a tail. In others, – like 虎, tiger – it is hard to see the image even after you know what you are looking for.

2. Ideograms

In these, a combination of pictures suggests an idea. 好 shows a woman on the left and a child on the right and means "good". The idea is that it is *good* for a woman to have a child and certainly *good* for a child to have a mother, and a wife and child are *good* things for a man to have. 鮮 shows a fish on the left and a sheep on the right and means "delicious." 看 shows a hand above an eye and means "look".

3. Phonetic loan (= rebus) characters (PLC)

It is hard to draw a picture of "can" as in "I can do that." In English, we could use a picture of a tin can to represent the verb "can." Once upon a time, the Chinese word for "bear" was similar in sound to the word for "can," so the Chinese used a picture of a bear to represent the verb meaning "can." Today, the

---

2   The sixth type, "mutual explanatories" is now usually regarded as useless; characters once regarded as being of this type are now classed under one of the other five.

picture of the bear has become so formalized that you might not recognize it in 能 néng. The feet have slid around to the right side, the head is in the upper left corner, and the giant mouth with teeth appears in the lower left. The modern word for bear, 熊 xióng, has a totally different pronunciation but the picture of the bear has been returned to its original meaning by adding the fireB radical below it, presumably indicating a preference for encountering a bear roasted.

4. Indicatives

In these, a stroke emphasizes or indicates a part of the character to convey the meaning. For example, 木 is a picture of a tree. 本 adds a stroke in the root area and means *root, stem, origin*. 上 means *above*, while 下 means *below*.

5. Semantic+phonetic or radical + phonetic

The number of words and ideas that can be expressed by these methods is obviously fairly limited, so it long ago became necessary to add another type composed of two parts. One part (the phonetic) indicates – often only very approximately – the sound while the other part (the semantic or radical) indicates very, very broadly what the character has to do with. For example, the horse character, 馬, is pronounced *ma*. The word for "mother" is also pronounced *ma* and is written by combining the horse character with the woman radical, thus 媽. This method has proven very flexible and accounts for some 85 percent of the characters in common use. It must be emphasized that the phonetic is often very approximate. Moreover, pronunciation has evolved, and words which were once close together – but not identical – in sound and were written with the same phonetic may now be pronounced quite differently but keep the same phonetic. Thus, the phonetics are often helpful but also often unreliable indicators of pronunciation. The semantic part is usually but not absolutely always one of about a hundred signs – called *radicals*, to which it is useful to give English names such as *man, woman, child, horse, bird, fish, tree, grass*. We will start meeting these radicals in lesson 1.

Character Etymologies

The oldest examples we have of Chinese characters are remnants of an ancient form of fortune telling called scapulimancy. The king posed a yes-no question to his fortune tellers; they inscribed the question on a bovine scapula or the breast plate of a giant sea turtle, then thinned a small spot on the shell or bone, and applied heat to that spot until a crack appeared. From the shape of the crack, the fortune tellers read the answer to the king's question. In the late 19th century, some of these ancient bones began to be found near the surface of the ground and were sold to apothecaries as "dragon bones" to be ground up for medicine. That the scratches on them were ancient writing was first recognized in 1899. By 1928, the source of these bones had been discovered and official excavations were begun. They lasted until 1937 and collected some 20,000 bone pieces, many of them whole shells or bones covered with questions. These are now in Taiwan and constitute some 20 percent of the total which have been discovered.

These oracle bones, as they are often called, date from about 1250 to 1050 BC. At this stage, it was often fairly clear what the drawing depicted. Later, the character became so stylized that it was virtually impossible to say what it showed. But when the oracle bone characters became known, it was possible to see the connection of the later characters back to them and thus to see what the later character represented. Consequently, the oracle bones have totally revolutionized Chinese character etymology.

 It must be emphasized, however, that there is no reason to think that writing was developed for the purpose of fortune telling. Other writing, however, was on bamboo or other perishable materials and disappeared long ago.

In Chinese, the oracle bone writing is referred to as 甲骨文 *jiǎgǔwén, shell-bone* writing, and we will use that designation for them..

From the millennium before 221 BC, a number of inscriptions on bronze vessels have survived, which we will call *bronze* characters. In 221 BC, Qin Shi Huang overcame his rivals and became the self-styled "First Emperor" of China. (Our word "China" derives from his family name.) His minister Li Si undertook a standardization of characters which produced what is called the seal script because it was used in seals and chops for signing documents. It often has flowing curved lines; but despite the effort at standardization, there are many variations on most characters.

The most exciting recent discovery is of about 20,000 legible bamboo slips in a riverbank in western Hunan Province. They appear to date from the Warring States Period (475 - 221 BC) to the Qin and Han (206 BC-220 AD) dynasties. Work began on the careful excavation in 2002. Study will extend over many years, but some examples are already appearing on Wiktionary websites. A nice example appears in the section on 风, page 174.

In 100 AD, a scholar by the name of Xu Shen completed the first collection of Chinese characters to analyze their structure and group them under radicals. This work, with 9,353 characters (by Xu's count) is known as the 说文解字 *Shuōwén Jiězì* or simply the *Shuowen*. The title can be freely translated as *Analysis of the Characters Used in Writing Speech*. The work is based on the seal characters; the shelll-bone and bronze characters were unknown to Xu Shen. The *Shuowen* strongly influenced the future development of the characters, and we will be able to see its version of nearly every character. That version will nearly always appear in the top right corner of the story of the character.

At the time of the *Shuowen,* the usual writing tool was a sort of "fountain pen" with an ink container above a narrow bamboo tube that may have had a sort of wick in it. It wrote easily in all directions, and the lines of the Shuowen characters swirl around gracefully in all directions.

 In the years 200 – 500 AD, the "regular script" emerged which is very like the modern traditional script. It is this script which first introduces the limited number of different strokes which make stroke encoding – and stroke counting – possible. This change seems to have been due to the invention of a type of wooden pencil with a fibrous tip which was easier to use than the bulky pen but better for drawing straight lines than for making fancily curved figures. We need not show examples of this script, for it is nearly the same as the modern traditional character. During the Ming Dynasty, Liu ShuTong (六書通) (born 1580) made a collection of all the seal-type characters he could find; we shall refer to them as LST characters. Though the collection was made in the 17th Century A.D., bear in mind that the characters relate roughly to the period 200 B.C. to 200 A.D.

In the 1950's, the communist government of mainland China introduced some extensive simplifications designed to make writing faster and printed materials clearer. At the same time, the pinyin system of phonetic transcription with Latin letters was introduced. Pinyin has been a huge success, and is now used virtually everywhere. The simplified characters, however, have not caught on with the overseas Chinese nor in Taiwan nor Hong Kong. Had the simplifiers known how soon young Chinese would be writing by typing pinyin into their word processors and cell phones, I doubt that the simplifications would have be so drastic, for mostly they make the characters easier to write, not clearer to read. Personally, I like some of the simplifications but find others, such as the substitution of the broken-down cart 车 for the cart in good functioning order 車, unfortunate to say the least. (In 車, a two-wheeled cart is viewed from above. The vertical line is the axle; the two wheels are the horizontal lines at the top and bottom; the middle rectangle is the body of the cart.) I would like to use a mixture, but that is considered very bad form. Only simplified characters are used in Yong Ho's books. In this book, where the modern traditional character differs from the simplified version, the traditional is given in parentheses in the heading for the discussion of each character. And, as mentioned above, the conversations are printed in both fonts.

Huge collections have been made with over 50,000 different characters, but most of them would now be recognized by few people. Today, a college graduate probably recognizes 5,000 - 6,000 characters. Analysis of Internet documents containing millions of characters turned up about 12,000 different ones. The *Quick Guide* has the most frequent 7,000 from this study. Based on the frequencies found, 10,000 characters of typical text can be expected to have one character not found in the *Quick Guide*.

The era of character creation is now over. New words and ideas are expressed by combinations of existing characters. Many of these combinations were created in Japan and borrowed by China. An exception to the no-new-character rule seems to have been made for chemical elements, each of which has its own character.

Not only the writing but also the pronunciation of Chinese has changed over the years. Indeed, because the writing system did little to stabilize the pronunciation, it seems to have changed more radically than Latin did as it evolved into Italian. On the basis of rhymes, Chinese words borrowed by neighboring cultures, various modern dialects and other sources, it has been possible to reconstruct the pronunciation of the literate classes of about the year 1000 AD. This language is referred to as Late Middle Chinese, and Mandarin and all modern dialects (except Min) derive from it. Old Chinese is the language of about 600 BC. The *Shijing*, or Classic of Poetry, is a collection of poems from about that date. From its rhymes and the phonetic elements in the characters, a reconstruction of the pronunciation of that era has been attempted, with less certain results than the reconstruction of Late Middle Chinese.

A major feature of the evolution from Late Middle Chinese to Mandarin has been the elimination of final consonants. The final m became n, and final t, k, and p were simply dropped so that in Mandarin syllables are either open (ending in a vowel) or end in -n or -ng. Thus the number of audibly distinct syllables dropped sharply. In the spoken language, it became necessary frequently to use two syllables where one would serve in the written language. For example, to say "help" in writing, one could write 帮 bāng, which means "help" or 助 zhù, which also means "help". But the sound bāng had so many meanings – and zhù had so many meanings – that, in order to be clear, one said bāngzhù – help-help. Up until the early 20th century, it was considered bad form to let this bisyllablism creep into one's writing. After the end of the Qing Dynasty, however, it became quite acceptable to reproduce this aspect of the spoken language in writing.

Books on Chinese Etymology

The great classic, path-breaking work is Bernard Karlgren's *Grammata Serica Recensa*. Its final version appeared in 1957; the full, photo-copied text is now available on the Internet. It shows the early forms of many, many characters but in Karlgren's drawing of them, not photographs of the original – a technology not available to Karlgren at the time of writing. It is, however, difficult to find anything in it. In *Dictionary of Old and Middle Chinese*, Tor Ulving has indexed it by pinyin pronunciation of the modern character, but without the images of the early forms of the characters. The best illustrations are in *The Origins of Chinese Characters* by Wang Hongyuan (Beijing, Sinolingua, 1993) – cited as Wang. *The Composition of Common Chinese Characters: An Illustrated Account* (Peking University Press, 1999) – cited as CCCC – covers 651 characters with useful accounts in both English and Chinese.

There are several important sources in Chinese only. The 古代汉语字典 (Gudai Hanyu Zidian, Commercial Press, Beijing 2005) – a dictionary of classical Chinese cited as GHZ – with entries for over 10,000 characters, is a comprehensive, up-to-date, and complete source, as is the 2000-page 汉字源流字典 (*Origins and Evolution of Chinese Characters, a Dictionary*) （北京, 语文出版社, 2008 – cited as OECCD). The full text of the latter is available on the Internet. The 423-page 图说细说汉字大全集 covers 1,200 characters.

A word about the large, widely held book *Chinese Characteres* by Leon Wieger is perhaps necessary. The third edition, from which the English is translated, came out in 1916. The shell-bone (or oracle bone) characters – which revolutionized Chinese etymology – were just becoming known, but Wieger made no mention nor use of them. Thus the work is seriously dated and mainly of interest in showing how much thinking on this subject has changed over the last century.

Helpful Internet Sites

You can type in Chinese characters on Google Docs. Go to docs.google.com. Click *File* on the main menu. A menu drops down. Click *Language*. A long list of languages appears. Click on 中文（中国）. At the far right of the main menu you should see the items shown on the right above. Click on that tiny downward-pointing triangle to the right of the keyboard icon. A list drops down. Click on 拼 拼音 (which reads "pin pinyin") Now type in pinyin and you are offered a selection of characters to represent the pinyin you have typed. Pick one and continue.

For setting up Chinese language support and Chinese input on your computer, I recommend consulting *www.pinyinjoe.com*, I use the Ubuntu Linux operating system, and installing Chinese language support included a number of Chinese fonts. The seal character font used here, however, required special installation. It is from: *http://www.ibiblio.org/chinesehistory/contents/08fea/c02.html* and is called HYZhuanShuF.ttf . Installing it in Linux was easy. In a terminal window:

(1) go to /usr/share/fonts/truetype and create a subdirectory.
(2) Copy the .ttf file of the font to be installed into this subdirectory.
(3) Type: fc-cache -fv

A most helpful site on etymology is Richard Sears's *www.chineseetymology.org* which has thousands of images of earlier versions of characters. It is cited as Sears. The explanations, however, are quite terse and sometimes totally different from the Chinese sources cited above. Images of early versions of characters used here are from this source unless otherwise indicated. The French Wiktionnaire is sometimes very helpful in understanding a character's origin and evolution. Wiktionary is also useful but terse.

Typing the special characters used in tonal pinyin is a pain. If you must do it, make a table such as the following and then select, copy and paste as necessary.

ā á ǎ à
ē é ě è
ī í ǐ ì
ō ó ǒ ò
ū ú ǔ ù
ǖ ǘ ǚ ǜ

Better still, mark each syllable with its tone number – 1, 2, 3, or 4 – at the end of the syllable. This method is older, clearer, and much easier to type than the marks above the letters. We will use it exclusively beginning in Lesson 2.

Lesson 1. Greetings

We will take the characters in an order different from that of their appearance, but we have at least a few words about each of the 30 characters in the conversation on pages 31-32, namely:

你好吗我很呢也爸妈他她王先生吗虎张小姐怎么样不错这是认识高兴.

The Form of the First Line for Each Character

On the left of the first line appears the character in the simplified version. If the modern traditional version is different, it comes next in parentheses. Then comes the pronunciation in pinyin, then the radicode, then a small-type version of the character, then the principal meanings. The purpose of the small type version of the character is to make it easy to create both radicode and pinyin indexes that show the character. Just think of it as punctuation before the English meaning.

Tone Indications

In this chapter, but only in this chapter, the tone marks will be written over some letter of the syllable, as required in standard pinyin. This system, while it may have some visual appeal in large fonts, plays havoc with alphabetical indexing, is a pain to type, can be hard to discern in small fonts, and requires memorizing some rather arbitrary rules for getting the mark on the right letter in dipthongs. Indication of tone by the numbers 1, 2, 3, or 4 at the end of the syllable is an older system which avoids these problems. It will therefore be used exclusively beginning in the next chapter. In this chapter, we introduce it by giving the pronunciation both ways in the first line for each character.

好 **hǎo hao3 woman 51** 好 **good**

This character contains two radicals, a **woman** on the left and a **child** on the right. The rule that the left radical is stronger than the right makes **woman** the character's radical while stroke coding of the right side gives 51. The character is one of a fairly small number of ideograms. The idea is that it is *good* for a woman to have a child, and certainly *good* for a child to have a mother, and *good* for a man to have a wife and child.

The *woman* radical, on the left of 好, is a horizontal contraction of the modern character for woman, 女 nǚ. The evolution of this character is shown on the left, beginning from a shell-bone version (top) through a bronze casting version (middle) to the *Shuowen* version. The shell-bone character shows the woman kneeling and serving in the traditional way. Between the *Shuowen* and the modern versions, the woman was rotated 90 degrees counterclockwise, so that her body became the horizontal stroke, while her two arms became the crossed 6 and 3 strokes of the modern character.

16

While the shell-bone and bronze characters shown here are fairly typical, there is great variety and the reader is warmly encouraged to have a look at Sear's website at www.chineseetymology.org. It is easy to use, but since there are presently no instructions on how to do so, let me quickly describe how it works. Input the the character you want to research into your word processor, select it, copy it to the clipboard, and open Sears's site if not already open. On the left, about two inches below his picture, you should see the word "Etymology" in black letters in a white box. To the right of that box is another, smaller white box which may have a character in it. Click in that box and paste in (Ctrl V) your character. Tap "Enter", and images of historical versions of the character should appear on the right while information on current meanings appears on the left.

 The story of the child character 子 begins from a picture of a baby with legs wrapped in swaddling clothes, its arms waving, and a head large in relation to its body, as is characteristic of babies. The heads are mostly rectangular because it is hard to scratch a nice oval into a turtle shell. Other shell-bone versions emphasize the baby's sparse hair.

The 子 character is often taught as having three strokes, so that its stroke code should be 551. In the radicode system, however, we have followed its Chinese originators and considered 了 a single 5 stroke, which is certainly the way it is made in ordinary handwriting.

马 （馬） mǎ ma3 horse horse

The wonderful expression 马马虎虎 mǎma hūhu, meaning "so-so", is literally "horse horse tiger tiger." If that seems a bit strange, remember that Chinese has no plural forms and often leaves out the verb "is" or "are," so you can think of it as almost literally, "Oh, horses are horses and tigers are tigers." It remains colorful but somehow comprehensible.

The shell-bone horse characters are mostly recognizable as horses. I picked the one on the top left because of the characteristic shape of the head. The bronze figures mostly emphasize the flying mane, four legs and a tail. The *Shuowen* character, on the right, preserved these characteristics, as did the modern traditional, though they have been become more abstract. The neck and head, formerly important parts, have been reduced to a vertical line. The modern simplified version has sacrificed vividness for speed in writing by hand – but not in typing on a computer.

妈 （媽） mā ma1 woman 551 mother

This is our first example of a radical-phonetic compound character with a radical having something to do with the meaning and a phonetic element usually having – or having once had – something to do with the sound. Some 89 percent of the characters in common use are of this sort, and this one is a good example. The meaning of the character is "mother," and the woman radical on the left is clearly appropriate. The sound is fairly well approximated by the horse on the right. Here, however, the *ma* has the first tone; while for horse, the *ma* is third tone.

吗 (嗎) ma ma mouth 551 (a question marker, see text. No tone.)

This *ma* is the interrogative particle pronounced without tone. The radical is the square on the left, which depicts a human mouth. There are a number of particles in Chinese which have a grammatical function, just as a question mark or an exclamation point do, but no specific meaning; they are not nouns or verbs or adjectives or adverbs. Most of them are written with the mouth radical as here. The horse phonetic is clearly helpful in remembering the pronunciation of the character. Like 吗, most of them were not written in the early texts, and Sears found no examples, not even in the *Shuowen*.

呢 ne mouth 53163 (No tone)

Like 吗, this character is a particle with the mouth radical. Its function is explained in the text. As a character by itself, the right side, 尼, goes back to the seal characters, as exemplified by the *Shuowen* version on the left. It shows two people close together and probably indicated closeness and warmth. If those two pieces don't yet look like people to you, just wait. The upper one is facing to the left and the lower one to the right. In modern character, 尼, the upper person has turned into a door, 尸, and the lower one has sat down under the door. This character, 尼, with the pronunciation ní, now means a Buddhist nun but in no way depicts the nun or implies any connection between the original meaning of this character and the nun. Instead, it is what is known as a phonetic loan character, or PLC, as explained in the introduction. It has given up its original meaning to function solely as an indicator of sound. Sometimes a radical has been added to return the character to its original meaning; in this case, it was the sun radical in the character 昵 nì, which means close, intimate. Maybe the sun indicates a warm relation.

我 wǒ wo3 lance 351 I, me

If, when you first saw this character, you thought it looked vicious, you were right. The shell-bone drawings show a weapon with three teeth, some sort of battle ax. It was as easy to draw a picture of it as it was hard to draw a picture of the pronoun I. But the weapon and the pronoun had the same or similar pronunciation, so the pronoun was represented by a picture of the weapon. Thus, we have another PLC. There is great variety in the numerous bronze versions, but the one in the middle on the left preserves the original idea; the cross line near the bottom of the handle is a hand guard. In the Shuowen version (bottom left), the weapon is still visible if you know to look for it. And indeed you can still see it in the modern version. In this PLC, however, the weapon went out of use and there was no need for a character with a radical returning the drawing to its original meaning.

The right-hand side of the character is the **lance** radical in the radicode system and appears in such characters as 戬 *annihilate*, 战 *war*, 划 *cut with a knife* and 戕 *kill*, though not all of its characters are so vicious. (Sears thinks he sees a *rake* in the shell-bone versions. I can't see the rake, nor is a rake consistent with the meanings the *lance* characters.)

18

你 **nǐ ni3 man 35534 you, thou**

The element on the left is the ***man* radical**, which dominates more characters than any other radical. As a character, it is written 人 and pronounced *rén*. The shell-bone version shows the head and arm with one stroke at the top. The bend in the man's body became more pronounced in many of the bronze castings, such as the one shown in the middle on the left. The Shuowen version, bottom, bent the man over at the waist to touch the ground. In modern characters, the radical form 亻 has straightened him up at the waist and provided a head and arm by the 3 stroke at the top. The full character 人 is a further evolution of the seal character and actually shows the man touching the ground with his hands, though you may prefer to see him as legs walking along with minimal torso and head, looking rather like Shakespear's forked radish (Henry IV Part 2: Act 3 Scene 2).

The right side of 你 is a simplification of 爾 ěr, but this simplification was made before the sweeping simplifications of the 1950s. Thus, 你 is used in texts in both the traditional and the simplified script. In fact, the character 爾, though in standard computer fonts, is not found at all in many modern dictionaries.

Unfortunately, there is considerable doubt about exactly what 爾 depicts. Wang Hangyuan suggests that it was some sort of device used in the spinning of silk and presents the collection of pictures (see below) which certainly seem to support that idea. I gather, however, that their connection with the pronoun is unclear. To complicate the matter, there are two second-person singular pronouns with quite different pronunciations, 尔 ěr and 你 nǐ, but both containing 尔. (The 尔 ěr form is now very rare.) The 尔 picture turns up in several rare characters pronounced ni or mi, but in no other character pronounced *er*. It is also suggested that in early times *er* was used for *I* and *ni* for *me*. For practical purposes, when you see 你, just remember spinNIng.

From Wang Hangyuan, The Origins of Chinese Characters, *(Sinolingua, 2000) p. 134.*

19

hǔ hu3 tiger 36　　tiger

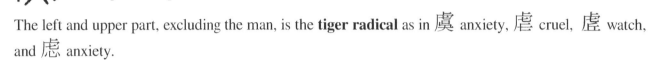 We can now return to the second character of 马马虎虎 mǎma hūhu, the tiger. The shell-bone drawings show a vicious animal with open mouth a big front teeth. The bronze figures emphasize the mouth, and the seal character (bottom lwft)has turned the whole left side into a giant open mouth. Strangely, a man has appeared seemingly under the tiger. Perhaps he is an actor or soldier wearing a tiger mask, or the front half of a dancing tiger team. The Shuowen version, top right, gives equal space to the man below and the tiger mask above. (Sears sees the man as a transformation of the tiger's legs in the bronze character, a not unreasonable idea.) The modern character has turned the tiger around but kept the emphasis on the mouth and the man below.

The left and upper part, excluding the man, is the **tiger radical** as in 虞 anxiety, 虐 cruel, 虗 watch, and 慮 anxiety.

 xiǎo xiao3 aa 534　　small, little

 The shell-bone and bronze characters show three seeds or grains, suggesting by their size the idea of *small*. A number of bronze characters add a baby to make an ideogram, as in the top character on the right. What do grains and baby have in common? Obviously that both are *small*. It was a nice idea, but it did not survive. Like a number of the LST seal characters, the Shuowen version on the bottom right seems to show something being cut in half, making it smaller.

 **jiě jie3 woman 251**　　elder sister

We recognize the woman radical and are not surprised to learn that the character by itself means "elder sister" and that the combination 小姐 means "Miss," though the phrase is used in addressing waitresses or sales clerks of any age. The 且 is presumably a phonetic. In the shell bone and bronze writing, 且 shows a monument to ancestors, or perhaps a tablet on the monument, as shown in the upper left. It remained essentially unchanged in the *Shuowen* character, lower left. In modern Chinese, 且 is a phonetic loan character pronounced qié and used in grammatical constructions such as "and … as well" or "for the time being." But it is also returned to something like its original meaning by adding the *altar radical* in the character 祖 zǔ, grandfather, ancestor. 祖 is probably not a radical+phonetic character, but rather the combination altar+monument used to indicate *ancestor*. Nevertheless, scribes must have interpreted it as implying that 且 on the right indicated that a character was pronounced *zu*, and we now have 组, 阻, 诅, 租, and 姐 all pronounced *zu*.

先 xiān xian1 ox 135　before

First, let's introduce the ox radical. Here are some examples:

牛 cattle, bovine, ox, cow, bull

物 things

犁 plow

告 accuse (= to gore like an ox, but with the mouth)

Our character, 先 xiān, is not etymologically an ox character, but now looks so much like one that it would confusing not to classify it under the ox radical.

In the shell bone script versions (top left), 先 appears as a footprint above a man. The large footprint was left by someone who had gone ahead, gone *before*. The primary meaning is "before" in position or time. Hence it occurs in combinations meaning "teacher", "master" or "mister", "vanguard", "guide". In many bronze version, such as the middle example on the left, the idea is still evident. But by the time of the seal characters, most scribes missed the idea. The footprint turned into the earth radical and the man fell apart, as in the *Shuowen* character, bottom left. In the transition to the modern character, someone must have seen the horns of an ox on top where once there was the footprint. Maybe he was thinking that the character represented someone who "plowed" on ahead.

生　sheng1 aa 3711 生 living being, life, to be born, to give birth.

In this stroke encoding, the "whisker" rule is applied. If two strokes begin at very nearly the same height but one is well to the left and not structurally below, it is coded first. Hence the 3 is before the 7.

The shell-bone character shows a seedling sprouting. Some of the bronze versions, like the middle character on left, add dot or line between the bottom line and the seedling leaves. The *Shuowen*, bottom left, turned the dot into a horizontal line. The modern character has become, well, more abstract. The character means living being, to come to life, to be born, life, grow, and so on. It forms many compounds, such as our 先生, which means something like "advanced being," a very complimentary way of saying "Mister."

是 **shì shi4 sun 1231** to be (in all grammatical forms: am, art, is, are, was, were)

In its present meanings, this is a phonetic loan character. The earliest versions of this character are from the bronze inscriptions of which the figure to the left is typical. The lower part is clearly a foot (see below), 止 zhǐ, and is likely a phonetic element. There is no agreement among etymologists on what the upper part represents. Wang Hongyuan (page 193) believes that it is a "a tool for measuring the sun." What the use of such a tool would be is unclear. On the other hand a tool for running a *straight* line in land surveying, a sort of transit, is very useful. Moreover, the earliest versions of the character meant "straight, not bent." I see in the figure just such an instrument. It is a bamboo tube on a pole; we are looking through the tube (the circle) at a point (the dot) on the line. The surveyor, positioned at the last known point on the line, would line the tube up with the line being run by looking back at the previous point on the line. Then he would walk around to the other side of the instrument and look forward along the line, just as does the modern surveyor. To turn angles with the device, it would need a horizontal plate, and that it is indicated by the horizontal line. In Taiwan, the 是 is to this day a unit of land measurement. (Perhaps I should add that during high school and college, I worked as a surveyor and ran many a line in just this way, though my tube – a transit – had lenses and cross hairs in it.)

The character was then borrowed for its sound to represent the verb "to be" though it still also means *right, correct*. In later versions, the horizontal line slid down to rest on the foot, and the vertical line merged with the vertical line of the foot, leaving only the tube with the dot, which looks just like a sun.

The modern sun character, 日, is derived from a circle with a dot in the center, a natural representation of the sun.

As for the foot, the basic character is 止 zhǐ whose evolution is shown in the shell-bone, bronze, *Shuowen* sequence on the left. In modern Chinese, however, it is a phonetic loan character and means "stop." It appears in red octagonal stop signs all over China. This usage would seem to be some combination of phonetic borrowing and meaning: "Put your foot down and keep it there." In the form in which it appears in 是, 正 zhèng, it retains the meaning of "straight, upright, correct." I think of it as "toeing the line." Like many pictograms whose form has been borrowed to write similar sounding words, 止 has been returned to its original meaning of "foot" by adding a radical, in this case the leg radical, to make the character 趾 zhǐ, which also means "toe".

"Foot" appears as a radical in such characters as

肯 ken3 foot 2511 肯 agree, consent

The **leg radical** shows the knee cap (the square) above the foot, and thus the leg from the knee down.

22

Apparently, many Chinese have forgotten that 止 is a foot and more commonly use for "foot" the unrelated character 脚 jiǎo.

很 hěn hen3 road 56 very

First, we need to introduce the **road radical** 彳 chi. It is the left side of the character 行 xíng meaning "walk, go, act, all right, OK." In the shell-bone script, the ancestor of 行 (top left) shows a crossroad, and that image remained fairly clear in the bronze characters (2nd on left). Some of the LST preserved the idea (top on right), but the *Shuowen* (2nd on right) got very fancy and even blocked the horizontal cross road. The modern version at least removed the roadblock. The road radical is just the left side of 行.

What does a road have to do with "very"? The earliest meaning of the 很 character is "to **go** one's own way, to **go** against against orders, to separate, to err, to disobey." And since disobedience was tantamount to evil, 很 came to mean "evil, wicked." And what does evil have to do with "very"? Well, if you want to say that someone runs very, very fast, you might be tempted to say he runs *damn* fast." Or if a baseball pitcher has a *very* fast fastball, might you not say he has a *wicked* fastball? So, whenever someone says to you, 你好吗? and you politely answer, 我很好 you are really saying "I'm damn well."

The phonetic in 很, 艮 gèn in the *Shuowen* version (on left) shows an eye 目 over a man facing right, 七. According to the GHZ, 七 is equivalent of 比 bi3 showing two men side-by-side and meaning to compete. Thus the original meaning was quite literally eyeball-to-eyeball struggle. The present meanings of 艮 are *tough, leathery* (of meat) and one of the Eight Trigrams of the I Ching. But for our present purposes, the meaning of 艮 does not matter, only the sound. Some other characters with the *gen* sound are

	radical	meaning
跟	leg	follow; heel
根	tree	root, take root
茛	grass	buttercup

and two with the *hen* sound are

	radical	meaning
恨	heart	hate, regret
狠	dog	ruthless, ferocious

These are good examples of how the radical+phonetic system works. The phonetic usually gives some indication – often imprecise – of the pronunciation while one of the 98 meaningful radicals used in the *Quick Guide to Chinese Characters* hint at some sort of connection between the meaning of the character and the object or action used to name the radical. The connection of 很 with a road is about as convoluted as the meaning-to-radical relation gets.

不 **bù bu4 aa 1324   no, not**.

This is a PLC. In the shell-bone drawings it depicts a seedling plant with its roots below the ground and first leaves above ground. The form has remained remarkably stable, while the meaning changed totally. There is perhaps a memory of its original meaning in the character 苤 pie3 meaning kohlrabi and in 芣 fou meaning the herb plantain (*plantago*). The top part of these two characters is the **grass radical**, which appears in many plant names. We will be properly introduced to it in Lesson 6.

认识 **rèn shí to know (a person)** (French *connaître*)

认 （認） **rèn ren4 speech 34** to recognize

This is our first character with the *speech* radical. As a character by itself, 言 yán, it means *speech* and *to speak*, and the simplified character is the same as the traditional. The shell-bone version on the left shows a mouth at the bottom with a tongue, projecting from it and presumably *speaking*. A bronze version, second from left, adds a line at the top, which the CCCC authors interpret as meaning that the tongue is flapping. The *Shuowen* version, right, keeps the flapping tongue. The modern version reduces the tongue to three horizontal lines. Folk etymology sees in the modern character a mouth at the bottom and *words* rising out of it.. The simplified version when used as a radical on the left keeps the top stroke and reduces the rest to a single stroke.

The phonetic of the simplified 认 character, 人 rén, is a definite improvement on the traditional. It gets the sound right except for the tone, is quickly written, and looks nice. Since the simplified version was created in the 1950's without regard to the previous phonetic, there is no need to consult the oracle bones for its origin.

The use of the "speech" radical in 认 is interesting. Perhaps it was used because when we recognize someone, we are likely to say his name.

识 （識）   **shí shi2 speech 034 to recognize, to know**

Here also a complicated traditional phonetic has been replaced by the simplified form of a common character, 只 zhǐ, which has the meaning "only, just, merely." The traditional form of 只 is 衹, so possibly 只 is a simplification of its phonetic, 氏 shi4, which is the name of a clan. Again, the simplification was so radical that shell-bone forms will not help in learning this character.

高兴 **gāoxìng   happy, glad**

高 means "high, tall" and rather clearly depicts a *high*, Chinese-style tower. The "hat" radical is at the top of the character. It is one of two radicals in the radicode system which have nothing to do with the radicals name. It is not a picture of a hat, and characters with this radical have nothing to do with hats, but it looks a bit like a hat and appears only at the top of a character, so "hat" seemed a good name for it.

兴 （興）   **xìng xing4 aa 44313 to rise, prosper, be popular, in fashion; to found, start, promote; to begin; to be excited.**

The shell-bone forms of 兴 (top left) show four hands lifting something. Some of the bronze forms (2ⁿᵈ on left) have added a mouth, suggesting that the workers lifting the object are singing. That suggestion has led to the idea that they are doing some sort of rhythmical work, perhaps lifting a tamping plate, for tamping earth into wall or foundation, and thus perhaps having some connection with the meaning "to found." Also, the plate "rises." The character does not appear in the *Shuowen*, but several of the LST seal characters (such as the 3ʳᵈ on the left) continue this idea. A different LST seal version (top right) shows the upper hands flipped around, the mouth on the plate, and the lower hands merged to look like a sort of table. The modern traditional character stays very close to this plan. The modern simplified version keeps the bottom of the traditional but just indicates that the top had three components. In other words, it is meaningful only if you know the traditional! Not a good simplification.

错 （錯）   **cuò cuo4 metal 721   incorrect, wrong , disorder**

Here we meet the **metal radical** on the left. In the traditional form, it is a horizontally compressed version of 金, which is a picture of an arrowhead or a combination of an arrowhead pointing upward and an ax with its blade pointing down. Both arrowhead and ax were made of bronze. The simplified version 钅 is faster to write but looks contorted and confusingly like the simplified "eat" radical 饣 in 馆.

The character 错 has had, according to the DHZ, a long history with major changes in its meaning. Originally, it seems to have meant *metal* ornaments, then ornamented, gilded knives, then whetstones for knives, then "crossed" or "staggered" (perhaps from decorative X-like patterns on the knives) – a meaning which it still retains – then to correct errors, and finally the errors themselves. If that seems implausible, suppose that an teacher marks errors in his students' work with an X (a cross pattern), and every error so marked must be corrected. Then one student may ask another, "How many X's did you have?" or "How many corrections did you have?" or "How many errors did you have?" and all the questions have the same answer, so X = correction = error. In any event, 错 which originally meant metal ornaments now means "error, incorrect, mistaken, wrong" but also "staggered". The meaning "bad" is pretty much confined to the expression 不错 "Not bad" in answer to the question 你好吗? There it seems to mean "no correction (needed)."

I once wanted to answer the 你好吗? question of a Chinese friend with "Not too bad" which I translated as 不太错, 太 tai4 being the standard word for *too*. I was met with absolute incomprehension. He knew English well and understood "not too bad" perfectly. But he insisted that what I had said made no sense whatsoever in Chinese. I now think that I had said, "Not too correction," which indeed makes no sense.

怎么样 zěnmeyàng how is? how are?

怎 zěn zen3 heartB 312   How?, Why?, What?

The bottom half of the character is the **heartB radical**, suggesting "a question of the heart." This radical is just a compressed version of the character 心 xīn meaning "heart, mind, feeling." The earliest known forms are bronze characters, such as shown in the drawing on the left. Possibly it represents the chambers of the heart, or possibly it shows the entire human torso with the breasts at the top and the navel marked by the dot. There is great variety among the LST seal characters. The *Shuowen* version is shown on the right and to me looks a little more like a cross section of a heart than like a chest. In the transition to the modern 心, the line that reaches down below the others becomes the big 6 stroke in the middle, and the other three lines become the three dots. As a radical in modern characters, a heart may appear on the bottom as in 怎 – where it is called the heartB radical – or on the left as 忄 as in 恨 hèn – where it is called the heart radical. 恨 , by the way, means "hate, regret".

The top of 怎 is phonetic. 乍 zhà means "first, at first, suddenly." It is a phonetic loan character; what it originally depicted is uncertain, but it may have been a garment.

么 (麼) me   aa 364 么 麼

The combination 怎么 zěnme means "how? why?" Like 吗, which it can replace, this particle indicates a question. The simplified character is taken from the bottom of the inside of the traditional character. All the rest of the traditional character is the phonetic component. By itself, the phonetic component expands slightly to 麻 má, and means "hemp, flax, sesame" and shows plants under a shed, 广. Perhaps the hemp plants are being dried and stored. This phonetic appears in such characters as:

麋 mí cooked rice – the rice radical is added a the botom.

摩 mó rub, scrape, touch, stroke; – a hand is at the bottom

26

魔 mó evil spirit – a ghost is at the bottom.

磨 mò mill, millstone; grind; turn around – the stone radical is at the bottom.

The 幺 at the bottom of 麼 is probably a further phonetic and is a slightly simplified version of the top part of 糸 mì, a picture of a skein of silk and now meaning "fine silk". The seal character version of 糸 is 糸 and of 幺 is 幺. The character has not been identified in bronze or shell-bone inscriptions.

样（樣） yàng yang4 tree 4317   to mold, form, pattern; shape.

The radical is the tree on the left, and the phonetic is the sheep, 羊 yang, on the right. The **tree radical** is a compressed version of the character 木 mu, meaning tree, and fairly clearly depicting the vertical trunk, the horizontal branches, and the roots sloping down to either side. This radical is often used for items traditionally made of wood such as molds, forms, and patterns.

 The phonetic , 羊 yáng, is a picture of a sheep. In the shell-bone version (top left), the horns are at the top, below them the eyes; then the mouth, and the neck extends downwards. The elegant bronze version, lower left, preserves the idea. In the modern version, there is a third horizontal line; maybe it represents ears. Once you see it, it looks very like a sheep. The seal character, 羊, already looks almost exactly like the modern character.

The literal meaning of 怎么样? is something like "What shape (are you in)?" In seal characters, it looks like this: 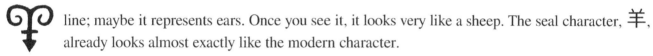 怎么样.

这 （這） zhè zhe4 go 417 this

Etymologists shy away from this character, in part, no doubt, because it is a fairly recent addition to the Chinese lexicon; it appears in neither the *Shuowen* nor LST. But the structure also seems to make little sense, either for meaning or for sound. The radical on the left and along the bottom is known as the **go radical** because it usually indicates motion. It is a combination of 彳, the road radical and 止, the foot radical. Road and foot certainly suggest *go*. The traditional shows clearly the "speech" radical, 言, yan, being used as a "phonetic." The simplified keeps the top two strokes of 言 but reduces the remaining five to two.

Why was the *go* radical chosen for a character which means *this*? The scholars offer no explanation, so I will just suggest the mnemonic "*This* moment is always *fleeting*." In Middle Chinese, 言 was pronounced something like "zen" and served as usable though inexact phonetic for 這. The pronunciation of 言

evolved into "yan" (which rhymes with English "hen") while the pronunciation of 這 evolved into "zhe." Although 這 does not appear among the genuine seal characters, the seal character font used in this book has a nice "modern" seal character for it, namely 这 which shows, on the left, the seal character version of the go radical and on the right, the seal version of 言.

爸 **bà ba4 aa 34756   father, papa**

Bàba corresponds directly to English Papa and is derived from baby talk. The formal word for "father" is 父 fù, which appears in the top part of 爸 as the meaning component. It, in turn, is a PLC from a picture of a hand holding a stone ax or celt and meaning "ax". Its evolution from shell-bone through bronze to the *Shuowen* is shown on the left. The 3 stroke on the top left corner of 父 is the stone; the rest of the character is the hand. This drawing is returned to its original sense by adding the **ax radical** below it in the character 斧 fǔ, meaning ax. The ax radical is a picture of a hatchet.

The phonetic element, 巴 bā, as it is now used, is itself a PLC. The seal character from which it is derived, 巴, may be a drawing of the palm of a hand, though the traditional explanation is that it depicts a boa. The current meaning of 巴 is "to hope earnestly".

它 **tā ta1   roof 63**   Meaning: it

他 **tā ta1   man 265**   Meaning: he, him

她 **tā ta1   woman 265**   Meaning: she, her

也 **yě ye3   aa 265**   Meaning: also

These four characters have a common origin. First, we should note that spoken Chinese has but one word for *he, she,* and *it,* namely *tā.* Of the four characters, 它 is the most primitive; its evolution is shown on the left. It is a PLC depicting a hooded, cobra-like snake. All of the numerous shell-bone examples show the foot above the snake, suggesting that the snake strikes the foot. The bronze character emphasized the hood and the foot completely disappeared. The seal character kept the emphasis on the hood but restored a short tail. The sign is returned to its original meaning by adding the **worm** radical in the character 蛇 shé which means *snake.* The modern 它 character, though superficially very different from the seal character, is almost stroke-for-stroke equivalent. The top stroke and the curving oval below have turned into the **roof radical**; the stroke that starts inside the oval on the left and ends as the snake's body has become the big 6 stroke, and the other lower line has become the 3 stroke.

When used as a phonetic element in 他 and 她, the "roof" slides down to coincide with the 3 stroke of the lower half, and the hook at the right end and the 4 stroke on top of the roof become exaggerated. These two characters are good examples of the use of an "appropriate" phonetic (它, *tā*), which contributes both to sound and meaning.

The 也 yě character seems to have started off quite independently of 它 as a picture of a bowl for washing hands, but the drawings were similar, and it became identical to the phonetic in 他, although there is no similarity of sound.

We have now covered all of the characters in the "Words and Expressions" list except the proper names 王 and 张 which we will cover when we have meaning to go with them. The "Supplementary Words and Expressions", however, have important characters which need to be learned now. Here are some of them:

中国美日本来去喜欢累忙老师学医律

中 **zhōng zhong1 aa 20**

Basic meaning: *middle* or *central.*

This character clearly suggests the idea of middle by the line through the *middle* of the rectangle. Old versions of the character, however, almost always look something like the bronze version shown on the right. This figure has been interpreted as a circle drawn on the ground with a pole in the center with flying banners. The shadow of the pole, shown by the lower half of the line and lower banners, could have been used to tell time. Like most peoples, the Chinese thought of themselves as living in the center of world, so China was – and is – the Middle Kingdom. The character is frequently used with the meaning of "Chinese."

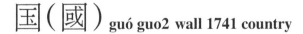

国（國） **guó guo2 wall 1741 country**

In 国 the radical is □, which I have called the **wall radical** because it suggests an enclosed area, though it is not the character or "wall". The inside component of the traditional character is 或 huò, a PLC now meaning "or; perhaps; probably; someone" and is still close enough in sound to broadly suggest the pronunciation of *guó*. These modern meanings of 或 have no obvious connection with the meaning of 國. Originally, however, there was a much better reason for using it as the phonetic. The seal

character and the earlier bronze and shell-bone characters show it as 或, a battle ax protecting a town, represented by the circle, and perhaps land outside the town, represented by the line under the circle. (Or the line may be the remnants of a second ax shown in some examples.) In the battle ax, the shaft is vertical and fits through the head; the blade of the head projects out mainly to the left. Between the shaft and the blade on the right is a hook. The line crossing the lower end of the shaft is the hand guard. A country is thus an area □ filled with towns and land protected by force of arms, 或. Thus, we have a beautiful example of an appropriate phonetic; it wasn't perfect phonetically, but it was close and contributed beautifully to the meaning. After being phonetically borrowed to mean "or; perhaps; probably" 或 was given an earth radical to form 域 yù to return it to its original meaning of "territory, region, land with certain boundaries". In the Internet age, it represents "area" in "local area network" and "domain" in "domain name."

The key to understanding the simplification of 國 to 国 lies in noting that the pronunciation of a number of characters with 或 as a phonetic is yù, not hou or guo as you might expect. The reconstructions by Bernard Karlgren of Old Chinese pronunciation of 或, 國 and several related characters – and their modern pronunciation, meaning and radical – are as follows:

	Old Chinese	modern	radical	present meaning
或	g'wak	huò	lance	or, perhaps
惑	g'wak	huò	heart	be puzzled; delude, mislead
國	kwak	guó	wall	country
域	giwak	yù	earth	territory
緎	giwak	yù	silk	bundle of threads, a seam
蜮	giwak	yù	worm	water demon
罭	giwak	yù	net	fishing net
棫	giwak	yù	tree	oak
淢	giwak	yù	water	a swift current
閾	giwak	yù	gate	a threshold
恧	giwak	yù	heart	heart pain

域 giwak	yù	jade	(occurs only in personal names)
稶 giwak	yù	grain	vast, luxuriant (of crops)

Thus, in Old Chinese, 或 (then pronounced g'wak) was an exact phonetic for 惑, and now as then the two characters are pronounced exactly alike. It was a close but inexact phonetic for 國 (then pronounced *kwak*) and for ten characters then pronounced *giwak* and now pronounced *yù*. What had been only slight differences in the pronunciation evolved into quite marked differences.

All but the first of these last ten are quite rare but are used enough to claim a place in standard computer Chinese fonts. Notice that, to one who knows the spoken language, these characters are not at all arbitrary. The character 棫, for example, says "the *yù* that means some kind of tree." And that, the speaker of Chinese would know, is the tree we call in English "oak." Learning several thousand such characters is by no means an impossible task if you already speak the language.

Though mostly rare, the *yu* characters shown above were certainly known to the 20th century scholars who produced the simplified characters. Thus, when they looked at 國, they saw *yù* inside the wall. Now there is another *yù* that is simpler and much more common, namely 玉 *yù*, jade, derived from a picture of a string of jade beads with the dot added to distinguish it from 王. So the simplifiers replaced one *yù*, 或, with another *yù*, 玉, and came up with 国. In Old Chinese times, 玉 was pronounced *ngiuk*, and was not a possible candidate for the phonetic.

Thus, the simplified form would seem to mean "jade in a box" and to be pronounced *yù*. Both of these deductions are, of course, quite incorrect. In other words, this simplified character makes little sense as an ideogram or phonetically. But history provides some rationale for it.

美国 méi guó America

美 méi mei2 aa 4313 beautiful

The basic meaning of the character is "beautiful", but it catches the "me" sound in *America*. The Chinese names of western countries were given by missionaries who chose nice words that picked up some element of the country's own name for itself. Germany (Deutchland), Deguo, is the virtuous country; France, Faguo, is the lawful country.

The 美 character is a combination of 羊 (a sheep) on top and 大 below (depicting a man with arms outstretched to look big and meaning *big*). In making up the code part of the radicode, the component rule comes into play. After taking three strokes, 431, from the top component, we moved to the lower component to get the 3 stroke. Scholarly etymology sees in 美 a man wearing a sheep or goat headdress (shell-bone version on left) and looking very *handsome*. Thus 美 originally indicated masculine beauty. Gradually, it came to mean beauty and beautiful in general. Folk etymology asks, What could be more *beautiful* than a Big Sheep?

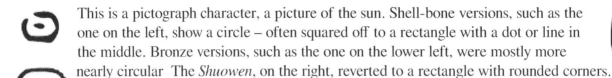

日本 **rì běn Japan**

日 **rì ri4 sun (the whole character is the sun radical) sun**

This is a pictograph character, a picture of the sun. Shell-bone versions, such as the one on the left, show a circle – often squared off to a rectangle with a dot or line in the middle. Bronze versions, such as the one on the lower left, were mostly more nearly circular The *Shuowen*, on the right, reverted to a rectangle with rounded corners.

本 **běn ben3 aa 7341 origin.**

This character is one of a small group called "indicatives." It begins from the tree character, 木, and adds a line pointing to the root area, so the character means "root, origin." Because Japan lies to the east of China, it was the land of the rising sun, or the origin of the sun, 日本.

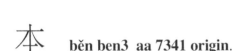

来 (來) **lái lai2 aa74313 to come, arrive**

The character now means *come, arrive*. Etymologists disagree about what it originally depicted. Some say it shows fruit which has *arrived* and is hanging from a tree when the harvest season has *come*. Others observe that the oldest forms in the shell-bone characters lack the top horizontal stroke necessary to make a tree, and that instead the drawing represents a wheat plant and was borrowed phonetically to write *come*. The second example on the left is a typical bronze version, which has, however, acquired the crossbar. The *Shuowen* version is at the bottom on the left; the modern traditional remains quite close. The wheat plant is now written 麥 mài and has a footprint below the original picture – which, however, has acquired the crossbar. You can take either or both explanations.

去 **qù qu4 earth 64   go**

The shell-bone and the bronze versions all clearly show a man with legs spread over a mouth. One bronze version (2ⁿᵈ on left) adds a foot at the bottom, suggesting that the man is moving, presumably *leaving, going* away. The mouth, either his or someone else's, is, we may suppose, saying goodbye. In the *Shuowen* (right) and other seal characters, the man is still recognizable, but the mouth has lost its characteristic shape and perhaps represents the house the man is leaving. In the modern character, the man and the mouth are still there but no longer immediately recognizable. The man's arms and legs have turned into horizontal lines and made him into the earth radical, 土 tǔ, which we will deal with when we encounter a more genuine example of it.

喜欢 **xǐ huān to like**

喜 **xǐ xi3 sir 0430 joy**

By itself, this character means "happiness, joy; to like, be fond of; related to weddings." In the center is a drum on a stand; the heads are on the front and back sides. Below is a mouth, suggesting singing or sound in general. Above is container with festive flowers or feathers. Altogether, the elements suggest the celebration of a joyous occasion. The three components are very clear in the shell-bone version (top left), are preserved in the bronze character (bottom left) and in the *Shuowen* version (right). The top part has evolved into the **sir radical**, though 喜 has no historical connection to this radical.

欢 (歡) **huān huan1 ab 5435**   merry, joyous; active; like, love.

The left side is the phonetic and is a picture of a great horned owl, 雚 huán. Its evolution is shown on the left, from a shell-bone version (top) to a fantastic bronze example, to the *Shuowen* (bottom). The modern traditional version has remained quite faithful to the *Shuowen* – and to the owl, for that matter. What of the simplified version? Well, you can see for yourself. The meaning element, 欠 qiàn, is on the right and shows a man with his mouth open, as seen in the seal character on the top right. One modern meaning of 欠 is *yawn*, but we can also imagine that the man is singing for joy.

So 喜欢, joy + joy = joy = like, and we have another example of bisyllabism.

累(纍) **lèi lei4 field 664   tired**

This character, when pronounced with the fourth tone, as in the text, means "tired, weary"; but the same character pronounced with a first tone means "to tie, to bind together." That meaning explains the **silkB radical** at the bottom, which is used not only for fine silk but for string, thread or rope. It is the meaning component. The "field" 田 at the top is the phonetic component, but is unrelated to the 田 character (which is pronounced *tian*) but rather is a fragment of the character 雷 léi meaning *thunder*. In this character, the 田 is essentially a picture of an explosion, a bang. The seal version of the thunder character was 雷 showing rain above and below: bang! boom! pow!

 The **silkB radical**, mentioned in Lesson 1 in connection with 厶, is a character, mi4, meaning *fine silk*. A shell-bone version is shown on the left. Sears sees in it a twisted thread; Wang sees a skein of silk. The bronze versions, such as the lower example on the left, preserve the original idea, whichever it was. The *Shuowen* version, on the right provides a link to the modern version. On the left of a character, 糸 becomes the **silk radical** 纟 in simplified characters and 糹 in traditional characters.

忙 máng mang heart 416 busy

This character is relatively new; it is not in LST or the *Shuowen* or earlier sources. We met the heartB radical in discussing 怎 (page 26). Being busy is a matter of how you feel, a matter of the heart. The 亡 is an inexact phonetic element pronounced wáng and meaning "to perish; flee; lost; dead." This character appears all the way back to the oracle bones, but it is unclear what it depicts.

老师 lǎo shī teacher

老 lǎo lao3 old 63 老 old

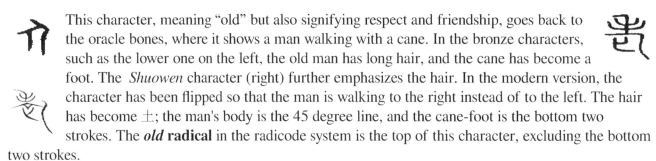

This character, meaning "old" but also signifying respect and friendship, goes back to the oracle bones, where it shows a man walking with a cane. In the bronze characters, such as the lower one on the left, the old man has long hair, and the cane has become a foot. The *Shuowen* character (right) further emphasizes the hair. In the modern version, the character has been flipped so that the man is walking to the right instead of to the left. The hair has become 土; the man's body is the 45 degree line, and the cane-foot is the bottom two strokes. The *old radical* in the radicode system is the top of this character, excluding the bottom two strokes.

师 (師) shī shi1 ab 231 师 troops, division; master, teacher, expert

Basic meaning: teacher, master

I have not found a convincing story of how this character suggests its meaning or sound. A typical bronze version is shown on the right, but there is no agreement about what the two sides depict. The oldest meaning seems to be *army, troops, division*. Today, it retains that meaning but has added the meanings of *teacher, master, specialist*.

学生　xuéshéng student

学 (學)　xué xue2 child 44 学 school, study, learn

The origin of the traditional form of this character must be all too obvious to many a Chinese child. The lower part is a child under a roof. Above the roof, two hands are cramming stuff (the x's) into the head of the hapless child. In the simplified, all that remains of the hands and curriculum are three lines to remind us that there were once three parts there. The shell-bone characters all omitted the child, but the one shown top left got the other three elements. The bronze characters nearly all added the child (2ⁿᵈ left), and the *Shuowen* version (top right) was close to the modern traditional. The *Shuowen* had a second version (bottom right) that adds an element to clarify the teaching methods used in the school. The added element is a hand with a stick.

医生　yīshéng physician

医 (醫)　yī yi1 aa 1631 医 heal

The key to this character is the 矢 shǐ character, meaning "arrow". Its evolution is shown to the left. The bone-shell character clearly shows the arrowhead, the shaft, and the feathers. The bronze adds a dot on the shaft to emphasize it (or perhaps show its circular cross-section) and to distinguish it from the forms of 大 then being used. The *Shuowen* character (right) enlarges that dot to a line and swells out the feathers. The modern character keeps those features but rather blunts the point of the arrowhead.

Once we recognize the arrow, the seal character for 医, 醫 , tells a nice story. In the upper left corner is a man's chest with an arrow in it. On the right, the hand of the 医生 pulls out the arrow. The pot of healing, antiseptic ointment is ready below. The little figure in the upper right corner may be an instrument but it could also be the physician kneeling beside his patient. The modern traditional character keeps all the elements of this story. The simplified character, while clear, is a little strange; it shows the man's chest pierced by the arrow but with no help in sight.

律生　lùshéng lawyer

律　lù lü4 road 25111 律　 to control, restrain; law

We meet again the *road* radical on the left. The basic meaning 律 is *to control, restrain*, hence, law. The seal character version on the right clearly shows, on its right, a hand holding a writing brush. Sears suggests that the hand with the brush may be mapping out the road to be followed, thus *controlling*. (In typing characters using pinyin input, the *ü* is typed as a *v*.)

Here are the conversations from pages 31-32, but without the pinyin so you can practice reading characters without danger of falling back on the pinyin. And, just for fun, the seal character version follows.

你好！

你好！

你好吗?

我很好，你呢?

我也很好。

你爸爸好吗?

他很好。

你妈妈呢?

她也很好。

王先生，你好吗?

马马虎虎。你呢，张小姐?

我也马马虎虎。

你怎么样?

不错，你呢?

我也不错。

这是张小姐。

这是王先生。

认识你我很高兴。

认识你我也很高兴。

Here are the conversations in modern traditional characters.

你好！

你好！

你好嗎?

我很好，你呢?

我也很好。

你爸爸好嗎?

他很好。

你媽媽呢?

她也很好。

王先生，你好嗎?

馬馬虎虎。你呢，張小姐?

我也馬馬虎虎。

你怎麼樣?

不錯，你呢?

我也不錯。

這是張小姐。

這是王先生。

認識你我很高興。

認識你我也很高興。

And here are the dialogs in a font using the *Shuowen* form of the character where it exists and a modern "reconstruction" of the *Shuowen* form where it does not. This is known as the HYCuZhuanf font.

Lesson 2. Names

Here are the new characters, 47 in all:

姓 名 字 朋 友　工 公 司 叫 有　谢 再 见 客 气　知 道　您 贵 没　什 们 的
但 银　行 校 餐 馆 男 同 事 板 市 长　经 理 儿 问 题　文 书 面 条 看　吃 都

您 nin2 heartB 3235 您 **you** (especially respectful)

Let's start with an easy one. We know 你 and we want to show heartfelt respect, so we add the heartB radical (which we also know) below it to get 您.

姓 **xìng xing4 woman 3711 姓 family name**

We have already met the woman radical and 生 as a character. Its sound, *sheng*, is close enough to *xing* that its use as a phonetic is not surprising. What is surprising is the woman radical in the word meaning *family name*. Chinese women do not change their family name when they marry, but the children get the name of their father. Perhaps the idea is that our birth determines our family name, and 女 suggests birth.

名字 **míngzì name**

名 **míng mouth 354 名 name**

A shell-bone version shows a mouth and a crescent moon. The story goes that the crescent moon means it is a dark night; the person approaching the sentry is challenged and his *mouth* gives his *name*. Shell-bone, bronze and seal characters are shown on the right.

字 **zì roof 51 字 Chinese character**

By itself, 字 means a Chinese character, or sometimes a word. Thus, 名字 means a name-word = name. This is an instance of bisyllablism. The character shows a child under a roof. We met the child on the right side of 好 and also under a somewhat truncated roof in 学. Here, in the seal character, 字, we have a proper, very sheltering roof. It is a picture of a baby in a house. If there is a baby, there must have been a birth; and the original meaning of the character was "giving birth" and was extended to mean "raising" and "multiplying." Originally characters consisting of one picture were called 文 wen, while composite characters – multiplied characters – were known as 字. Gradually the distinction was dropped and all characters are now known as 字. The original meaning of "giving birth" has disappeared. (See CCCC, p. 58)

朋友 péngyǒu friend

朋 péng moon 251 朋 friend

The modern character for *moon*, 月 yuè, is called the ***moon* radical** in the radicode system. It is derived from a shell-bone form such as we saw in the evolution of 名; in the seal script it looks like 月 and then evolved to 月. Obviously, 朋 must be classified under the moon radical. But it has nothing to do with the moon. Rather it evolved from a picture of two strings of cowrie shells which were used as money. The earliest pictures are in the bronze characters, such as this one: 丰丰. Most of the seal characters kept a recognizable resemblance to this version, but the *Shuowen* came up with the elegant one shown on the top right of the paragraph. From it, by leaving off the top curling line, the modern character was developed. The cowrie strings were also used as money. A line in the *Classic of Poetry* reads, "Encountering a friend, a hundred peng I was offered." (CCCC p. 273). Perhaps under the influence of this line, 朋 now almost always means *friend*.

友 yǒu aa 3154 友 friend

From the shell-bone form on the left through the *Shuowen* form on the right, this character clearly showed two hands, plainly hands together in friendship. The modern character slides the upper hand of the seal form to the left and straightens the wrist-middle-finger line. 朋友 = friend-friend is a good example of the bisyllabism that became necessary as the final consonants were dropped.

工 gōng aa 121 工 work

The shell-bone form, shown on the right, depicts a tool, probably an earth tamper, for heavy *work*.

公司 gōngsī company

公 gōng aa 3464 公 public, common.

The shell-bone form on the right shows a mouth speaking with a loud voice, perhaps with hands used to make it carry far. Thus, a *public* expression or statement. The bronze characters, such as the one shown lower left mostly remained faithful to this idea. In the *Shuowen* version, shown on the right, the mouth is no longer recognizable as a mouth and the "hands" have become exaggerated. In the modern form, the mouth looks more like a nose and the "hands" like a broken stick. In fact, folk etymology says that the erstwhile mouth is, in fact, a nose and means *private* and the "hands" are a broken stick and mean "not" so the character reads "not private" = *public*. This is, of course, etymological nonsense, but I find that it works mnemonically.

司 **sī aa 510** 司   **to take charge, manage**

By itself, the character means *take charge of, manage,* and the shell-bone version (on the left) shows a man on the right pointing and directing with one arm and his mouth barking out orders on the lower left. The *Shuowen* verion on the right the commander is bent way over and his arm has fallen off but is still present. The modern character is unchanged except for style of drawing. Because 公司 means "company" and is used like "Inc." it is one of the most frequently seen words on the street in China.

叫 **jiào mouth 26**   叫   **to call, to be called, shout**

This radical+phonetic character goes back only to the *Shuowen* form shown on the right. The mouth radical on the left clearly fits the meaning. The phonetic element on the right is an earlier form of the modern character 纠 jiu1 meaning *to entangle*. This element, by itself meaning *to entangle*, goes back to shell-bone (upper left) and bronze (lower left) forms. If you get entangled, *call* for help. (Images on the left from English Wiktionnary.)

有 **yǒu meat 31**   有   **have**

Here we meet the *meat* radical in the lower part of this character. As a character by itself, it looks like this 肉 and depicts a pork chop. (You will see it often on menus in Chinese restaurants. Unless otherwise qualified, it means *pork*.) Above the meat is a hand. There could hardly be a clearer picture of the idea of "to have, possess" than the hand that *has* the meat. There are abundant bronze examples such as the one on the left above. The Showen version is on the right.

The radicode system distinguishes between this *meat* radical which has a straight 2 stroke on the left and the *moon* radical 月 which has a curving 3 stroke on the left. A quick glance through the *moon* pages of the *Quick Guide* reveals, however, that most *moons* are, in fact, *meat* etymologically.

谢谢 **xiè xiè thank you**

谢（謝） **xiè speech 3255**   谢   **thanks**

In the code part of the radicode, notice that after taking three strokes – the 325 – from the middle component, 身, we follow the component rule and move to the 寸 component to take a fourth stroke – the second 5. The meaning is *to thank, apologize.* Either action requires speech, so it is not surprising to find the speech radical. The phonetic is 射 shè, meaning *shoot, send out*. One could easily suppose that 射 comes from 身 shēn (meaning *body*) plus 寸 cùn, the *inch* radical depicting a hand with a finger on the wrist. But, in fact, the true origin is simpler, as we see from the bronze version of 射 above left, which is clearly a hand *shooting* an arrow. By the time of the seal characters, however, many scribes were apparently getting confused and were replacing the bow and arrow by a 身. Even the *Shuowen* has 射.

再见 zài jiàn Good bye! (Literally: Again see!)

再 zài aa 127   再   again, more

The stroke code requires a word of explanation. As spelled out in the introductions to *The Quick Guide*, a 2 stroke does not make a 7 when crossed by a 5, but it loses the power to make a 7 with a 1 stroke below the 5. Thus, the second stroke is just a 2, not a 7. The 7 in this character's stroke code comes from the cross between the 2 stroke on the left side and the lower 1 stroke. The meaning of 再 is *again, more, even more, in addition*. The *Gudai Hanyu Zidian* says plainly that the origin of 再 is not clearly known. The Witionnaire authors believe that it shows hand-held scales or balance, a view consistent with the only known shell-bone example, shown top left. Sears believes that it shows two fish on a stringer. The fisherman caught one fish and then *again* caught another. Of the various versions his web site offers, the lower one on the left above which best supports this idea. It is an LST version; the earlier bronze versions look very like the *Shuowen* version on the top right.

见 (見) jiàn see   见   見   see

This entire character is the *see* radical and occurs in such characters as 览 and 规. The top of the traditional, 目 mù, is the *eye* radical and occurs in such characters as 看 and 瞬. The oracle bone characters, of which a good example is shown on the left, show a man with a huge eye for a head, clearly suggesting *to see*. In the *Shuowen* version, top right, the eye has rotated to become vertical, and the rest of the man has become stylized. In the modern traditional character, the eye, 目 mù, is clearly visible. The simplified is less vivid and harder to remember.

The expression 再见 therefore literally means "again see".

客 kè roof 3540　客 guest

A guest is someone who sits down and talks and eats under your roof. That is exactly what the shell-bone versions of this character show, as seen on the top left, where a mouth under a roof is fed by a woman. Some of the bronze characters, such as the one on the lower left, show the same elements. The woman has been reduced to her arms and a single line for torso and legs. The similar *Shuowen* version is on the right. In the modern character, the woman has been further reduced to a hand holding something and presumably offering it to the mouth below.

气（氣）　qì air　气　氣　breath, air, gas; vital force

The basic meaning 气 is *breath*, from which modern meanings such as *air, gas*, and *airs* (as in *to put on airs*) derive. Oracle bone and bronze versions show simply three horizontal lines. Some seal-character scribe added the mouth, as shown on the top left right, but this version did not become standard. Another sense of the character is the Qi or vital force of traditional Chinese medicine. The *Shuowen* version is shown on the right.

To this *Shuowen* version was added in the modern traditional character a 米 mi (rice) to get 氣. The reason may lie in the expression 客氣 "guest airs" meaning *politeness*. The politeness, the "airs" included, above all, offering the guest food, at least some rice. Hence the addition of the rice component in the modern traditional version. The rice was removed again in the simplification.

The Chinese do not say 谢谢 to one another nearly as much as Westerners say "thank you" or its equivalent in other languages. In particular, family members seldom say 谢谢 to one another. Guests in the home, however, might say 谢谢. So the expression 不客气 – which functions like "you are welcome" – literally means "Don't [put on] company airs" like saying 谢谢. If, however, you actually did go to some trouble and don't want to scold your guest for saying 谢谢 you can say 客气了 meaning something like "It was was no more than common courtesy."

知 zhì arrow 0　知　to tell, to know

We have already met both components, the arrow. page 35, and the mouth. The basic meaning is "to tell, inform, speak straight to the point, wisely and well." But to inform, one must know, and *to know* is now the most common meaning. It may help to remember the English idioms "straight talk", "straight as an arrow", and "speak to the point."

道　**dào go 43130** 道　**way, road, truth; Taoism; say; think; doctrine.**

The character is one unified ideogram. Among the many LST versions, the one on the left is particularly clear, both in meaning and relation to the modern character. In the top left, we find the road, the way. Below it, the foot traversing the way. On the right is a foot above an eye, indicating going forward with vision on the way, just what Daoism (=Taoism) is about. That the fragment in the upper left corner indeed represents the road or way is made certain by several bronze versions such as the lower character on the left. The two sides show a crossroads, as we shall see later in this lesson (page 23). Just the left half of the crossroads – as seen in the upper caracter on the left – is sufficient to represent the road. (This bronze version of 道 also has four elements – the road, the foot (top center), the eye (center), and a hand instead of a second foot.) The *Shuowen* version is on the top right.

The expression 知道 basically means "know the truth" and is yet another instance of bisyllabism.

Perhaps you are wondering why 道 is often written Tao in English. Before the introduction of pinyin, an earlier system of Chinese transcription into the Latin alphabet, known as the Wade or Wade-Giles system used *t* to represent the sound expressed by *d* in pinyin. The *t* sound was written as *t'*. The same change of phonetic transcription system explains how Peking became Beijing. Thomas Wade, the creator of the Wade system, was a British army officer who served in various parts of China, learned the language and many of its dialects thoroughly, and later became the first professor of Chinese at Cambridge. The Wade system, while more complicated than pinyin and more subject to misinterpretation by those who do not know the system, is also more flexible and can be used to write dialects that pinyin cannot write. Anyone who understands the Wade system will look at *Peking* and pronounce it exactly as one who knows pinyin will pronounce *Beijing*.

贵 (貴) **gùi shell 20** 贵 貴 **expensive, precious**

The radical here is 贝 (貝) bèi, which is a picture of a cowrie shell. The bronze version on the left depicts the shell; the *Shuowen* version 貝 added the animal projecting from the shell. These shells came to be used as money, so the radical is used in many characters, such as our 贵 to convey the meaning of *precious, costly, expensive.* The *Shuowen* version of 贵, shown on the right, depicts, at the top, *hands* full of something. The figure between the hands indicates that what they hold is shown below, namely cowries. Note how the top part evolved into the top of the modern character; the two hands are still there but joined to make a rectangle. So the whole character means *handfuls of cowries*, or *really expensive.* In the expression 贵姓, it is best translated *honorable.*

没 méi water 3654 没 not; mo4 sink

In its original meaning of *to sink, submerge*, this character is pronounced mò. In the sense of *not* in 没有, it is a phonetic loan character. Its etymology comes from its original meaning. The *Shuowen* version, shown at right, has flowing water on the left, a whirlpool at top right and below the hand of the *sinking* man reaching up desperately for help.

什么 shénme what?

什 shén man 7 什

In Lesson 4, we will learn that 十 means *ten*. It is like the Roman numeral X rotated 45 degrees, and, indeed, a number of bronze versions of 十 are an X. Recall that 5 in Roman numerals is a V, a picture of a hand with the four fingers together and the thumb extended. Then notice that an X is two V's, one opening upward and one downward. The Chinese seem to have come independently to the same idea. The character 什 originally meant a squad of 10 men. It was phonetically borrowed for the interrogative word *shén*.

们 (們) men man 452 们

The *man* radical follows naturally from the grammatical use explained in the text. The phonetic is 门 (門) mén. The traditional form pictures clearly a Chinese *gate,* which is what the character means. It appears not only in the well-known name 天安门 Tiananmen (Gate of Heavenly Peace) but in many of the station names of the Beijing metro line which runs where there was once the city wall.

的 de white 35 的

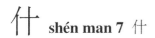

This is by far the most frequent character in Chinese. It alone accounts for some 4.4 percent of written Chinese. Nearly all of that use is in its grammatical function explained in the text, where it is close to the English *'s*. In this use, however, it is a phonetic loan character. Pronounced dì, it means a *target*, a goal. It does not appear in the *Shuowen* – a commentary on how much the language has changed – but the LST collection of seal characters shows several versions like the one on the right, which clearly depicts the target and the bow that will shoot the arrow into it. The target has turned into 白, which means *white*.

但 dàn man 011 但 but

This is a radical+phonetic character. The phonetic, 旦 dàn, is a picture of the sun 日 rising and means *sunrise, dawn.* Just why *man* is the appropriate radical is less clear; maybe it's just human to object and say "but." 但 by itself means *but*; 但是 , literally "but is", trranslates as "but" and is another example of bisyllabism.

The following characters are from the "Supplementary Words and Expressions."

银行 **yìnháng bank**

银 **yìn metal 561** 银 **silver**

We have already met the *metal* radical in 错 and the phonetic in 很 hen. The meaning of 银 by itself is *silver.*

行 **háng road 115** 行 **line, row; occupation, line of business; seniority among siblings**.

Yes, we met 行 before (page 23) , and it was pronounced *xing2*. Most characters have only one pronunciation but some have more than one with different meanings going with the different pronunciations. You can tell which pronunciation only by the context. Here 银行 is to be understood as the "silver line of business" i.e. a bank. We learned that 行 depicts a crossroads. There is certainly some similarity between a road and a line. One can understand why a scribe, already having a picture for a road might use it for a line, although the spoken words were quite different.

校 **xiào tree 413** 校 **school**

 The tree radical for a character meaning *school* may refer to teaching under a tree or the wooden school house, though doubtless it seemed to many a Chinese boy that it referred to the teacher's stick. The phonetic, 交 jiāo, means *to cross*. A typical bronze example is shown on the left, a picture of a man with crossed legs. The *Shuowen* version of 校 is on the right.

餐馆 **cānguān restaurant**

餐 **cān eatB 2** 餐 **dining**

 The **eatB radical** at the bottom is 食 shí, meaning *eat, meal, food, feed*. The shell-bone version shown on the left depicts a wide open mouth over a bowl of rice on a stand. This idea survived fairly well to the *Shuowen* character on the right, which adds a hand in the upper right corner reaching for a bone in the upper left. (See Wang, p.184 for the bone.) In the transition to the modern form, it seems to have fallen under the influence of our friend 艮. My impression of the difference between 餐 and 食 is that 餐 is more likely to be used in the sense of *dining,* not just eating.

馆 (館) guān eat 445 馆 館 inn, hall, embassy, legation, consulate, shop, private school

Here is the *eat* **radical** again, but now as it appears on the left side of the character. The traditional form is a compressed version of 食 minus only the small 3 stroke on the bottom right. All traditional characters with this radical on the left have had it simplified as shown in this character.

馆 is a character where the right side has been phonetically borrowed for a different meaning but then returned to its original meaning by the addition of a radical. The right side of the character is 官 guān. The seal character version, shown on the right, has under the roof a "mound" element which the GHZ says means *many* and Sears adds "many rooms" in the house. So the original meaning of 官 is a building with many rooms. But 官 has been phonetically borrowed to mean *a government official,* someone who works in a big building, so the *eat* radical was added to restore 官 to its the original meaning of a building with many rooms, in particular, to one where people eat. The other meanings of 馆 – *hall, embassy, legation, consulate* – come from the original meaning of 官 and have little to do with eating. The word for restaurant, 餐馆, is a "dining-eat-house".

男 nán field 35 男 male, masculine

田 tián is the field radical and shows a rice paddy with dividing ridges. Below the field is the character 力 lì which means *strength.* Thus 男 is the strength that works the fields, namely, men. It now means also *male, masculine,* and is very important to know when choosing a restroom. (The other one is marked 女.) A typical bronze version of 男 (top left) shows the field and a strong arm emphasizing the biceps area. In most of the numerous LST versions, the arm is reduced with the hand emphasized (lower left). In the *Shuowen* version (upper right), the arm has lost all resemblence to an arm and the hand has been strangely squared off. The modern version dropped all of the arm above the wrist and the left half of the hand. The scribes had lost the picture, but we can enjoy restoring it in our mind's eye every time we see 男.

力 is the *force* radical in the radicode system.

同事 tóngshì colleague

同 tóng aa 2510 同　same, equal, alike, together; agree

The shell-bone and bronze characters, such as the one on the left, show a molding box (seen from above) and below it a mouth. The molding box suggests the idea of *same, equal*; everything made in the mold is the same. And if all *mouths* say the same thing, they *agree*. Many of the LST seal characters preserve this idea, but in the *Shuowen* version, right, a side fell off of the molding box and looks like an 一 floating above the mouth, while the rest of the molding box has turned into sort of a hut or roof. It was a shame to loose the molding box, but perhaps the idea of everyone under a roof being "of one mouth" is good enough for mnemonic purposes. .

事 shì aa 5105 事　matter, affair, business, work, event.

A 同事 is someone who has the same work, a colleague. The shell-bone versions of 事, such as the one at the top left, clearly show a hand below holding something that extends above. Just what is being held is not clear. Wang believes it to be a net made from a branch and used for catching a boar; he adduces a shell-bone drawing complete with boar. Sears shows some 90 shell-bone drawings of which the one shown here (lower left) is typical. It is not unlike what Wang shows but lacks the boar. It may be a three-way forked branch which has had cross pieces added (the horizontal line) to make a net for catching animals. Catching a boar with such a device would certainly be a tricky *business*, a piece of *work* and a big *event*. But the bronze (lower left) and *Shuowen* versions (upper right) all lack any boar and look more like a writing brush. Sears sees a mouth between the hand and the brush and believes the hand and brush are writing what the mouth has said, thus recording a business matter or agreement.

老板 lǎobǎn boss

板 bǎn tree 3354 板　plank, board; stiff, ridgid; stern

This is a relatively new character not found in the *Shuowen* or earlier sources. Its literal meaning is *plank, board,* so the tree radical fits. By extension, the character means *stiff, rigid, stern.* To call the boss 老板 is to say he is the *stern old plank.* Remember, however, that 老 carries the connotation of affectionate respect.

The phonetic, 反 fǎn is used in a number of characters pronounced fan or ban. It goes back to shell-bones times (left) and shows a cliff and a hand, possibly the hand is pulling something up the hill. The *Shuowen* version is at right. As a phonetic loan character, it means *to turn over, in the opposite direction,* but it is returned to something close to its original meaning by adding the hand radical in the character 扳 bān meaning *to pull.*

市长 shìzhǎng mayor

市 shì hat 225 巿 market, trade, buy, sell; city.

The most common meaning now is *city*, but more fundamental meanings are *market, trade, buy, sell*. The *Shuowen* seal character, right, may show a man with long hair using a shoulder pole to carry merchandise strung from either end of the pole. Even in the late 20th century, a man carrying goods on a shoulder pole was a common sight around a market in China.

长 (長) zhǎng aa 631 长　chief, head; grow; eldest

This common character has two different pronunciations with distinct meanings. Pronounced cháng, it means long, length. Pronounced zhǎng, it means grow, increase; eldest, oldest; chief, head. It is used in this last sense in the word 市长 used in the text.

The etymology relates to both senses, for it shows an old man with long hair, as is plainly seen in the shell-bone version on the left. The *Shuowen* version, top right) is a barely recognizable descendant but a plausible ancestor of the modern traditional character. The simplified has removed the last traces of the long hair. The Great Wall, by the way, in Chinese is 长城 cháng chéng, literally long city wall.

经理 jīnglǐ manager

经 (經) jīng silk 541 经　warp; meridian; main north-south road; to rule, regulate, manage.

This character basically means the warp of a loom or cloth, the long threads attached to the loom. It gives a good example of the silk radical as it appears on the left side of a character. The *Shuowen* version on the right has in the top right corner a picture of the warp threads and below a picture of the frame of the loom. The threads running in the other direction, the weft or woof are the 纬 (緯) wěi. These characters came to be used also for the meridians of longitude and the parallels of latitude, respectively. By extension, they came to be used for main north-south and east-west roads, respectively. From the main road idea, 经 came to mean *mainstream*, hence *rule, regulation,* and *to regulate, to manage*.

经 also means the "meridians" of acupuncture.

Economics is 经济学 iīngjì xué, 济 jì means *aid, help*. 经典 Jīngdiǎn the classics, scriptures.

理 **lǐ jade 071** 理 **reason, logic, science; manage.**

This is a radical+phonetic character. The phonetic, 里 lǐ is composed of the paddy field radical 田 above and the dry earth radical 土 below. The combination is a good place to live, and 里 basically means a village, though it is now more commonly used as a measure of length equal to 500 meters. The radical is jade, which we met in 国. Usually, it denotes something costly. Here it seems to suggest that reason, logic, and science have something of a jade-like crystalline beauty.

The bisyllabic word in the text, 经理, tells us to concentrate on the common meaning of the two characters, which is *manage*; so the combination means *manager*.

儿 (兒) **ér ab 36** 儿 child, son, person

This character has long been interpreted as showing a child with the fontanels of the skull still open. The GHZ and all Wiktionary sites repeat this explanation. While this interpretation is plausible for the *Shuowen* and modern traditional characters, the earlier versions – such as those on the left – have far too large a gap for this explanation to be plausible. The simplified character for *fontanel* is 囟 xin4, being very close to the *Shuowen* version on the lower right. The square is the baby's head and the lines are the fontanels, thus showing that the ancient Chinese correctly thought of the fontanels as lines, not great gaping holes. (The traditional character for *fontanel* is 顖 with the head radical on the right, a heart, xin, on the bottom left as phonetic and the picture of the baby's head in the top left corner.) Wang repeats this explanation as the "traditional" one – thus suggesting that he is unsure of it. Sears offers the explanation that these early versions, such as the shell-bone and bronze versions on the left, show a baby with arms uplifted wanting to be picked up. That explanation works fairly well for the old versions, though one might expect the hands to be either absent or more conventional. The *Shuowen* version on the right begins to fit the fontanel theory and is traceable in the modern traditional. The simplified version omitted the supposed head and thus – if we buy the fontanel theory – shows a decapitated baby. Or, if you like, it shows a being that is all legs – not a bad description for a three- or four- year-old.

问题 **wèntí question**

问 (問) **wèn gate 0** 问問 **inquire, ask**

From the shell-bone stage, left, to the *Shuowen*, right, and on to the modern versions, the character consistently shows a mouth at a gate. The mouth must be inquiring, asking, for that is what the character means.

题 (題) **tí head 011** 题　題　**forehead; subject, topic, sign**

A 问题 is an ask-subject, that is, a question. This is our first meeting with the **head radical**, 页. By itself, this character now means *page* but in 题 and many other characters it indicates something to do with the head, here the *forehead* or the *heading*, that is, the subject. An oracle bone version of 页 is shown on the left, while the *Shuowen* version is on the right. The phonetic is our friend 是 shì, which serves as a phonetic in several characters pronounced *ti*.

文　**wén hat 7** 文 **writing, literature, language, culture, learning, science**

The bronze characters, such as the one on the left, show a man with a tattoo on his chest. From that tattoo, or rather from the man sporting it, comes the character that means all culture that depends upon writing. Curiously, the tattoo has disappeared from nearly all of the seal characters, including the *Shuowen* version on the right, from which the modern character derives by simplification.

书 (書) **shū aa 245** 书書　**book.**

The character means *book*, and the LST character on the right shows a hand (above) holding a writing brush, with the book itself represented by the rectangle at the bottom. All this is still visible in the modern traditional, but in the simplified character the book is gone and hand and brush only faintly suggested.

面条　**miàntiáo noodle**

面　**miàn aa 1302** 面 **face, surface, flat, plane.**

Recall the *Shuowen* version of 页, 𧼭 , picturing an exaggerated *face* above a man. Now look at the *Shuowen* version of 面 shown on the right. The box around the central part seems to emphasize the flatness of the face. Also recall English sur*face*.

条 (條) **tiáo tree 354** 条條 **long and thin**

This character is a picture of a man testing the depth of water with a *long, thin* pole. In the first of the seal characters shown on the right, you see the water clearly on the left, the pole (shown as a tree) in the lower right corner, and the man in the upper right. In the second, the man has moved over to the left side and become very elongated; the stream of water is reduced to just one side of the stream, the tree is still in place, and a hand holding something is in the upper right. This is the *Shuowen* version and is the direct ancestor of the modern traditional, while the right side alone serves as the simplified.

The word 面条 – meaning *noodles* – literally means *flat long thin things.*

 kàn eye 331 看 **to look, see, read, look at; visit; consider, think; look out, be careful.**

Even in the modern version, the picture is clear: an eye with a hand above *looking*. The *Shuowen* version is on the right; the LST seal variant shown on the right makes the picture clear.

吃 (喫) **chī mouth 316** 吃 **eat; eat up; live off of; wipe out; suck; feel, suffer, bear**

 The mouth radical is natural for this character which means to *eat* – though a little surprising that it is not the eat radical.. The right side is phonetic. In the simplified, it is the character 乞 qi3 meaning "to beg for alms". In the traditional, the phonetic is the character 契 qi4 meaning "a written deed, contract or agreement". The top is phonetic 㓞 qì meaning "to engrave". It, in turn, shows a knife (for engraving) on the right and presumably the object engraved on the left. A shell-bone version is on the top left. If you are having trouble with the difference between chi and qi, you may find it consoling that the phonetic for this chi character is a qi character. 气氣

都 **dōu placeR 741** 都 **both, all, even, already**

Since the ideas expressed by this character are rather abstract, we immediately suspect that it it is a phonetic loan character, and that is indeed the case. So what is pictured has nothing to do with the current meaning. Exactly the same character pronounced dū means a *big city* like 成都 Chéngdū, the capital of Sichuan. It is in this meaning that the picture relates to the meaning. In this meaning, the character is of the radical+phonetic type with the PlaceR radical on the right. In the radicode system, we have kept the distinction made in the traditional radical system between 阝 when on the left – where is is called the *place* radical – and the same sign when placed on the right – where it is called the *placeR* radical and indicates a town. In the next lesson, we will meet the characters 那 and 院, where the left and right 阝 have the usual etymologies, which we will discuss more thoroughly.

The phonetic in 都 is 者 which serves as the phonetic in a number of characters pronounced *du*, though as a character by itself it is pronounced zhě and is a PLC meaning "a person who does (something)". It goes back only to the seal characters, where it shows some kind of food being put into a pot. In the LST seal character shown on the right, it appears to be a chicken going into the pot head first with feathers flying. Or perhaps it is not a chicken but an herb with roots as well as branches. As is often the case with phonetic loan characters, it has been returned to its original meaning of *to boil* by adding the fireB radical below in the character 煮 zhǔ.

We have now covered all the characters in Lesson 2. It's time to practice reading the dialog without the pinyin.

您贵姓?

我姓王。 你呢?

我姓张.

你姓什么?

我姓李. 你呢?

我姓黄。

你叫什么名字?

我叫马丁。你呢?

我叫安。

认识你我很高兴。

认识你我也很高兴。

有中国朋友吗?

没有。 你有美国朋友吗?

我有。

他叫什么名字?

他叫安迪。

你知道她的名字吗?

不知道。 你呢?

我也不知道。

你是学生吗?

不是。 我是工人。

你们的公司叫什么名字?

我们的公司叫海尔。

谢谢。

不客气。

再见。

再见。

Here are the conversations in modern traditional characters.

您貴姓?

我姓王。 你呢?

我姓張.

你姓什麼?

我姓李. 你呢?

我姓黃。

你叫什麼名字?

我叫馬丁。你呢?

我叫安。

認識你我很高興。

認識你我也很高興。

你有中國朋友嗎?

沒有。 你有美國朋友嗎?

我有。

他叫什麼名字?

他叫安迪。

你知道她的名字嗎?

不知道。 你呢?

我也不知道。

你是學生嗎?

不是。 我是工人。

你們的公司叫什麼名字?

我們的公司叫海爾。

謝謝。

不客氣。

再見。

再見。

And just for fun, here they are in the *Shuowen*-like font.

您貴姓?

我姓王。 你呢?

我姓張.

你姓什麼?

我姓李. 你呢?

我姓黃。

你叫什麼名字?

我叫馬丁。你呢?

我叫安。

認識你我很高興。

認識你我也很高興。

你有中國朋友嗎?

沒有。 你有美國朋友嗎?

我有。

他叫什麼名字?

她吃牛油。
你知道她的名字嗎?
不知道。 你呢?
我也不知道。
你是學生嗎?
不是。 我是工人。

你們的公司叫什麼名字? 我們的公司
叫機器。
謝謝。
不客氣。
再見。
再見。

At this point, you have met 94 characters and 40 of the 100 radicals used in the radicode system. Here is a list of the radicals you have seen: air, arrow, child, cloth, earth, eat, eatB, eye, field, gate, go, hat, head, heart, heartB, horse, jade, lance, man, meat, metal, moon, mouth, old, ox, placeR, road, roof, see, shell, silk, sir, speech, sun, tiger, tree, wall, water, white, and woman. Thus, after only two lessons you know 40 percent of all the radicals in the radicode system.

Flash cards are a common way to learn words in a foreign language, but in Chinese you need four-dimensional flash cards with the character on the first side, the pinyin on the second, the meaning on the third, and the radicode on the fourth side. The closest that I have been able to come to making such flash cards is to enter the four fields in four columns of a computer spreadsheet. Add a column of random numbers, then sort on the random numbers, cover up all but one column and try to fill in the others. Of course, there is no need to try to work back from radicode to character.

请 (請) **qing3 speech 7112** 请 **please; request, ask; invite**

This character is of the radical+phonetic type. Since asking and requesting involve speaking, the speech radical is natural. The phonetic, 青 qing1, means green, the color of young grass or leaves. In the *Shuowen* character shown on the right, we see at the top of the right side a 生 sheng1, a young plant growing. Below the 生 is a 丹 dan1, which pictures a dot of cinnabar on a tray for use as a red pigment. The modern meaning of 丹 is red or cinnabar, which is not the color indicated by 青 but perhaps the 丹 is used to indicate the idea of color itself, while the 生 tells what color is meant. Sadly, since the days of the seal characters, the scribes lost the picture and turned the 丹 into a pork chop.

作 **zuo4 man 3211** 作 **to do, to work**

The "man" radical is clearly appropriate for a verb meaning "to work" The phonetic, 乍 zha, we met in Lesson 1 in the character 怎 zen3 (page 26).

单 （單） **dan1 aa 4307** 单 **one, single, simple; unit, unitary.**

This is a phonetic loan character. The shell-bone character on the left shows some sort of weapon made from a branch possibly with stone points at the end and a net or shield below the fork of the branch. The bronze image on the right preserves that picture and adds what may be a hand guard at the bottom. It appears as a phonetic element in such characters as 弹 惮 郸 掸, all pronounced *dan*. A hint of its original bellicose meaning survives in the traditional character 戰 zhan4, meaning *war, battle* where it appears together with the lance radical 戈. (This graphic character with two elements related to meaning was "simplified" to the more conventional radical-phonetic character 战 by using the phonetic element on the right of the character 站 zhan4, which appears later in this lesson.)

位 **wei4 man 4143** 位　**place, position, status.**

Here we have the familiar *man* radical on the left and on the right a picture of a man *standing*. In the shell-bone version of this element, shown on the left, the man has his feet squarely planted on the ground, holding his *place* and *position* against all comers. (The modern fellow, in contrast, looks a bit shaky.) Recall, by the way, that our word *status* comes from the Latin verb *stare*, to stand.

在 **zai4 aa 3127** 在　**at**

The meaningful radical here is 土 tu2 *earth*, but because it does not occupy a whole side nor is it in the upper left corner, it cannot count as the radical in the radicode system. But for etymological purposes, it is certainly the radical. Where something is *at* is where it is on **earth**. In the shell-bone characters, 土 looked like a clod, a clump of earth, as shown on the top left. In the bronze characters, it often took on a more tree-like appearance, as shown on the right. By the seal-character stage, it is virtually identical to the modern character.

The two-part image on the left is a bronze version of 在. The earth radical on the right is clear. The phonetic element on the left is a picture of a dam. The vertical line is the stream; the horizontal line is the dam, and the blob is the water backed up behind the dam. In the *Shuowen* character on the right, the water has turned into a single sloping line. In the modern character, 在, the dam (the 丨 stroke) is still there, the backed-up water has become the sloping line, and the stream is visible only at the bottom. At the same time that this character was evolving, the dam and water picture by itself evolved into 才 but was robbed of its meaning when, by phonetic borrowing, the picture was taken over to represent the abstract word *cai2*, meaning *ability, capacity, talent*. The sound of the old word for *dam*, however, lives on in the word *se2*, meaning *to block* and in *sai1*, meaning a *stopper*. Here, however, the sound is represented by a totally different character, 塞. Modern words for *dam* use the earth radical, but nothing related to 在 or 才.

哪 **na3 mouth 53152** 哪　**Where?**

Having found the mouth radical on the left of the interrogative characters 吗 and 呢, we are not surprised to find it there in this interrogative meaning "where?". The rest of the character functions here as a phonetic for the sound *na*. This character, 那 na4, means *that* or *those,* as opposed to *this* and *these*. We will meet it in Lesson 5, but we can explain its origin here.

Since it is not easy to draw a picture of *that*, it is no surprise that 那 is a PLC. There were not, however, many things with names pronounced *na* whose sound could be borrowed to write this common word. But one of them seems to have been a town noted for clothing made of hemp. The *Shuowen* character for its name is shown on the right. The left side of the character is thought to represent the hemp. The right side is the standard seal-character sign for a town. Its shell-bone antecedent is shown on the left. The town is depicted by the rectangle at the top, which suggests the wall around the town. An inhabitant is squatting down making himself (or herself) at home in the lower part of the character. There are many of these town-name characters, which have often become family names. In the *Shuowen*, the right side is uniformly represented as shown in this example. (As far as I can ascertain, the location of the original 那 town is no longer known, though I found one 那 on the map of China.)

In the transition from seal characters to modern characters, the character for town,邑, became 邑 yi4, but the radical – always on the right – uniformly turned into the β-like figure which appears on the right in 那. In the *Quick Guide*, this radical is called *placeR;* and it accounts for about one percent of all characters in the *Guide.* Most of them, however, are surnames or place names of low frequency.

北 bei3 ab 2116 北   north

In the shell-bone script, this character always clearly shows two people sitting **back-to-back**, as seen on the left, and thus its original meaning is *back*. By phonetic borrowing, it became the character to express the concept *north*. By adding the *meat* radical (remember the character 有), it is returned to its original meaning of *back* in the character 背 bei4. It is possible, however, that in using the sound *bei3* for the concept *north*, there was some connection with the *back* idea. In cold weather, it is a good idea to keep one's back to the north. The emperor's throne put his back to the north. The *Shuowen* version of the character, top right, looked even less like the modern character than did the ancient shell-bone version. Something a little closer to an intermediate step is shown in the LST seal character on the right.

京 jing1 hat 0534 京   capital city

From the shell-bone character on the left – depicting a high building characteristic of the capital city – to the *Shuowen* version on the right there is a clear line of descent, though the older one looks more structurally sound. And even the modern version shows only the usual squaring off.

家 jia1 roof 135 家   family

 This delightful character, meaning *family*, shows simply a pig under a roof! A pig is 豕 shi3. Some shell-bone versions of the character, such as that shown on the left, make the pig look quite pig-like. The *Shuowen* version is on the right.

公 gong1 aa 3464 公   public

The shell-bone character on the left shows a mouth shouting out something *publicly,* with the hands on either side being used to project the voice. Some bronze and even seal characters, such as the one shown immediately to the right, preserved this idea, but the *Shuowen* character, shown on the far right, has obscured the picture. The modern character, derived from it, preserves some traces of the original idea.

城 cheng2 earth 6413 城 city, town.

 The finely-drawn bronze character on the left shows, on its left side, the city wall with towers all around and, on its right side, a battle ax, representing the defenders of the city. (We met the battle ax on page 30 in describing the traditional form of 国.) In the *Shuowen* version, on the right, the simple earth radical has replaced the elaborate drawing of wall and towers, though a simplified tower may have slipped into the battle ax. From this version to the modern version is a short step.

远 (遠) yuan3 go 113 远 **far, distant, remote; (of a difference) big, great; deep, profound**.

This is a radical+phonetic character. Both the traditional and the simplified have the *go* radical – the stretched foot which we met in 这 on page 27 – as is quite natural for a character meaning *far, distant.* In the simplified character the phonetic is 兀 yuan2. Though it may not be obvious at first, it is a picture of a man with the head emphasized by the line at the top. The *Shuowen* version is on the upper left. It can mean the head, the beginning, or various other things, but it is most common as the symbol for the Chinese currency, the yuan.

 In the traditional character, the phonetic is 袁 yuan2, now in common use only as a surname, but originally meaning a long, flowing robe reaching the feet. There is no known example of the phonetic by itself before the Shuowen version (on the right), but there are several bronze versions of 遠 such as the one shown on the top left of this paragraph. Note the foot at the bottom of its right side indicating that the garment (middle of the right side) reached the feet. It is not clear to me what is on the top of the right side. The scribes turned it into earth 土 tu3, but this may not be what was originally intended.

太 tai4 aa3144 太 **too, most, greatest**

Sears says that this character appears in none of his sources, but Wang Hongyuan adduces shell-bone examples of simply one man above another, smaller man, much as shown in the image on the left, which I created. Later, the lower man was reduced to a line and finally to just a dot. The bigger man is, presumably, the *greatest*, the *most*.

电 （電） dian4 aa 601 电 **lightning, electricity**

The *Shuowen* version on the right shows rain above and lightning splitting the clouds below. The modern traditional preserves the idea, and the simplified is just the bottom half to the traditional.

It is now used in many combinations to denote electrical devices, such as 电话 dian4 hua4 = electric speech = telephone.

话 （話） hua4 speech 370 话 **speech, language; word; talk; talk about.**

 The speech radical is to be expected. The right side is a picture of a tongue; the mouth is at the bottom and the tongue is sticking out. The combination speech + tongue pretty clearly means language, talk, speech. An LST character is on the left; there is no *Shuowen* version.

住 zhu4 man 4171 住 **dwell, live, reside; stop, cease; firmly; withstand.**

 This is a radical+phonetic character. The *man* radical is natural enough for a character meaning to dwell, live, reside. The right side 主 zhu3, is phonetic. Its original meaning is a lamp or a lamp wick, clearly shown in the *Shuowen* character on the left. Because a host carries a lamp to guide his guests to their rooms, it came to mean *host*. And from that meaning, it extended to *master*, and even *lord*. There is no *Shuowen* or earlier example of 住.

"Manhattan" and "New York" appear in the text because that is where the author teaches. The characters used to "spell" these names in Chinese, 曼哈顿 纽约, are used here solely for sound, not for meaning, so we will skip their etymology.

Supplementary words and expressions

商店 **shang1 dian4 store**

商 **shang1 hat 432** 商 **trade, business; merchant; consult, discuss**

Although this character is found in all stages of character evolution, there is no agreement about what it depicts. Four shell-bone versions are shown at left. The first suggests to me simply a table with goods piled on top and struts below to stabilize the legs: a good picture to represent *merchant, trade, business.* In the next two, the goods become more substantial, but in the last, there is only one pile and it is resting precariously on a point. At this stage, the character usually lacked the mouth in the lower center. But it appears in all the bronze versions, such as shown top right. It was added later and is likely busy negotiating price. The *Shuowen* has four versions; one is shown bottom right.

店 **dian4 shed 210** 店 **shop, store**

The fairly common *shed* radical, 广 guang3 (meaning *to expand, wide*), is basically a picture of a lean-to added to a house to expand it. (扩 kuo4, *to enlarge*). It appears in characters meaning *shop, store, room of house* (other than the main room), *kitchen, palace, wide, expand,* and numerous others. So it indicates the building used as the shop or store.

The element under the shed, 占, is the phonetic By itself, it is pronounced zhan1 and appears in several characters pronounced zhan, including 站 战 沾 粘. It also indicates a *dian* pronunciation, as here and in such characters as 点 點 玷 战. Sometimes it indicates a *nian* or *zhen* or *shan* or even *tie* pronunciation. Obviously, it was a favorite of the scribes. And for good reason. It means *to divine, to foretell the future,* especially by scapulimancy, as described in the introduction. The top element, 卜 bu2, depicts the crack in a bovine scapula or turtle shell caused by a hot coal. A shell-bone version is shown on the left. The mouth was added to represent the questioner. Sears found no version of 占 by itself but numerous examples, such as the one on the right, showing the a whole bovine scapula with the crack and the mouth on it.

Note that 商店 is redundant in writing. 店 means *shop* and 商店 "trade shop" likewise means *shop* but is easier to understand in speech than just 店.

电影院 **dian4 ying3 yuan4 motion picture theater**

影 **ying3 sun 41033** 影 **shadow.** (by extension) **copy, image, trace; movie, film.**

Note that here we have used the rule that if there is no radical occupying a whole side but there is one in the ***upper left corner***, it claims the character. (Radicals elsewhere not occupying a whole side do not claim the character.) The 京 jing1 in the lower left corner is the phonetic. The sun in the upper left corner and

61

its rays on the right are there because, without light, there is no shadow. Recall that in a traditional motion picture the viewer looked at the *shadow* on the screen of the image on the film in the projector. Surprisingly, there is no *Shuowen* or other early example.

院 **yuan4 place 4451** 院 **court, courtyard.**

 The phonetic on the right, 完 wan2, as a character by itself means *intact, whole, complete,* but here seems to function solely as a phonetic. In it, the phonetic is 元 yuan2, which we met on page xxx . (So actually 元 is a better phonetic than 完 is; the simplifiers missed a good opportunity.)

A 阝 on the left side of character, the *place* radical, has a totally different etymology from a 阝 on the right side, where, as we have seen on page 58, it means a *town*. On the left, however, it indicates that in the seal character there was something like the figure shown here on the left. It has been variously interpreted as a terraced hillside or as stairs. In a number of characters it indicates something about going up or down or being high or low, as in the following examples.

阶 jie1 steps, stairs; rank

除 steps; (by phonetic loan) eliminate; except, besides
阪 ban3 a slope
阼 zuo4 eastern steps leading to a hall
陟 zhi4 ascend, climb up
降 jiang4 to fall down, to drop, lower
陵 ling2 hill, mound, imperial tomb

It fits our character, 院, because a Chinese court was often elevated and had steps leading up to it.

医院 **yi1 yuan4 hospital**

We have had both characters previously. The combination "healing court" is reminiscent of the *asclepeia* of the ancient Greeks and is certainly an optimistic word for a hospital.

邮局 **you2 ju2 post office**

邮 (郵) **you2 placeR 70** 邮 郵 **post, postal, mail**.

The "town" symbol on the right is certainly appropriate for a character meaning "post office." The *Shuowen* version is on the right; there are no earlier known examples.

The 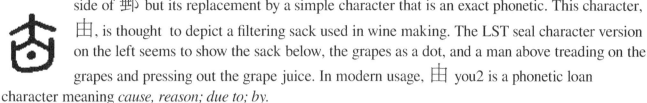 由 you2 on the left is a simplification introduced in the 1950s. It is not a simplification of the left side of 郵 but its replacement by a simple character that is an exact phonetic. This character, 由, is thought to depict a filtering sack used in wine making. The LST seal character version on the left seems to show the sack below, the grapes as a dot, and a man above treading on the grapes and pressing out the grape juice. In modern usage, 由 you2 is a phonetic loan character meaning *cause, reason; due to; by.*

The left side of the traditional character, 郵, is 垂 chui2, with the basic meaning of *droop, hang down,* which is exactly what the plant on the left side of the *Shuowen* ancestor of 郵 is doing.

局 ju2 door 50 局　government bureau or office; narrow, restricted; part of; situation, state

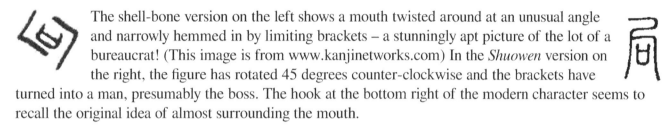 The shell-bone version on the left shows a mouth twisted around at an unusual angle and narrowly hemmed in by limiting brackets – a stunningly apt picture of the lot of a bureaucrat! (This image is from www.kanjinetworks.com) In the *Shuowen* version on the right, the figure has rotated 45 degrees counter-clockwise and the brackets have turned into a man, presumably the boss. The hook at the bottom right of the modern character seems to recall the original idea of almost surrounding the mouth.

公园 gong1 yuan2 park

园（園）yuan2 wall 11 园園 yard, garden, orchard; park

The difference between the *wall* radical and the *mouth* radical is that a *wall* always has something inside it and the *mouth* never does. Indeed, the *wall* surrounds the whole character. Interestingly, the English words *garden* and *yard* both derive from the proto-Germanic word *garda,* meaning an enclosed, *walled* area. The phonetic in 园 is familiar from page Error: Reference source not found.

图书馆 tu2 shu1 guan2 library

图（圖）tu2 wall 354 图圖 picture, drawing, plan, design, chart, map

This character is probably an pictogram showing a picture of something. The frame around the outside represents a surface on which the picture, plan or map is drawn. The inside is the picture. In the traditional, it may be a drawing of a granary. In the simplified, the drawing is clearly unrelated to whatever was inside the traditional. It is 冬 dong1 which means *winter.* Presumably, we are to think of a picture of a winter scene.

 The *Shuowen* version of 冬 is on the right. The two upside-down Y's at the bottom are probably ice crystals. The top presumably evolved from the shell-bone version of the character shown on the left. Wang believes that it is a picture of a quipu (see page 96) and in the sense of *winter* is a phonetic loan character.

In Lesson 2, we met both 书 shu1 (meaning book) and 馆 guan1 (meaning eat-house or inn). Thus a library, a 图书馆, is literally a map-picture-and-book eat-house. But don't try eating in a Chinese library!

办公室 ban4 gong1 shi4 office

办（辦）ban4 force 44 办 handle; do, act

We met the force radical, 力 li2, in the character 男 on page 47, where, however the field radical on top was dominant. A radical derived from a picture of a strong arm is clearly appropriate for a character meaning *handle, do, act*.

The 辛 xin1 element in the traditional character is phonetic and despite its current pronunciation, appears in several characters such as 辩 and 辨 pronounced bian or 瓣 辨, 辩, and 辯 pronounced ban. In these characters it appears on both sides of the radical. The combination 辟 pi4 is pronounced pi4 or bi4 in a number of characters. In the simplified version 办 of 辦, it has been reduced to just a dot, one on each side of the radical, so there is essentially no phonetic. As to what a 辛 is, there is no clear agreement. Some see a chisel, others a sword, others a knife, others a tool for tattooing, others some sort of instrument for punishing criminals or disobedient slaves or wives or concubines. There are many shell-bone examples; a typical one is shown top left. The Shouwen version is top right. There seem to be no bronze examples.

As to how a character pronounced *xin1* came to represent the sound *bian* or *ban*, the character 辟 pi4 and meaning *law* may possibly offer a clue. A typical bronze version is shown on the left. The usual explanation is that the man on the left has been or is about to be decapitated by the 辛 on the right, and that the circle shows his head. My alternative is that the circle shows a city; the man, a citizen; and the 辛, the ever-present authority keeping the man in line. So the whole represents *law*. But perhaps someone looked at it and said, "If 辟 is pronounced *pi*, then 辛 must stand for the sound *pi*." And *pi* easily slips over to *bi* and *bian*. (This is just my speculation; I have seen no authoritative discussion of the xin-to-bi problem.)

室 shi4 roof 164 室 room

The familiar *roof* radical is natural enough. 至 zhi4 is the phonetic component. By itself, it means *to arrive* and shows an arrow – with point down and feathers at the top – stuck into the ground where it has *arrived*. In the shell-bone character, on the top left, the picture is clear. In the bronze character on the lower left, the arrow head is rounding and isn't in the ground. By the *Shuowen* character for 室 (top right) the picture is lost unless you know to look for it, and in the transition to the modern character, the arrowhead was completely flattened while the feathers were rather strangely trimmed and flattened.

An office, a 办公室, is thus a public room for action.

公安局 gong1 an1 ju2 police station

安 an1 roof 513 安 peace, quiet

We readily recognize the elements of this character: a woman under a roof. Perhaps the idea is that the woman is at peace in her home; or perhaps it means that, in times of peace, women have roofs over their heads. 公安 is public peace and a 公安局 is the bureau responsible for preserving it. 天安门 (tian an men) is the famous Gate of Heavenly Peace in the heart of Beijing. But on it is written 門安天, for when it was built it was customary to write Chinese from right to left.

博物馆 bo2 wu4 guan2 museum

博 bo2 ab 77 博 extensive, ample; to obtain, win

In Lesson 2 we met 什 shen2 and learned that 十 means *ten*. In 博, 十 is the radical and suggests not just ten but *many*. The rest of the character, 尃 fu1, is phonetic. It is a rare character meaning *to announce*. The bronze version on the left shows a hand, below, ringing a bell, to get attention to the announcement.

物 wu4 ox 35 物 things, objects

We have already met the ox radical. It is appropriate here because one's cattle were the most important *things* one had. Recall that the English word *capital* comes from Latin *caput* meaning *head* and in particular, head of *cattle*. The *Shuowen* version is at right.

 The phonetic is most interesting. It depicts the sound emerging from a plucked bow string, which is a sort of *wooh*. This idea is fairly clear in the shell-bone version at the far left. The bronze version in the middle still distinguishes the bow from the sound waves. The seal version has lost the distinction. One would never guess the origin from the modern version.

勿 wu4 by itself means "Do not" and is common in signs but unusual in speech.

教堂 **jiao4 tang2 church**

教 **jiao1** and **jiao4 hit 73** 教 **jiao1 to teach; jiao4 education, religion.**

 The two images on the left show shell-bone and bronze examples, and *Shuowen* version is on the right. The key to understanding it are the lines from *School Days:*

    Readin' and 'ritin' and 'rithmatic,
   Taught to the tune of the hickory stick.

The right side is a hand holding the "hickory stick," and forms the *hit* radical. On the lower left is the child being taught; the two X's above its head are the subjects being taught. The hand with a stick in a seal character regularly transforms into the *hit* radical as shown here. The child also transforms as in this character. The two X's, being less pictorial, got turned into the old man whom we met in 老 lao3.

堂 tang2 roof3 071 堂 **principal room of a house; hall; court, courtroom;**

 The bronze version on the left shows a tall building with the earth sign in the center at the bottom. In the *Shuowen* version on the right, the building has been simplified and a mouth added inside to indicate a building for talking, speaking, teaching. It is then but a short step to the modern character.

汽车站 qi4 che1 zhan4 **bus stop**

汽 qi4 water 3116   汽   **steam, vapor, gas**

We met the *water* radical in 没 mei2 and the *air* radical in 气 qi4 in the expression 不客气, "don't put on company airs." In 汽, 气 does double duty to convey both meaning and sound. *Water* turned to *air* is *steam*. The combination in 汽 is a clever new character to mean *gas*. It is not found in the *Shuowen* or earlier sources. And the Chinese follow the American practice of saying *gas* to mean *gasoline*.

车 (車) che1 cart   车車   **cart, wagon, car, any wheeled vehicle**

The traditional character, 車, shows a two-wheeled cart viewed from above. The vertical line is the axle; the two horizontal lines are the wheels; and the square in the middle is the body of the cart. Very similar versions go back to the shell-bone age. The modern simplified version shows a badly broken cart.

站 zhan4 stand 210 站   **to stand, to stop, halt, a station, a stop, a stand**

The origin of the phonetic 占 zhan was described under 店 on page 61 above. The *stand* radical appeared earlier in this lesson on the right of 位 in 单位, where a picture of an earlier version was given.

火车站 huo3 che1 zhan4 **train station**

火 huo3 fire 火 **fire**

 This character is a picture of *fire*. The flames are clear in the shell-bone version on the left, and have survived fairly well to the *Shuowen* version at right. A little fantasy suffices to see the flames even in the modern character. A bus is a *gas wagon* while a train is a *fire wagon*. To anyone old enough to remember a coal-fired steam locomotive, that is a perfect picture. In a horizontally compressed form, 火 appears as a left-side radical in a number of characters, such as 烟 yan1, meaning *smoke*. This form is known as the fire radical.

飞机场 fei1 ji1 chang3 airport

飞 (飛) fei1 aa 534 飞 fly

 The character on the left, an LST seal version, shows clearly what is intended: a bird in flight with the wings emphasized. The *Shuowen* version on the right, shows abstraction setting in. The tuft of feathers behind the head has come to look like a third wing. In the modern traditional, the tuft wing and the wing on the right are drawn one above the other; the body is a straight vertical line, while the wing on the left is still there but quite different from the other two. The modern simplified is just one of the right wings of the traditional, but it also suggests a humming bird, poised in mid air, about to stick its long beak into a blossom.

机 ji1 tree 36 机 machine

In the first sentence of the next lesson we will meet the character 几 ji3 as a question word. Pronounced ji1, however, it means a small, low table, which is what it pictures. In 机, however, it is an exact phonetic. We have met the tree radical before in the 样 of 怎么样 and in 校. Basically our character says "something made of wood and pronounced ji1." Today, we think of machines as made of steel, but the early machines, especially looms, were made of wood and the character was highly appropriate. The character appears in the *Shuowen* but, not surprisingly, not in earlier sources.

An airplane, 飞机, is a *fly machine*.

场(場) chang3 earth 533 场 field

The earth radical is natural for a character meaning *field*. The right side is an inexact phonetic; its traditional form is a rare character 昜 yang2, meaning *bright, glorious, to open out, to expand*. One, somewhat atypical, bronze form shown on the left seems to depict clearly the sun sending down its rays, a good image for *bright, glorious, to open out*. In its further development – and even in many bronze versions – it seems to have fallen under the influence of 勿. The *Shuowen* version is on the right. The simplified form abbreviates the sun but its rays are still clear.

An airport, 飞机场, is a fly machine field.

饭店 **fan4 dian4 hotel**

饭 (飯) **fan4 eat 3354** 饭   **cooked rice or other grain; a meal. FR 935.**

The eat radical is natural. The phonetic, 反 fan3 is a phonetic loan character meaning *to turn over*. It shows a hand pulling its owner up a cliff and is returned to its original meaning in the character 扳 ban1, meaning *to pull*. The *Shuowen* version is shown on the right.

南京 **Nan2 jing1 Nanjing = South Capital**

南 **nan2 aa725** 南   **south. FR 307.**

 This is a phonetic loan character. It probably depicts an ancient suspended bell. The shell-bone version on the left shows the suspension mechanism above and a clapper in the middle. The clapper is very much present in the modern version but is absent in many shell-bone versions because many ancient bells were rung by hitting them from outside. The *Shuowen* version is shown on the right.

上海 **Shang4 hai3 Shanghai = On the sea**

上 **shang4 aa211** 上 FR 16   **xia aa124** 下 **FR 42.**

Basic meanings: 上 means *above, on* 下 means *below, under*.

These two characters are examples of the indicatives discussed in the introduction. When something, such as a book, has two parts, the first is marked 上 and the second 下.

海 **hai3 water 31** 海 **sea. FR 189**

 The water radical obviously fits. The right side is not a phonetic but rather contributes to the meaning. It is 每 mei3 meaning *each, every, all.* Thus, the sense of the character is *all the water.* 每 is a phonetic loan character whose original meaning was *beautiful* and depicted a woman wearing a feather headdress, as shown in the shell-bone version, top left. In bronze characters, the breasts became emphasized, as shown in the second character on the left. The modern character has detached the hair and rotated the bosom 90 degrees. The *Shuowen* version of 海 is on the top right. Meanwhile, mei3 meaning beautiful has come to be written 美, originally meaning masculine beauty, which we met in the name 美国 America.

Here are the conversations without the pinyin.

请问，你工作吗？

工作。

你的单位在哪儿？

我的单位在北京。

你妈妈在家吗？

不在。

她在哪儿？

她在公司。

请问，中国银行在哪儿？

中国银行在中国城。

中国城远吗？

不太远。

请问，你在哪儿工作？

我在公司工作。

你在什么公司工作？

我在电话公司工作。

请问，你在哪儿住？

我在曼哈顿住。

曼哈顿在哪儿？

曼哈顿在纽约。

你学中文吗？

学。

你在哪儿学中文？

我在纽约大学学中文。

你的中文老师是中国人吗？

是。

他叫什么名字？

他叫李华。

请问,这儿有厕所吗?

有,在那儿。

谢谢。

不客气。

请问,这让有中国餐馆吗?

没有。

哪儿有中国餐馆吗?

中国城有中国餐馆。

中国城有日本餐馆吗?

没有。

Here they are again but in modern traditional characters.

請問，你工作嗎？

工作。

你的單位在哪兒？

我的單位在北京。

你媽媽在家嗎?　　　　　　　　學。
不在。　　　　　　　　　　　你在哪兒學中文?
她在哪兒?　　　　　　　　　我在紐約大學學中文。
她在公司。　　　　　　　　　你的中文老師是中國人嗎?
請問，中國銀行在哪兒?　　　是。
中國銀行在中國城。　　　　　他叫什麼名字?
中國城遠嗎?　　　　　　　　他叫李華。
不太遠。　　　　　　　　　　請問,這兒有廁所嗎?
請問，你在哪兒工作?　　　　有,在那兒。
我在公司工作。　　　　　　　謝謝。
你在什麼公司工作?　　　　　不客氣。
我在電話公司工作。　　　　　請問,這讓有中國餐館嗎?
請問，你在哪兒住?　　　　　沒有。
我在曼哈頓住。　　　　　　　哪兒有中國參觀嗎?
曼哈頓在哪兒?　　　　　　　中國城有中國餐館。
曼哈頓在紐約。　　　　　　　中國城有日本餐館嗎?
你學中文嗎?　　　　　　　　沒有。

And here are the conversations in the *Shuowen-like* font.

請問，你工作嗎?　　　　　　不在。
工作。　　　　　　　　　　　她在哪兒?
你的單位在哪兒?　　　　　　她在公司。
我的單位在北京。　　　　　　請問，中國銀行在哪兒?
你媽媽在家嗎?　　　　　　　中國銀行在中國城。

中國城遠嗎？
不很遠。
請問，你在哪兒工作？
我在公司工作。
你在什麼公司工作？
我在電話公司工作。
請問，你在哪兒住？
我在曼哈頓住。
曼哈頓在哪兒？
曼哈頓在紐約。
你學中文嗎？
學。
你在哪兒學中文？
我在紐約大學學中文。

你的中文老師是中國人嗎？
是。
他叫什麼名字？
他叫李華。
請問，這兒有廁所嗎？
有，在那兒。
謝謝。
不客氣。
請問，這邊有中國館嗎？
有。
哪兒有中國餐館？
中國城有中國餐館。
中國城有日本餐館嗎？
有。

In this lesson, we have learned 41 new characters but only 8 new radicals, which are shown in bold in this list of radicals we have encountered: air, arrow, **cart**, child, **door**, earth, eat, eatB, eye, field, **fire**, **fireB**, **force**, gate, go, hat, head, heart, heartB, **hit**, horse, jade, lance, man, meat, metal, moon, mouth, old, ox, **place**, placeR, road, roof, see, **shed**, shell, silk, sir, speech, sun, tiger, tree, wall, water, white, and woman. It is a good idea to check that you can visualize each of these radicals.

Lesson 4. Family

We have a light chapter for etymology, only 28 characters needing to be explained.

历史 li4shi3 history

历(歷) li4 cliff 35 历歷 to go through

This simplified character is the successor to three different traditional characters all having the cliff radical 厂 , but none having having 力 li4 as a phonetic element. The one which is used to write 历史 li4shi3 (meaning *history*) in modern traditional characters is 歷 which means *to go through*. A shell-bone version is shown on the left. It shows a wheat field at the top and a foot at the bottom. Clearly, that foot is about *to go through* the wheat field, and that is exactly what the character means. *History* is what has been *gone through*. All of the LST seal characters and the *Shuowen* character, shown on the right above, have added the **cliff** radical of the radicode system. Why it was added eludes me.

The name *cliff* for the 厂 radical is a bit problematic. Wang (page 136 of the Chinese edition) quotes the *Shuowen* as saying " 厂 [han4] is a radical for mountains and rocks." But a glance at the characters under this radical in the *Quick Guide* fails to reveal any examples. Instead, many are characters that had the shed radical 广 in the traditional form and thus certainly have nothing to do with cliffs. In another group, 厂 seems to be functioning as a phonetic element for the *yan* sound. One of the remaining characters, however, is a nice example of the cliff idea. 厄 e4 shows a crumpled-up man under a cliff ; presumably he has fallen off. The character means *disaster*. 原 yuan4 shows water flowing from the face of a cliff, but is a phonetic loan character meaning *original*. It is returned to its pictorial meaning by adding the water radical to get 源 yuan4, a spring, fountainhead, source. The character 岸 means a *shore, bank, beach, or coast*, but the mountain radical on the top indicates that this is a rugged coast probably with *cliffs*.

史 shi3 aa304 史 history

There are numerous examples of this character in all stages of development. From the shell-bone version on the left to the *Shuowen* version on the right they all depict clearly a hand holding a brush and presumably writing. Maybe it is writing history, but maybe it is the hand that makes history: "The moving hand once having writ moves on. Nor all thy piety nor wit can lure it back to cancel half a line." — Omar Khayyam, *The Rubáiyát*

男孩 nan2hai2 boy

孩 hai2 child 416 孩 child, children

The *child* radical clearly fits. The right-hand side is 亥 hai4, a common phonetic. Exactly what it depicts is not clear. It is the last of the 12 "earthly branches" used in the Chinese traditional calendar. 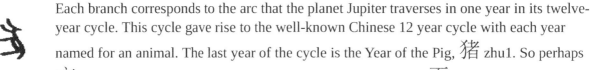 Each branch corresponds to the arc that the planet Jupiter traverses in one year in its twelve-year cycle. This cycle gave rise to the well-known Chinese 12 year cycle with each year named for an animal. The last year of the cycle is the Year of the Pig, 猪 zhu1. So perhaps 亥 has something to do with *pig*. Now *pig* can also be written 豕 shi1, which which looks a little more like 亥. That it is a picture of a pig as is clear enough in the big-mouthed shell-bone version in the upper left. By the bronze version, lower left, it has become more abstract on its way to the modern version. Our 亥 hai4 is shown in a bronze version on the bottom right and in a seal character above it. It seems not implausible that it also represents a pig, The *Shuowen* version, upper right, looks unlike any of these versions, and the modern version is far from the *Shuowen*. If you are confused, you are in good company, for so are the best minds in the field.

岁 （歲） sui4 mount 354 岁歲 year, years (of age), harvest.

The **mount** radical on top of the simplified version is a picture of mountains, as is clear in the shell-bone version of the full character 山 shan1 on the far left. The next character is an elegant bronze version. The seal characters became more abstract; the rather fanciful *Shuowen* version is on the right.

The original meaning of 岁 was *harvest,* and many instances of the character are found all the way back to the bone-shell stage. The example on the far left is fairly typical of that earliest stage.

Most of the drawing is, I believe, a scythe; the two short horizontal lines are what is cut. The next version, a bronze character, elaborates this idea and shows the curve of the scythe blade. The third version exaggerates the blade and clarifies the plants being cut. Finally, the Shouwen version on the right adds (on the top) the foot of the harvester walking through the field but reduces the scythe blade. This version was preserved fairly faithfully in the modern traditional character. The simplified looks vaguely like the traditional but the foot has turned into a mountain and the scythe into the moon. Mountain over the moon? Not in a million *years*!

做 zuo4 man 703 做 do, make, produce, act, cook

This is a fairly recently created character not found in the *Shuowen* or earlier sources. Perhaps it is too abstract in its meaning for early stages of the language. The *man* radical is natural enough since the meanings are all actions of man. 故 gu4 (**hit 70**) is an inexact phonetic. It has a number of meanings, among them *incident, cause* which may explain the *hit* radical. But it also has the meanings *old friend* and *die.* The phonetic in 故 is 古 gu3 (mouth 7) which means *old, ancient.* In the shell-bone versions, it is just a mouth with a straight line sticking out; the cross bar came in the bronze characters. No one is sure just how it came to mean *old*. Sears speculates that it may show the straight talk of *old* people. Or maybe it just means that *old* people talk a lot, or that *old* people should talk and young people should listen.

学习 xue2xi2 to study

习(習) xi2 aa 541 习習 to practice.

The *Shuowen* character on the right shows a pair of wings. Presumably, they are the wings of a young bird *practicing* flying. Below the wings is a cotton bobbin, which when used alone has evolved into the character 白 bai2 meaning *white*. For 白 to be a phonetic in a character pronounced xi2 would seem impossible were it not for the character 皙 xi1 meaning *white* or *f*air as applied to skin color. In this character, 白 relates to the meaning of the character, but some scribe must have mistaken it for a phonetic and added it to the wings in the traditional form of 習 . In the simplified form, 习, only one wing is left, so the scribe's mistake is irrelevant. We can just remember that it takes a lot of *practice* to fly with only one wing.

几 （幾） ji3 aa 36 几幾

In the use explained in the text, 几 is a phonetic loan character. Pronounced ji1, it means a small, low table, which is exactly what it pictures. The *Shuowen* version is on the left. The modern traditional character for this grammatical use obviously has a different origin. It is also a phonetic loan character. The *Shuowen* version, shown on the right, pictures a loom rigged with silk thread.

多少 duo1shao

Meaning: how many? Note the similarity of the question form "Many few" with the 好不好 "good-not-good" form.

多 duo1 aa35435 多   many, too many, much

The *Shuowen* character on the right clearly shows two moons, and that is *too many* moons. There are many instances of the character back to the shell-bone texts; all show clearly two moons.

少 **shao3 aa 2343** *少* **few, little, lack, lost, missing, a little while;**

(pronuncced **shao4 it means** *young*)

In all the shell-bone versions, there are simply four dots, as shown on the left. Later scribes must have found this character too simple for their taste and elaborated it. In the bronze and later versions, the top and especially the bottom dots are emphasized, as shown in rather extreme form in the *Shuowen* version on the right. Probably the dots represent *little* grains of sand, for the modern character for *sand*, 沙 sha1, appears to have restored the pictograph to its original meaning by adding the water radical to show where the sand is found.

谁（誰） shei2 speech 34127 谁 誰 who? anyone

The speech radical on the left indicates that this character serves some function in speech that is not readily pictured. The 隹 zhui1 on the right is phonetic. It shows a short-tailed bird nicely pictured in numerous bronze versions such as the one on the left. In the *Shuowen* version (on the right) the little bird has become quite a formidable creature. In the radicode system, 隹 is the *fowl* radical. In most characters where it is present it is dominated by something on the left, but it claims thirty or so characters such as 隼 sun3 fowl 7 隼 falcon.

零 **ling2 rain 3445** 零 **zero**

This is a phonetic loan character whose original meaning was *mist, light rain.* In its original meaning, it was a radical + phonetic character. The *Shuowen* version is on the top right, and there are no earlier versions. It is our first instance of the **rain radical** in a simplified character. (We saw it before in the traditional form 電 of 电, electricity.) Even in the modern version, the full character meaning rain, 雨 yu3, clearly shows the heavens above and the raindrops falling down. In 零, below the rain radical is the phonetic 令 ling4, shown in its *Shuowen* form on the lower right. It means order, command, and shows an inverted mouth above barking orders to an underling crouched below.

四 **si4 wall 36** 四 **four**

In the shell-bone characters, 4 is represented by four horizontal strokes as shown on the left. Most bronze versions are likewise four strokes. Most seal characters look somewhat like the Shuowen version shown on the right. This seems to be a picture of the human nose as seen from below and to have been used to mean *nasal mucus.* When it was phonetically borrowed to represent the number 4, it was also returned to its original meaning by adding the water radical in the character 泗 si4. Note that 四 and 泗 have exactly the same pronunciation. The Shuowen version of 泗 is shown on the right.

All the higher numerals are probably, like 四, phonetic loan characters.

五 wu3 aa 1251 五 **five**

From the earliest shell-bone characters through the *Shuowen*, 5 was represented by something always very close to the *Shuowen* character on the right. Why this symbol was chosen seems to be a mystery, and various mystical interpretations have been offered. For example, the top and the bottom represent heaven and earth (or maybe yin and yang) and the X represents all that is in between, and everybody knows that that is the **five** (Chinese) elements earth, metal, water, air and fire. The modern character seems to derive from it by converting the \ stroke into the 5 stroke in the center. And if the two straight-line parts of this stroke are thought of as two separate strokes, then 五 has five strokes.

六 liu4 hat 34 六 six

This is a phonetic loan character. It is a picture of a hut or cottage. Shell-bone and bronze versions are shown on the left. The *Shuowen* version is on the right. (In pronouncing liu4, remember that the dipthong sound *iou* is written *iu* following an initial consonant. The sound of *liu* is very like that of the name Leo.)

When the hut was phonetically borrowed to represent 6, a rather different and fantastical character 廬 lu4 was invented to replace it. We recognize our old friend 虎 hu3 the tiger working as a rather inexact phonetic. This character was simplified to 庐 lu4, meaning hut or cottage.

七 qi1 aa 61 七 seven

七 is a phonetic loan from a character meaning "to cut" and now restored to its original meaning by adding a knife on the right, to get 切 qie1. Early versions of "to cut" were simply a cross such as the bronze shown on the right where one line *cuts* the other..

八 ba1 ab 34 八 **eight**

Another phonetic loan character. The *Shuowen* character on the right meant separation and must have had a pronunciation similar to that of the number eight. The concept of separation is now represented by 分 fen1, where to 八 has been added 刀 dao1, a knife. Thus, both elements of 分 relate to meaning and neither to sound.

九 jiu3 aa36　九　**nine**

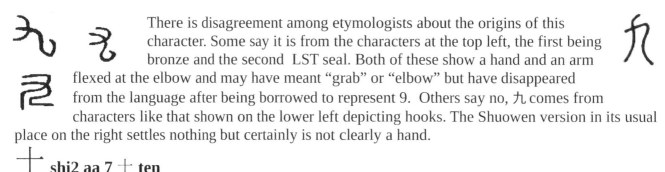

There is disagreement among etymologists about the origins of this character. Some say it is from the characters at the top left, the first being bronze and the second LST seal. Both of these show a hand and an arm flexed at the elbow and may have meant "grab" or "elbow" but have disappeared from the language after being borrowed to represent 9. Others say no, 九 comes from characters like that shown on the lower left depicting hooks. The Shuowen version in its usual place on the right settles nothing but certainly is not clearly a hand.

十 shi2 aa 7 十 **ten**

In traditional Chinese counting, a horizontal line, 一, is one but a vertical line ｜ is ten. One ten is 十 shi2, and in traditional counting two tens is 廿 niàn4, three tens is 卅 sa4, four tens is 卌 xi4. See also 什 page 45.

和 he2 grain 0 和 **and, with; harmonious.**

On the left is the **grain** radical 禾 he2. Distinguish it carefully from the **rice** radical 米 as in 粘 and from the **tree** radical 木 as in 杠. The grain radical pictures the grain at the seedling stage with two horizontal leaves above ground and well developed roots below. The rice radical shows the mature grain. In the tree, the horizontal line represents branches.

The character goes back to bronze versions such as shown on the left. The *Shuowen* version is on the right. The top stroke of the rice radical is missing in the former but is emerging in the latter. Sears tells us that in 和 the mouth means that the character is pronounced like the other component, here 禾 he2. A more folksy mnemonic is that "*grain **and** mouth harmonize* with one another."

个 （個） ge4 top 2 个個　a *classifier* or *measure word.*

In the traditional form we recognize our *old* friend 古 gu3 functioning as a phonetic. Since 个 is in the first place a classifier for people, the man radical of the traditional form is appropriate and the simplified character looks like just a slightly augmented version of this radical.

本 **ben3 aa 7341** 本 **r**oot, stem, origin; book.

This character was already encountered in the word 日本 Japan on page Error: Reference source not found. The meaning "book" is so remote from its other meanings that one suspects a phonetic loan, which, however, did not surpress the original meanings. The *Shuowen* version is on the right.

口 **kou3   mouth** 口 **mouth, classifier for family members.**

口 is clearly a pictograph of a human mouth.

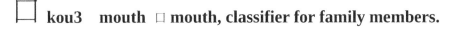

爷爷 ye2ye paternal grandfather

爷 （爺） **ye2 aa3475** 爷 **paternal grandfather**

We have already met 父 fu4 in connection with 爸 on page 28. The phonetic 耶 in the bottom of the traditional form is used to represent the ye sound in transcribing foreign words, but has no meaning in Chinese. It would appear to mean "ear town" and is used in some Korean place names and is phonetic in 椰 ye2 *coconut*. The figure in the bottom of 爷 appears to be just a graphical simplification of 耶. I have not noticed it in any other characters. There is no *Shuowen* or earlier version.

奶奶 **nai3nai paternal grandmother**

奶 **nai3 woman 53** 奶 **breasts, milk, suckle, breastfeed**

This is a phonetic loan character, 乃, returned to its original meaning. One of many similar bronze versions is shown on the left. As a phonetic loan, 乃 nai3 has a plethora of meanings: just, only, then; even; to be; right after, therefore. As we have seen, a phonetic loan is often returned to its original meaning by addition of a radical, in this case the woman radical. Cow's milk is 牛奶 niu2nai3. There is no Shuowen or earlier version. One of a few LST versions is shown on the right. The woman on the left is clear; on the right we seem to have an er-machine such as we met in connection with 你 on page 19.

外公 **wai4 gong1   maternal grandfather**

外 **wai4 ab 35424** 外 **outer, outside.**

The left side is a moon, as is clear in the *Shuowen* version on the right. The right side depicts the crack in the bone or shell used in fortune telling, as described on page 11. Sears suggests that the idea is "*out* of this world."

In the traditional Chinese family, the wife went to live with her husband's family, so her father was the "outside" grandfather. 公, which we have already had in the meaning *public* (page 59), is also used as a term of respectful address for an elderly man.

外婆 wai4po2 maternal grandmother

婆 **po2 woman 44125** 婆 **old woman, husband's mother**

The woman radical is as to be expected. The top half is an inexact phonetic 波 bo1 meaning *waves, ripples, surges*. The reason for the water radical in it is equally evident.

Its phonetic element is 皮 pi2; it has a number of meanings of which the original is *to skin* (an animal that has been killed). By extension, it came to mean *to peel* (fruit or vegetables). It was further extend to mean the skin that had been removed from the animal, hence *hide, leather, cover, wrapper, sheet, rubber, soft, soggy* and finally *naughty*. This range of meanings has garnered it a place in 1000 most common characters. The bronze version on the left shows a hand with a stone tool skinning an animal with horns. The three elements are still visible in the *Shuowen* version, though the animal has become rather abstract. Actually, all three are present in the modern version if you know to look for them. Do you see them?

百 **bai3 white 1** 百 **hundred.**

We met the *white* radical 白 bai2 in the discussion of 习 earlier in this lesson. The word for *hundred* is bai3, the same except for the tone, so 白 is a good phonetic for it.

We can think of the horizontal stroke above as a *one*, so 百 becomes one hundred. There are many examples at all stages of character evolution. The one on the left is shell-bone; the one on the right is the *Shuowen*.

千 **qian1 aa 37** 千 **thousand**

It is thought that, in shell-bone times, 人 ren2 and 千 qian1 sounded more alike than they do now, so a picture of a man plus the *one* stroke, as shown on the left, became the symbol for *one thousand*. An LST seal version is shown on the lower left. In the modern character, the long horizontal line is the added *one* stroke, while the vertical line is the man's body and the sloping stroke at the top is his arm on the left and his head on the right. The Shuowen version, right, seems to be a bit of a detour.

80

万 wan4 aa 135 万 ten thousand

万 is a simplification of the Buddhist symbol 卍, which was given the same pronunciation, wan4, as the character 萬, a PLC picturing a scorpion but meaning, *innumerable* or *ten thousand*. A shell-bone version of 萬 is on the left and is plainly a scorpion. Since 卍 was a lot easier to write than 萬, it soon replaced the indigenous character but was transformed by the scribes to something better suited to Chinese writing practice. (See *Wiktionary* entry for 万.) There seems to be no *Shuowen* version.

Here are the conversations without the pinyin.

你家有几口人？我家有五口人。他们是谁？

他们是我爸爸，我妈妈，我姐姐，我弟弟和我。

你家有几口人？我家有四口人。他们是谁？

他们是我太太，我女儿，我儿子，和我。

你女儿是不是大学生？不是。她是中学生。

你儿子呢？　他是小学生。

你有没有孩子？　有。你有几个孩子？

我有两个孩子。一个男孩，一个女孩。

你儿子多大？我儿子七岁。你女儿几岁？她五岁。

她太太在哪儿工作？　他在学校工作。

他做什么工作？她是老师。她忙不忙？他很忙。

她有多少学生？她有五十学生。

你有哥哥马？有。　你有几个哥哥？我有一个哥哥。

你哥哥工作吗？他不工作，他是学生。

他在哪个学校学习？他在纽约大学学习。

他学什么？他学历史。

他喜欢历史吗？很喜欢。

Here they are again but in modern traditional characters.

你家有幾口人？ 我家有五口人。他們是誰？

他們是我爸爸，我媽媽，我姐姐，我弟弟和我。

你家有幾口人？ 我家有四口人。他們是誰？

他們是我太太，我女兒，我兒子，和我。

你女兒是不是大學生？ 不是。她是中學生。

你兒子呢？　 他是小學生。

你有沒有孩子？　 有。你有幾個孩子？

我有兩個孩子。一個男孩，一個女孩。

你兒子多大？ 我兒子七歲。你女兒幾歲？ 她五歲。

她太太在哪兒工作？　 他在學校工作。

他做什麼工作？ 她是老師。她忙不忙？ 他很忙。

她有多少學生？ 她有五十學生。

你有哥哥馬？ 有。　 你有幾個哥哥？ 我有一個哥哥。

你哥哥工作嗎？ 他不工作，他是學生。

他在哪個學校學習？ 他在紐約大學學習。

他學什麼？ 他學歷史。

他喜歡歷史嗎？ 很喜歡。

And here they are in seal characters.

We added five radicals in this lesson: fowl, grain, mount, rain, and rice. Our list now has 53 members; we are past the half-way point in learning the radicals. Here are the ones we know so far:

air, arrow, cart, child, door, earth, eat, eatB, eye, field, fire, fireB, force, **fowl**, gate, go, **grain,** hat, head, heart, heartB, hit, horse, jade, lance, man, meat, metal, moon, **mount**, mouth, old, ox, place, placeR, **rain, rice,** road, roof, see, shed, shell, silk, sir, speech, sun, tiger, tree, wall, water, white, and woman.

Lesson 5: Time

现在　xian4zai4　now

现 (現) **xian4　jade 2536** 现 **to show, reveal; *now*, the present; in stock, on hand**

This is a rather recent character not found in the *Shuowen*, LST, or earlier sources. It is of the radical+phonetic type. The thought behind it seems clear enough: beautiful *jade* is something to *show* or *reveal*, while the see radical 见 = 見, serves as the phonetic. We encountered it in Lesson 2 in the expression 再见, where it had the pronunciation jian4, but it also has the pronunciation xian4 and is thus a good phonetic for 现. Moreover, it is not just any old phonetic, but is a good example of an *appropriate* phonetic, one that contributes also to meaning. For it is the "eye on legs" which is looking at the jade which is being revealed. The transition from "reveal" to "now" is also interesting. Maybe the thought goes something like "The present is revealed to us; the past and future are wrapped in mystery."

点 (點) **dian3　fireB 2** 点 **spot, dot, drop; point; item, part; drip; some; *o'clock***

This is a radical+phonetic character, the radical at the bottom and the phonetic on the top. The simplified character has obviously been made by taking the bottom of the left side of the traditional character and putting the

right side above it. So for the etymology, we must start from the traditional character. Its left side is 黑 hei1 meaning *black*. A bronze version is shown on the far left and a LST seal version to the right of it. The *Shuowen* version is on the far right. It shows something above a fire. Some think that that something is a window, as looks possible from the LST version. But it hardly matters; whatever it is, it is surely turning *black* with soot. The four strokes at the bottom of 黑 are derived from the four at the bottom of the *Shuowen* version and are known in the radicode system as the fireB radical.

The right side of the traditional character and the top of the simplified is 占 which we discussed under the character 店 dian1 in Lesson 3, page 61,

Thus a 点 is something that is *black* and pronounced *dian*. In other words, a spot, dot, point.

The much-loved small dishes of tasty food known in Cantonese as *dim sum* is written 点心. Remember that 心 (page 26) means *heart*, and make your own translation.

分　**fen1　aa 3453** 分 **divide; allot; distinguish; branch; *minute*; fraction**

This is a pictograph. On the bottom we have a knife, 刀, dao1 which is dividing, while on the top there is what is being divided. We have already met 刀 twice and asserted that it is a knife but have not shown its development. Perhaps you don't think it looks like a knife. How could such a device cut anything? Even its shell-bone version on the left above may not look much like one of your knives. But look again. Grab the knife by the handle at the lower end. Don't be afraid of cutting yourself; the hand guard branching off to the left will prevent your hand from slipping up onto the sharp, curving blade at the top. By the time of the *Shuowen*, the picture had reached the stage shown on the right. The handle and hand guard are dominant, but the curving blade is still there. The modern character is all handle and hand guard with almost no blade. You were right; this modern knife without a blade won't cut anything!

 **ban4   aa 743   半 *half*; in the middle; very little; semi-**

There is only one bronze version of the character, and it is very like the *Shuowen* version shown on the right. It clearly shows a cow or bull on the bottom and something split apart to the left and right at the top. One might suppose that the bull, like the knife in 分, has split the something apart with its horns. The etymologists of the CCCC, however, see it the other way around. They interpret the "something split apart" to mean that the cow has been split apart, **halved**, presumably lengthwise.

今天   **jin1tian1   today**

 jin1 top 45 今 now, present, current

Sears has found no less that 186 versions of this character among the shell-bone inscriptions. They all look very similar to the one shown on the left. It is hard to draw a picture of *now*, so we may expect that we are dealing with a phonetic loan character (PLC). According to Wang (page 142), that is indeed the case. The character pictures a bell, with the clapper shown by the line at the bottom. (Over the years, a rope has been tied to the clapper.) A PLC, as we have seen, is often returned to its original meaning by adding a radical. In this case, that has not happened to 今 but to the very similar character, 令 ling4, which derives from a shell-bone character such as that shown on the right above depicting a man sitting under a bell and presumably giving orders, for the character means *order, command, law*. Adding the metal radical to it gives 铃 ling2, which means *bell*. Why was 令 rather than 今 restored to mean bell? The fact that the word for *order* and the word for *bell* still have the same pronunciation indicates that they have always had the same pronunciation. Maybe the commander sat next to the bell, gave an order and rang the bell, so that the orders were known as *bells*. To make clear that in a particular case the metallic bell itself was intended, a scribe added the metal radical to 令. On the other hand, the phonetic similarity between the word for *bell* (ling2) and the word for *now* (jin1), while perhaps greater at the time of the borrowing than now, was not perfect and the pronunciation of the two words diverged. It would therefore not make sense phonetically to "restore" 今 jin1 to mean "bell" ling2.

86

tian1   aa1314 天   **sky, heaven; natural;** *day*; **climate; season; over; most**

  This character is a picture of a man with his head – or what is above his head -- emphasized. Two shell-bone versions are shown on the left. In the first, the head is emphasized, and the character presumably meant *head.* In the second, the head has shrunk to a short line and what is above it, the sky or heavens, is emphasized. This version presumably meant *sky* or *heaven.* In the bronze characters shown below the shell-bone versions, the two versions persist, with most examples lacking the "sky". The *Shuowen* version, on the right, is ambiguous. Is that line on the top the sky fallen to rest on the man's neck or is it his head, flattened but emphasized? Given the meaning of the character, I see it as the sky. I would like to see in the character an assertion of the direct connection between man and the heavenly world, but I have to admit that there is slim etymological support for this idea.

The step from meaning *sky* and all its phenomena to meaning *day*, the chief of those phenomena, is easily understood. The word for astronomy, by the way, is 天文 tian1wen4, and 天气 tian1qi4 "sky air" means *weather.* The names for the seasons all begin with 天. And the most famous gate of Beijing is 天安门, Tiananmen, Heavenly Peace Gate.

明天 **ming2tian1 tomorrow**

明 **ming2 sun 3511** 明 **bright, clear; eyesight; gods;** *next* **(of days, weeks, months, years)**

 The component on the left, 日, we had in Lesson 1 and means *sun*. The component on right, 月 yue4, means *moon.* There are many shell-bone examples, of which the one on the left is fairly typical. The bronze characters are primarily of this form but a few examples, such as the lower figure on the left, hint what will happen with the *Shuowen* character, shown on the right, from which the modern version derives by the usual squaring off. In the radicode system, 月 is called the *moon* radical, although it usually represents etymologically not the moon but a piece of meat.

That the combination of sun and moon should mean *bright* seems a perfect example of an ideogram character, as explained on page 10. 明 has traditionally been so explained, but with the great increase in the number of known early examples there have arisen two problems. First problem: in the shell-bone inscriptions, the character, as shown in the upper example on the left, usually means *daybreak,* when the sun comes up and outshines the moon, which may, according to its phase, set. Second problem: the "sun" component often looks more like a window than the sun. This second problem is particularly pronounced among the bronze characters and LST seal characters such as the lower one on the left. These characters mean *bright*, but it is from the brightness of the room with the moon shining in the **window**.

The *Shuowen* gave characters of both types, both meaning *bright,* and both shown on the right. The window-moon version went out of use and the sun-moon version prevailed, perhaps precisely because of the seemingly evident ideogram etymology.

The fact that the Chinese use *bright day* and *bright year* to refer to tomorrow and next year certainly indicates a cheerful outlook.

昨天　**zuo2tian1　yesterday**

昨　**zuo2 sun 312** 昨 **yester- (as in yesterday, yesteryear), last (as in last week, last month)**

The sun radical alerts us that we are dealing with a time period, while the phonetic 乍 zha4 we met in the character 怎 zen3 (page 26).

时间　**shi2jian1　time**

时(時)　**shi2 sun 514** 时時 **o'clock;** *time;* **times, era; epoch; season; period; hour; sometimes**

 Traced back to the shell-bone stage, all the examples are very simple and very clear: a foot above the sun, as seen on the left. The foot represents movement. Time is movement of the sun. Only one bronze version is known; it preserves the idea of the foot over the sun. The *Shuowen* version on the right is typical of the seal characters. The sun has moved to the left and a hand has been added below the foot. The horizontal line at the wrist of the hand is a finger (from the other hand) on the pulse. One is reminded of Galileo using his pulse to time the swings of the chandeliers of the cathedral. Unfortunately, the *foot* is in the process of turning into *earth* 土 in the modern traditional. One could, of course, argue that time is measured by the position of the sun relative to the earth, so maybe the modern traditional is not so bad. The simplified kept the essence: the sun and the pulse.

 Meanwhile, a character originally meaning "to measure the motions of the sun and moon" has undergone a similar evolution. There are no known shell-bone examples, but there are several very similar bronze versions such as the one on the top left, showing a foot over a hand. An LST seal version, the middle character on the left, shows the addition of the finger on the pulse of the hand while the top remains arguably a foot. By the *Shuowen* version on the right, however, the *foot* has undeniably turned into *earth.* Another LST seal version, the third on the left, shows an interesting innovation, a gate radical enclosing the original two-component character. Although the gate did not catch on, it shows that the scribe who invented this version thought of the character as meaning a place behind a gate. Indeed, that was what the character had come to mean, and that place was a t*emple* or *monastery,* precisely what its modern descendant, 寺 si4 , has come to mean.

While this 寺 si4 can be thought of as a phonetic for 時 shi2 (the traditional form of 时) it clearly represents more than just sound. The modern simplified, 时, makes some sense as "checking the pulse of the sun," but it makes no sense phonetically, because 寸, meaning "inch, very short, very little" is pronounced cun4. It is, by the way, called the **inch radical** in the radicode system. The inch idea is said to come from the pulse being best felt an inch above the wrist.

间　jian1　gate 01 间　**between, among; space, room; classifier for rooms**

jian4, interval, space between two things.

The sun is peeking through *between* the gate posts. The character is not in the *Shuowen*, and no earlier examples are known. Perhaps that is why its origin is so clear.

时候　shi2hou time

候　hou4　man 25131 候 **wait, a period of time, season, visit**

In the radicode, the 2 stroke just to the right of the man radical is a component by itself and is therefore coded before the component on the right.

This is also a relatively new character not in the *Shuowen* or earlier writing. Its original meaning, according to the GHZ, was a *sentry* or *guard*. A sentry stands guard, waiting patiently, for for a set peried, and is then relieved. It was therefore a fairly short step to meaning *wait, a wait*, and thus *a period of time, a season.* Since a sentry is a man, the creator of the character knew it had to have a 亻 on the left. Casting about for a nice phonetic, he no doubt quickly decided on 侯 *hou2,* which had, as we shall see, a long and noble history. But the combination 亻 + 侯 looked strange with the two 亻 right together, so the second one was turned into just a vertical line. But the phonetic is for sure 侯.

This 侯 has a long pedigree with numerous examples from earliest times forward. A shell-bone version is on the left; it shows an arrow flying towards a target and means *target.* The bronze versions stayed close to this pattern, but the seal characters began to add a man at the top or on the left. The *Shuowen* did both, as can be seen in its version on the right above. The addition indicates a change in the meaning of the character, as explained in detail in CCCC. Men good at hitting the target came to be called *targets.* They were valuable to the kings or emperors, and were appointed into the nobility. In fact, *target* became the second highest noble rank, roughly equivalent to marquis. So addition of the *man* radical became quite appropriate. Use of the character in the normal sense of *target* disappeared, and that meaning of the character is not found in dictionaries of contemporary Chinese.

The combination 时候 "time + a period of time" to mean "time" is a typical example of bisyllabism. A more interesting use of 候 is 候鸟 hou4 niao3, a "period bird", a migratory bird that spends one period (or season) in one place and another period in a different place.

89

 **xing1qi1　week**

星　xing1 sun 371 星 **star, planet**

There are several shell-bone examples, such as the one on the left, showing stars as little squares combined with a 生 sheng1 to hint at pronunciation. In the one and only bronze example, the stars have become little suns and are directly connected to the 生 expressing their close relation to the plant world. The *Shuowen* gave three versions, one very like the bronze version, one similar to the first but without the lines through the circles, and finally the one shown on the right with only one star, the direct ancestor of the modern character.

期　qi1　moon 7213 期 **a scheduled time, issue number of a publication; hope; expect.**

The radicode is an example of the component rule. Three strokes were taken from the left half and then one from the right half.

期 is a radical+phonetic character. The left half is phonetic and appears in such characters as 其, 旗, 琪, 欺 and 棋, all pronounced qi. The connection of the moon with time seems natural enough, especially in a country where the traditional calendar relates to both the sun and the moon.[3] The question is, What is that phonetic picturing?

The key to this question lies in the last example, 棋, which is the only one to have a known bone-shell version. It is shown on the left. The character means wooden chess pieces. In the modern version, the tree radical – which we met on page 68 and indicates something wooden – is on the left. In the shell-bone version, it is at the top; and everything else is phonetic. At the bottom are two hands and above and between them something which according to the GHZ is a 簸箕 bo³ji¹, a winnowing basket. (簸 means *to winnow* and *winnowing fan*; 箕 means a *winnowing basket*. 簸箕 is bisyllablism.) In the modern character, the fingers of the two hands merged into one horizontal line while the wrists have become completely detached from the fingers. 其 qi2 by itself is now a phonetic loan character meaning *he, she, it, they* and *his, hers, its, their.* As you would expect, its frequency rank is high, and indeed, it is 85.

For our character, 期, the earliest examples are bronze and all fairly similar to the example shown on the left. The fingers of the two hands have already merged into a

---

3　In the traditional Chinese "lunisolar" calendar, the day begins at midnight, and a month begins on the day of the new moon. Thus some months will have 30 days and some 29 days. The winter solstice must occur in the 11th month giving year n 12 months would cause the solstice to occur in the 12th month of year n+1, then year n is given Thus, the calendar does not "crawl" significantly relative to the solar year, as did the Julian calendar. The new always on the first of the month and the full moon on the 14th or 15th of the month, so the tides are almost the same on the same day of any month. Some years, however, are a month longer than other years. This calendar is used in setting the dates of Chinese New Year and other festivals. Government and business in China use the Western Gregorian calendar.

straight line, but the wrists are still attached to the fingers. The basket is prominent, and the moon is the circle at the top. In the *Shuowen* version, on the right, the moon has moved to the right, the basket is clear, and the wrists are still attached to the fingers. An LST version lower right shows a step in the transition to the modern version.

We would not, however, know that the bottom of the figure had ever been two hands rather than some kind of stool or table were it not for the shell-bone version of 棋.

号 （號） **hao4 mouth 15** 号號 **number**

This character has two pronunciations with widely different meanings. Pronounced hao2, it means *to howl, shout, wail, cry*. The mouth radical makes perfect sense, and the howling tiger phonetic – remember 马马虎虎 ma3 ma hu3 hu – fits the sense wonderfully. The figure below the mouth is thought to represent the breath (the lower zigzag line) cut off by some blockage. In the Shuowen version on the right and in most other seal-character versions, it looks very like it does in the modern traditional character, except that the tiger has turned around. This hao2 pronunciation has the meaning that seems to best match the structure of the character.

The other pronunciation, hao4, basically means some sort of identification, thus a *mark, sign, date, house number, signal*. And from the signal idea, a *bugle*. This is the sense used in the text One sees it frequently in China preceding telephone or house numbers.

月 **yue4 moon** 月 **month, moon**

We have had 月 meaning *moon*, so it is no surprise that it also means *month*, which is really a *moon*.

上午 **shang4wu3 morning**

午 **wu3 aa 317** 午 **noon**

A phonetic loan character. It pictures a wooden pestle as in the shell-bone version on the left. It is returned to its original meaning by adding the tree radical in the character 杵 chu3 meaning precisely a wooden pestle.

下午 xia4wu3 afternoon

晚上 **wan3shang evening**

晚 **wan3 sun 350** 晚 **evening, night, late, younger, junior**

The Tale of the Tailless Rabbit

The sun radical is not surprising for any character related to the time of day, even if it is the time when the sun is *not* shining. The mystery of this character lies in the right side, 免 mian3, a rather remote phonetic. 免 always has something to do with *free*. It can mean, avoid, evade, escape, remain *free*. One common meaning is to remove someone from office, thereby setting him *free*. 免冠 mian3guan3 means bareheaded, *free* of a cap. 免费 mian3fei4 means *free* of charge. But what is 免 picturing?

The almost incredible answer is: a hare or rabbit without a tail! It is <u>not</u> a phonetic loan character but rather an ideogram. The idea is that the rabbit runs *free*; it survives by *escaping* and *evading* danger. The modern character for rabbit is 兔 tu4, the same as 免 except for the dot in the lower right corner, which is the remnant of the rabbit's tail. Now you may say that rabbits must look very different in China.

  They didn't used to. Two shell-bone versions are shown on the left. We recognize the first as a rabbit by the gesture of its paws; the second, by its big eyes and long ears. There are no bronze examples, but by seal-character times the rabbit had undergone a surreal transformation to emerge in the *Shuowen* as shown on the right. The big eyes are evident. The two leftmost lines reaching the bottom are the paws with the characteristic rabbit gesture; the tail is in the lower right corner; a floppy ear tops off the character. Or maybe the hook at the left end of the ear is really the second ear. Yes, the more you look at it, the more it looks like a rabbit. Certainly the scribe who wrote it knew that it was a rabbit. The big eyes, the two pairs of legs, the ears and the tail are all still in 免 once you see them. Next time you see a rabbit, think 免！

Presumably, the tail got dropped from 免 to distinguish the two characters.

And by the way, the fact that the rabbit is a nocturnal animal makes 免 fit all the better in 晚.

明年　　**ming2 nian2**　　**next year**

年　**nian2**　**aa 3172** 年 **year**

 This character is a picture of a man carrying grain, 禾, and originally meant *harvest*, from which it is a short step to meaning *year*. The shell-bone of the grain character is shown at the top on the left, and below it is a shell-bone version of 年. The idea of the man carrying grain can still be seen in some bronze characters such as the one on the bottom right. Here a short horizontal mark has been added to the man's body. Maybe it shows the burden in relation to the man, or a strap that holds the grain to his back. The *Shuowen* version, top right, preserves the grain element at the top, while the the horizontal line has been strengthened, as in a number of other seal characters. In the modern character, 年, the top two strokes appear to be a remnant of the grain. The central stalk of the grain has been joined to the man's body. The horizontal line has been emphasized while the man's arm has been cut off below the level of the line.

生日　**sheng1 ri4 birthday**

日　**ri4 sun**　日 **sun, day, daily, time; Japan.**

　The many shell-bone sun characters are mostly quite rectangular, but the one on the top left shows an effort to round the corners. Several of the bronze versions, such as the one on the lower left achieve a quite round sun, The *Shuowen* (top right) returns to a rather rectangular sun, and the line stretches all the way across. All of the early characters show the dot or line in the center, presumably to distinguish between a sun and a mouth.

课 (課)　**ke4 speech 071** 课 課 **class, lesson**

This is a radical+phonetic character. The speech radical seems natural enough for a character meaning *class, lesson*. The phonetic, 果 guo3, shows a tree bearing fruit and means *fruit,* also in the metaphorical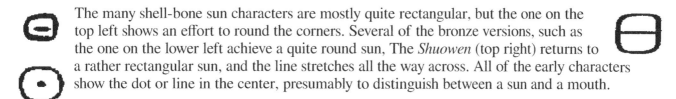

sense of *fruits of labor*. The examples are, left to right, shell-bone, bronze, and *Shuowen*. While guo3 seems rather remote from ke4 phonetically, the restored pronunciations of 果 in middle and old Chinese all begin with k.

手表　**shou3biao3 watch** (the time-keeping instrument)

手　**shou3 aa 3511** 手　**hand; handy; hold, engage; with one's own hands;**

someone good at something

The basic meaning is *hand*. The *Shuowen* version on the right is typical of most earlier versions.

表　**biao3 aa711346** 表 **outside, surface, show, a meter or watch.**

This is an ideogram. The top half of 表 is from 毛 mao2, *hair, fur, feather, down*. The bottom half is from 衣 yi1, *clothing, dress*. The picture is of a fur coat with the hair on the *outside*. The *Shuowen* version is on the top right; there are no examples before the seal characters.

　The 毛 character begins from a picture such as the bronze example on the left, which shows a *feather,* one of the meanings of the character. The *Shuowen* version is on the right. Folk etymology sometimes explains 毛 as a *beard,* which works for mnemonic purposes but is not accurate historically.

衣 **yi1 dressB** 衣 **clothing, dress.**

 The evolution of 衣 begins from numerous shell-bone examples such as the one on the left. It is thought to depict the top of a hooded jacket, with the hood above and the neckline below. By the *Shuowen* version, right, it was little changed. Obviously, there was a big step to the modern 衣.

 As for the combination of 毛 and 衣 into 表, it does not go back of seal characters. One of them, shown on the left, seems to be the ancestor of the modern character. The *Shuowen* version, on the right, puts the "feather" between the hood and the neckline, but the transition to the modern character pulled it back on top.

The 衣 character is the base of two radicals in the radicode system. In a contracted form, it appears on the left of a number of characters such as

袍 pao2 dress 35561 袍 robe, gown

where it is known as the **dress** radical. In a dozen or so characters, however, it appears in full form at the bottom of the character and is known as the **dressB** radical. A good example is 装, zhuang1, meaning to dress up, pretend, load, install, bind (a book), frame (a picture).

上班   shang4ban3 go to work

班   **ban3 jade 3417** 班 **class, team, a group of people organized for work or tudy; place of work or study, a work shift; classifier for groups of people.**

 The bronze version on the left shows a knife between two pieces of jade. The knife has cut or divided the jade. Hence the fundamental meaning of a division of something larger, usually a subgroup of people from a larger group. The *Shuowen* version, right, kept exactly the same idea, as does the modern version, except that the knife is no longer immediately recognizable as a knife.

下班   xia4ban3   leave work

看书   kan4shu1   read

每   **mei3   aa 31165** 每 **every, each**

We met and explained this character in the course of explaining the character 海 on page 69.

对不起   **dui4buqi3   sorry, excuse me (Lit.: right not happen)**

94

对 (對)   dui4   inch 54 对對 to set, adjust; right, correct; answer, respond; facing; mutual.

There are numerous elegant bronze versions of this ideogram character, all similar to the one on the left and showing a hand setting up or adjusting something, presumably making it *right* or *correct*. Wang thinks the something is a column; Sears thinks it is foliage. There are also LST seal versions fairly similar to the bronze versions, but there is no *Shuowen* version. The simplification replaced the ornamental 11-stroke left side of the traditional with a meaningless two-stroke placeholder. But since we don't what the that left side was, the loss is not great. The hand on the right is represented by the inch radical, though none of Sears's many examples have the "finger on the pulse" below the hand.

起   qi3 run 526 起 happen, occur; stand up, get up; begin; raise, build, set up

Here we meet for the first time the *run* radical, 走 zou3. While it is supposed to mean "walk, walk quickly, run", the fellow in the bronze version on the left hardly appears to be walking, so it is called the "run" radical in the radicode system. Below the runner is a foot or footprint, which often indicates motion. The *Shuowen* version, shown on the right, was little changed.

Our character has as a phonetic 己 ji3, which is thought to have originally meant "to unravel". In the *Shuowen* version on the right, the phonetic does indeed look like an unraveled thread.

As a mnemonic, try "You have to stand up to run; then things happen."

The expression 对不起 literally translated is "right not happen" or maybe "it is not right that this happened".

没关系   mei2 guan1xi4 don't mention it, it's all right

关 （關 関）   guan1 aa 431314 关 關 関 close, shut; frontier; critical juncture, link; connected.

This ideogram character is a picture of a double-doored gate blocking a road at a frontier barrier, or toll house, or customs collection point. The gate is shown from the inside. There are no known shell-bone examples. In the bronze version on the top left, two sticks prop the door shut. In the LST seal character below on the left, several elements have been added. The sticks are still there, and at the upper end of each there is a plate attached to the door to catch the upper end of the stick and prevent it from sliding upward if someone pushes against the door from the outside. Above the plate, there is a ring for opening the door. Below the plate is a crossbar that runs across the two door panels of the gate, thus bolting it shut. Once you see it, all that is very clear in this example. Sadly, not all scribes saw the picture so clearly. In the LST seal example on the top right, the scribe has seen in the ring and plate on each side a silk skein, bent the sticks into an utterly useless shape, and left only the cross bar to hold the gate shut.

Something like this version became the basis of the modern traditional form 關, where the silk skeins have turned into 幺 as they usually do in characters such as 糸 mi4. The bolt is broken; and the sticks, well, you can see for yourself. The next step, also modern, was from 關 to 関, where the picture under the gate is a contraction of what was previously there. With some imagination, you can still see the sticks, the bolt, the bottom line of the silk and the rest of the skein reduced to a dot. In the final simplification of the 1950s, the gate is swept away leaving only bent sticks, a bar and some silk thread to guard the frontier. To me, this is one of saddest character stories. A beautifully worked out picture was corrupted and virtually destroyed. The meaning, however, survives: close, shut, frontier, and a guarded mountain pass. Extended meanings include: critical juncture, link, and to be linked or connected.

系(系， 繫， 係)　　xi4 silkB 3 系 **bear on, relate to, connection, a school or university department**

The simplified character 系 represents three different modern traditional characters, each having its own meanings. In the first place, as a traditional character itself, it means *system, series, university department,* so something made of connected parts.. As the representative in simplified characters of 繫, it means *tie, bind, fasten, relate to, worry about,* and *lock up in prison.* As the representative of 係, it means *be, bear on, relate to.*

 The shell-bone ancestors of the traditional 系 include the one on the left and numerous others like it. The CCCC authors see this figure as showing that the hand is holding together knotted chords and hence the idea of binding together.

Wang has a much more intriguing explanation. He sees it as a hand above knotted chords tied together at the top. In the 16th century, the Spaniards found the Incas operating an empire without writing but with such bunches of knotted chords called *quipus.* The type and position of the knot recorded a number. Although no quipus have been found in China, our character and some literary references give reason to believe that similar devices were once used there. Among the literary references is a line from chapter 80 of the famous *Dao de Jing* (traditionally dated from the 6th century BC) where the sage is advocating imposing a simple life on people:

使人復結繩而用之、

There are various interpretive translations such as "Make the people return to the use of knotted cords instead of the written characters." A very literal, one-character-one-word translation would be: "Make people complex knot chord and use them."

The quipu theory fits well with the idea of something composed of connected parts, as well as with the idea of tying and binding.

 Bronze versions of the character remained very similar, such as the one on the left. The *Shuowen* version, on the right, kept a simplified hand, one chord with two knots but with an indication at the bottom that there might be more than one chord. From this version to the modern 系 is a short step. It is also clear why the scribes saw a silk radical below the hand, although historically what was there was not a skein of silk but a *quipu*.

The expression 没关系, idiomatically translated as "Don't mention it" or "It doesn't matter" might more literally be translated as "There's no connection" or perhaps, "There are no consequences."

早上   **zao3shang   early morning**

早   **zao3   sun 7 早 dawn, early morning**

甲   The GHZ says that this character is a ideogram combining a sun above with a helmet 昻
below. The *Shuowen* version of 甲 jia3, the helmet, is shown on the left. The
combination with the sun in the *Shuowen* version of 早 appears on the right. Now an ideogram has to combine features of the two components. So how does the *sun* combine with a *helmet* to indicate *dawn*? Well, see that T in the helmet? That is the man's face *peeking out,* just like the sun *peeks out* at dawn. (I didn't make this up; it is straight from the GHZ.)

中午   **zhong1wu3 midday, noon**

夜里   **ye4li   night**

夜   **ye4 hat 32 夜 night, evening**

夾   This character is connected etymologically with the rather different looking but similar sounding character 亦 yi4. From shell-bone forms down to the *Shuowen*, 亦 always looked essentially the same, a man with lines to emphasize the armpits, as shown in the in the *Shuowen* version on the left. And it meant *armpit.* Then it got phonetically borrowed to mean *also* in literary Chinese.

夾   Meanwhile, our character, 夜 ye4 meaning *night*, started off among the bronze 夾
characters as shown on the left. The moon is the meaning element and all the rest is phonetic, namely, the similar-sounding armpit character. This idea reached the *Shuowen* intact, as shown on the right. But the transition to the modern version was drastic. The man's head and arms flew off to make the *hat* radical across the top. The armpit mark on the left became a whole *man* radical, the moon became the 夕 on the lower right corner of 夜 and presumably all the rest of the man's body jumped into the moon, where it is now just a dot.

Now the *armpit* character, having been pressed into service as a PLC, had lost its original meaning. But armpits were still around, so a new character had to be created for them. While it would have made sense

97

to restore 亦, it was in fact our character, 夜, which got "restored" to mean something it had never meant. To indicate *flesh*, 月 was added to give 腋 ye4, meaning *armpit*. As we have mentioned before, 月, while meaning *moon* by itself, most frequently means *meat* or *flesh* in compounds.

里　li3 field 71 里　village, 500 meters, inside

In simplified characters, 里 is used in place of three traditional characters: 里, 裡, and 裏. The first, identical with the simplified character, is an ideogram, a combination of a rice paddy 田 on top and dry land 土 on the bottom. The original meaning was *village,* a place that had both types of land. It also came to mean a unit of length, now standardized as 500 meters. A bronze version is shown on the left, and there has been little change.

The other two characters, in which we recognize the *dress* and *dressB* radicals, both mean *inside*, presumably originally the inside of a coat or other garment, but now *inside* generally. They are of the radical-phonetic type, with the phonetic of 裡 being precisely our *village* character.

Thus, 夜里, "night inside" means simply "at night."

早饭	zao3fan4	breakfast
中饭	zhong1fan4	lunch
晚饭	wan3fan4	supper
去年	qu4nian2	last year
周末	zhou1mo4	weekend

周　zhou1　aa 35710 周　circumference, circle, cycle; week

There are numerous shell-bone examples of this character, all – like the one at the far left – showing a subdivided field with crops indicated by dots. In the bronze versions, such as the next example, a mouth has been added, presumably to eat those crops. There is great variety in the LST seal versions, but many add a border and replace the field by a simpler earth. The one shown on the left leads directly to the modern character. The addition of the border indicates that the emphasis was now on the boundary of the field, in line with the modern primary meaning of *circumference*. The *Shuowen* version is on the right, but it does not seem to lead to the modern character.

末　mo4 aa7134 末 tip end, end; minor details; dust

Just as in 本 a line was added to a picture of a tree to emphasize the bottom or *origin*, here we add a line to the top of the tree to emphasize the tip top.

起床　　**qi3chuang2 get up**

床　（牀）　**chuang2　shed 734**　　床 牀　**bed**

The object on the left of the traditional character is a bed stood on end. If it does not look like a bed to you, take the *Shuowen* version on the right and rotate it 90 degrees counter-clockwise. Now do you see the bed? The long line is the sleeping surface and beneath it are the feet of the bed. The tree is there, of course, because the bed is made of wood. The authors of the CCCC lament 床 as a vulgarism; it seems to show a tree growing in a shed.

睡觉　**shui4jiao4 sleep**

睡　　**shui4　eye 377**　睡　**sleep**

We met the eye radical 目 on page 42 in connection with the character 见 or 見. The idea here, of course, is that sleep is what we call in slang *shut-eye*.

The phonetic in 睡 is 垂 chui2, which we met on page 63. Recall that it means *to hang down, to let fall*. The hanging plant interpretation of the Shuowen version works fairly well. The pot is at the bottom, which happens to be the earth radical, the wire comes up the middle to a hook at the top, and the graceful foliage waves in the air. The foliage got a bit crushed in the transition to 垂. In 睡, it is another example of an appropriate phonetic; when our eyelids *hang down*, we go to *sleep*.

觉　（覺）　**jiao4 see 44**　觉 （覺）　**sleep**

This character has a dangerously split personality. Pronounced jiao4, as here, it means *sleep*. Pronounced jue2, it means *to sense, feel, wake up, become aware*. The structure of the character goes with the jue2 pronunciation. The bottom is the *see* radical, the eye on legs. The top shows hands cramming sensations into the eye. Perhaps the explanation of the contradictory meaning is that one wakes up, feels very aware, goes to class and falls asleep.

睡觉 *sleep-sleep* = sleep is, of course, bisyllabism.

开始 **kai1shi3 begin**

开（開） **kai1 aa 137** 开 開 **to open, start, begin, liberate, exploit, expand, develop**

The *Shuowen* has two forms, one is essentially the modern traditional, while the other, shown on the right, better reveals the sense. It shows two hands reaching up to remove the bar that keeps the gate shut. A vivid way to draw a picture of *to open!*

始 **shi3woman 640** 始 **begin, beginning**

 In this radical+phonetic character, the idea is that our physical bodies begin inside a woman. Two bronze versions are shown on the left. The upper one shows the woman plus a ladle-like figure; the second adds a mouth. The ladle-like figure became the modern 厶 si1, and is a quite good phonetic. (The *Shuowen* version of 厶 is on the right. It depicts not an object but an idea: being self-enclosed, private, shut off from the outside, complete in one's self.) Not content to let well enough alone, other scribes – still in the bronze inscriptions – added a mouth as in the lower figure on the left. The combination makes 台 tai1, which is a poor phonetic. It is an obsolete character meaning *private, not public*. The equivalent modern character is 私 si1, which is etymologically "private grain" but is used in the general sense of *private*. Just why the mouth was put into 始 is unclear. Maybe the combination on the right simply means "say 厶."

结束 **jie2shu4 end**

结 **jie2 silk 710** 结 **knot, tie, weave, conclude**

The silk radical is natural for the meaning. The right side is a phonetic 吉 ji2 meaning favorable, auspicious.

束 **shu4 aa 7034** 束 **bind, tie, hinder, restrain**

 The shell-bone version on the left seems to show a sheaf of grain bound in the middle, with the binding exaggerated for emphasis. The *Shuowen* version on the right has remained close to its origins, as has the modern version.

一般　yi1ban1　generally, usually

般　ban1 boat 365　般　way, like; sort, kind

This is an ideogram character. It shows a boat on the left and a hand with a stick propelling it on the right, as seen in the bronze version on the left. Older senses of 般 included *to move, to carry, to return.* To represent these ideas, the boat and the hand propelling it were a good picture. From those ideas, came the sense *way,* and from it, the other modern senses. But perhaps that thing on left does not look like a boat to you.

Well it is a boat all right – indeed it is the boat radical 舟 zhou1 – but it is standing on end. A bronze version of the boat character is shown on the left. From it we can see that the intention was to show only what was above the waterline and to represent a boat with a considerable structure above the deck, not a simple rowboat. On the right is the *Shuowen* version, which you must rotate nearly 90 degrees clockwise to make it look anything like a boat. You can see how the modern version was derived from it, though there seems to have been no effort to make it look like a boat.

星期　xing1qi1　week

A week is a "star period" because of the names of the days in the Roman calendar: Sun day, Moon day, Mars day, Mercury day, Jupiter day, Venus day, and Saturn day. The seven day week, with Babylonian origins, was used in the calendar introduced by Julius Caesar. The "star" names of the days were in use by the 2nd century AD. Although the star names are not used in China except for Sunday, the week remains a "star period."

Here are the conversations without the temptation to look at the pinyin.

请问，现在几点？现在七点三十分。谢谢。不客气。

请问，现在几点？对不起，我没有表，我不知道。没关系。

你每天几点上班？我每天八点上班。

你每天几点下班？我有时五点下班有时五点半下班。

你今天上午作什么？我今天上午在家看书。

下午呢？下午我去学校。

你昨天晚上在不在家? 不在。你在哪儿? 我在图书馆。
今天星期几? 今天星期三。今天记号? 今天二十八号。
你的生日是几月几号? 我的生日是十二月四号。

你星期几有中文课? 我星期三五有中文课.
你什么时候去中国学习? 明年。

Here they are in modern traditional characters.

請問，現在幾點？現在七點三十分。謝謝。不客氣。

請問，現在幾點？對不起，我沒有表，我不知道。沒關系。

你每天幾點上班？我每天八點上班。

你每天幾點下班？我有時五點下班有時五點半下班。

你今天上午作什麼？我今天上午在家看書。

下午呢？下午我去學校。

你昨天晚上在不在家？不在。你在哪兒？我在圖書館。

今天星期幾？今天星期三。今天記號？今天二十八號。

你的生日是幾月幾號？我的生日是十二月四號。

你星期幾有中文課？我星期三五有中文課.

你什麼時候去中國學習？明年。

And in the *Shuowen* font they are:

請問，現杜幾黠？現杜十黠三十分。謝謝。不客氣。

請問，現杜幾黠？對不起，我得有事，我不知道。沒關系。

你每天幾黠上班？我每天八黠上班。

你每天幾黠下班？我有時五黠下班有時五黠半下班。

你今天上午作什麼？我今天上午杜家看書。

下午呢？下午我去學校。

你昨天晚上杜不杜家？不杜。你杜哪兒？我杜圖書館。

今天星期幾？今天星期三。今天記號？今天二十八號。

你的生日是幾月幾號？我的生日是十二月四號。

你星期幾有中文課？我星期三五有中文課.

你什麼時候去中國學習？明年。

New radicals in Lesson 5: 走 run, 衤 dress, 衣 dressB, 寸 inch, 舟 boat

The total is now 57. air, arrow, **boat,** cart, child, door, **dress, dressB,** earth, eat, eatB, eye, field, fire, fireB, force, fowl, gate, go, grain**,** hat, head, heart, heartB, hit, horse, **inch,** jade, lance, man, meat, metal, moon, mount, mouth, old, ox, place, placeR, rain, rice**,** road, roof, **run,** see, shed, shell, silk, sir, speech, sun, tiger, tree, wall, water, white, and woman.

Lesson 6. Nationalities and Languages

英 **ying1 grass 325** 英 **flower, outstanding; English, England, British, Britain**

英 is an example of a country name represented by a character with a nice meaning and a sound somewhat reminiscent of the country's own name for itself. 英明 ying1 ming2 is *wise, brilliant*; 英雄 ying1 xiong2 is *hero,* 英勇 ying1 yong3 is *brave, bravery.* (And 勇 is the given name of our author, Yong Ho.)

艹 cao is the **grass radical**. It appears only at the top of a character. The names of most plants not big enough to have the tree radical (as on the left of 机) have the grass radical. Chinese is rich in these plant names; the *Quick Guide* has some 400 characters with this radical, about six percent of the total. In the full form of the grass character, 艸 cao, the roots and blades of the grass are still quite recognizable. The *Shuowen* version is shown on the right. No earlier forms are known. Though common as a radical, 艸 is rare as a character. In Jun Da's sample of 19 million characters from documents on the Internet, it appeared once.

The *Shuowen* version of 英 is shown on the right. The bottom of the character is the phonetic. It is the character 央 yang1, meaning *center, centered,* and showing a man carrying something on a shoulder pole. The man is in the *center* and must be careful to keep the load *centered* on his body. This character goes back to shell-bone origins where it appears as shown in the top character on the left. Rather strangely, the burdens seem to be *above* the pole. The LST seal version, bottom left, has adopted the more conventional system with the loads hanging down from the pole. The *Shuowen* version is identical to the bottom of the character on the right.

语 （語） **yu3 speech 125** 语 **language, tongue, proverb, say, speak , talk, gesture**

The speech radical fits the meaning. The phonetic, 吾 wu2, means *I, we*. In it, 五 is phonetic while the mouth is the mouth of the speaker, thus suggesting the meaning of *I, we.* 五 by itself would be an adequate phonetic for 语, but adding the mouth makes it more appropriate. The earliest known examples of 语 are bronze versions such as shown on the leftl; the *Shuowen* version is on the right. Recall the etymology of 五(page 77) and note its form on the top right of this *Shuowen* form.

法（灋）　fa3 water 716 法 law, way, dharma; standard, model; France, French

This is yet another example of naming a country with a nice character that faintly echoes the sound of its own name for itself. In this case, the character is deeply rooted in Chinese mythic history. In *The Chinese Unicorn*, Jeannie Thomas Parker writes:

> According to an ancient Chinese legend, long, long ago, before history began, the land was ruled by the great Emperor Shun. He was the last in the series of five culture heroes who ruled prior to the establishment of the first historical dynasty, the Xia. Each of his predecessors was famous for inventing rules and regulations designed to improve the organization of human society. But Shun's innovation was perhaps the greatest of all. For, with the able assistance of his Minister of Justice, Gao Yao, he formulated the first law code. Gao Yao was a very wise counsellor, but sometimes, when even his acumen was baffled, he would appeal to his infallible one-horned goat, 廌 zhi4, to butt the guilty person with its horn.[If the accused was guilty, it would butt; but if innocent, it would not.]

> An early version of this ancient tale, which dates to the first part of the Eastern Han Dynasty, appears among the writings of the scholar Wang Chong (c.27-100 C.E.) His account is found in Lun Heng (The Scale of Discourse) Part 2, in the Shi Ying (Auguries Verified) section, Book 17, Chapter 2, (Forke, 1962), and its new translation by James Hsü reads as follows:

> "At present in the courtyards of public buildings, Gao Yao's 解廌 xie4zhi4 is painted, and scholars declare that the xiezhi is a goat with one horn, which by instinct knows the guilty. When Gao Yao, administering justice, was doubtful about the guilt of a culprit, he ordered this goat to butt it. It would butt the guilty, but spare the innocent. Accordingly, it was a sage animal born with one horn, a most efficient assistant in judicial proceedings. Therefore did Gao Yao held it in high respect, using it on all occasions. Consequently, it belonged to the class of supernatural creatures of good omen." (Chinese characters added.)

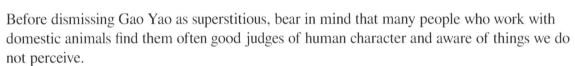

The *Shuowen* ancestor of 法 is shown on the top right, while the *Shuowen* version of Gao Yao's goat is just below it. In the top right corner of the character meaning *law,* there is the goat! If the *Shuowen* version of 廌 does not look to you like a goat, compare it element-by-element with the one of its numerous shell-bone ancestors shown below it. The horn is at the top; the head has become the horizontal U and the neck extends down the lower left side. The back, four legs, and tail are in the lower right. What more should a goat have?

Before dismissing Gao Yao as superstitious, bear in mind that many people who work with domestic animals find them often good judges of human character and aware of things we do not perceive.

Returning to the whole *Shuowen* character at the top right, we see on the left opposite the goat, *water*. And at the bottom, a *man* above his footprint, representing his deed – or misdeed. The character is a beautiful ideogram. The *law* is above the individual man and his actions; it should have the evenness of water and the unerring judgment and force of Gao Yao's goat.

In the transition from the *Shuowen* to an early modern traditional, 灋, the water idea survived, the horn and neck of the goat turned into the *shed* radical (an idea totally extraneous to the original), the head and body of the goat survived fairly well, and the man and his deed slid under the shed and turned into the earth radical over something. In the simplified character, 法, sad to say, all trace of the wonderful goat is gone.

The legend of the one-horned goat, however, moved on to India, Arabia, and Europe, where it appeared as the wonderful Unicorn which you can see in the great tapestries in the Cloisters museum at the north end of Manhattan.

Gao Yao's goat as the Unicorn in Captivity. The Cloisters. Image from Wikipedia.

德 **de2 road 70** 德 **virtue, good conduct, morals, heart, mind, kindness; Germany, German (Deutsch)**

  Another nice name for a country. There are three components, the road radical (page 23), the heart (page 26), and the component in the upper right corner meaning "straight". This is another ideogram. To go one's way with a straight heart, that is surely virtue, good conduct, and a life filled with kindness. We need to trace only the "straight" component. In the shell-bone characters it is an eye looking *straight* ahead, as indicated by a line jutting out from the eye (top left). The *Shuowen* character (lower left) has rotated the eye 90 degrees and crossed the line that emanates from it and added yet another line at the bottom, which, however, is strangely not straight. The modern descendant of this character is 直 zhi2, meaning *straight.* In it, the bottom line has fortunately been straightened but unfortunately merged with the eye. In our character, 德, however, the eye was not rotated and the added line was made straight. Its *Shuowen* version is on the top right.

西班牙 Xībānyá   España (Spain)

The characters are used solely for their sound. We have had 班(page 94) and will come back to explain the other two when their meaning matters. The meaning, however, is not so complimentary as in the case of Germany, France, England and America; it is West Class Tooth!

广州 Guang3 zhou1 Guangzhou = Canton (the city)

广（廣） guang3 shed 广 vast, wide, numerous, spread, Guangzhou.

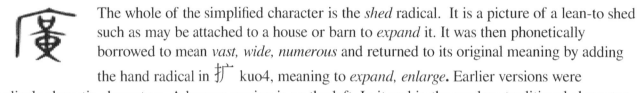

The whole of the simplified character is the *shed* radical. It is a picture of a lean-to shed such as may be attached to a house or barn to *expand* it. It was then phonetically borrowed to mean *vast, wide, numerous* and returned to its original meaning by adding the hand radical in 扩 kuo4, meaning to *expand, enlarge.* Earlier versions were radical+phonetic characters. A bronze version is on the left. In it and in the modern traditional character, under the shed is the phonetic element 黄 huang2, meaning *yellow,* which we will discuss when discussing its meaning.

州 zhou1 aa 3224 州 a former administrative division which survives in place names.

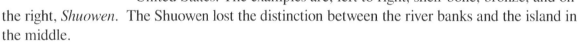

A pictograph showing an island in a river, hence a separate area, a state or administrative district. The Chinese use 州 to refer to the states of the United States. The examples are, left to right, shell-bone, bronze, and on the right, *Shuowen.* The Shuowen lost the distinction between the river banks and the island in the middle.

广东 Guang3 dong1 Canton (the province)

东（東） 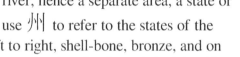 dong1 aa 615 东 east

xi1 aa 1360 西 **west**

The two characters, 東 and 西, have rather beautiful folk etymologies. 東, it is said, shows the sun behind a tree. If you arrive at night in an unfamiliar place and look out the next morning and see the sun behind a tree, you know you are looking *east*. Even the *Shuowen* says that 西 shows a bird on a nest, and "The bird is on its nest when the sun is in the *west*." Unfortunately, both etymologies are quite wrong and break down as soon as we look at earlier versions of the characters. The shell-bone, bronze and *Shuowen* versions of 东 are shown down the left side of this paragraph and the corresponding versions of 西 are shown down the right. Both characters are PLCs and depict *things* wrapped up for carrying. In the Shouwen version of 西, the long line probably represents the cord for tying the pack, not the bird above its nest. Neither 东 nor 西 seem to have been returned to their original meaning by adding a radical, but the common bisyllabic expression 东西 means, not *east-west*, but *thing*. The "simplification" from 東 to 东 is from both an aesthetic and etymological perspective most unfortunate. The beautiful and beloved symbol of the Orient has been smashed. The well-tied bundle has been ripped open, the *things* have all spilled out and are lost, and only the torn bag is left.

四川 **Sichuan, a province in southwest China (formerly spelled Szechuan).**

While most people suppose that the name refers to the four major rivers in the province, historical scholars believe that it refers to circuits on four plains.

 chuan1 ab 322 川 **river, plains**

The first of the oracle-bronze- Shouwen sequence on the left shows that in this pictograph the middle line represents the water and the outer two lines are the banks of the river.

香港 **Xiang1 Gang3, "Fragrant harbor" = Hong Kong.**

"Hong Kong" approximates the Cantonese pronunciation. The name 香港 was originally applied only to a harbor, now called Aberdeen, at the west end of the south side of Hong Kong island where the shore was once lined with shops producing incense.

香 **xiang1 grain 01** 香 **fragrant, tasty, appetizing, spicy**

 The shell-bone version of the character shows grain over a mouth (not a sun), as shown on the left. The connection between grain+mouth and "tasty, appetizing" is clear enough. Since things that are tasty and appetizing are also often fragrant, the extension to that meaning is also natural. In all of the known seal characters, including the *Shuowen* version on the right, the mouth has turned into a sun.

港 **gang3 water 7215** 港 **harbor, port**

The water radical is natural for the meaning. The right-hand side, 巷 xiang4, is a fairly remote phonetic, but it also contributes to the meaning. A 巷 is a narrow lane, an alley. Some harbors – and in particular, the Aberdeen harbor on Hong Kong island – are just that: a water lane. 巷 is a combination of two parts. On the bottom is a simplified version of 邑 yi4, meaning town, which we met on page 58 in connection with 哪. The top of 巷 is 共 gong4, meaning common, shared, showing two hands lifting something together. The Shouwen version is on the right; there are numerous similar bronze and seal versions. So a 巷 is the common, shared parts of a town, namely, the streets. And a 港 is a water street, that is, a harbor.

言 **yuan2**

We met this character in connection with the speech radical on page 24.

普通话 **pu3 tong1 hua4, the standard national language of China; Mandarin.**

The etymology of the word *Mandarin*, by the way, has nothing to do with Chinese. It was picked up in the 1580s by Portuguese traders from Malaysian traders who had gotten it from Hindi traders as a word for Chinese officials and advisers. The Sanskrit root is *mantri*, meaning basically *thinker*. Mandarin as the name of a color comes from the color of the robes of these officials. And the mandarin orange gets its name from its color.

普 **pu3 sun 431** 普 **universal, general**

This is an ideogram. The Shouwen character on the left, ancestor to the top of 普, shows two *equal* men and means *equal, on the same level*. The Shouwen version of 普 on the right shows *equal* above the sun. So the meaning of the character is *equal to the sun,* that is to say, *universal, general.* (The Shouwen character on the left evolved into the traditional character 並 bing4 meaning *side-by-side, even, together, and, furthermore.* As a very common character (frequency rank 141) *it* got simplified to 并, but the simplification was not systematically carried through to 普.)

通 **tong1 go 542** 通 **open, through, connect, understand, clear, accessible**

The *go* radical (page 27) certainly fits the basic senses of *open, connect*. The 甬 is a picture of a bell and appropriately represents the sound *dong* or *tong*. (甬 is now pronounced yong3 and is a PLC meaning 5 pecks.)

话 **hua4 speech 370** 话　**speech, language, word, talk**

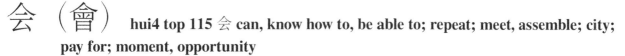

The speech radical (page 24) is clearly appropriate. The right-hand side, 舌 she2 is the **tongue radical,** and is a picture of a mouth with a tongue sticking out. A shell-bone example is shown on the left and the *Shuowen* is on the right. Rather strangely, the tongue is forked or crossed in all examples.

国语 **guo2 yu3 national language**

Both characters have already been covered.

会　(會)　**hui4 top 115** 会 **can, know how to, be able to; repeat; meet, assemble; city; pay for; moment, opportunity**

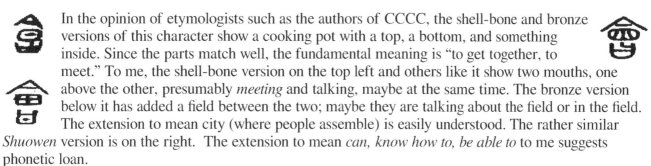

In the opinion of etymologists such as the authors of CCCC, the shell-bone and bronze versions of this character show a cooking pot with a top, a bottom, and something inside. Since the parts match well, the fundamental meaning is "to get together, to meet." To me, the shell-bone version on the top left and others like it show two mouths, one above the other, presumably *meeting* and talking, maybe at the same time. The bronze version below it has added a field between the two; maybe they are talking about the field or in the field. The extension to mean city (where people assemble) is easily understood. The rather similar *Shuowen* version is on the right. The extension to mean *can, know how to, be able to* to me suggests phonetic loan.

说 **shuo1 speech 430** 说 **speak, say, discuss, explain**

The speech radical is natural. The right side is 兑 dui4, meaning to exchange, barter. Shell-bone versions such as the one on the left show a man with a very big mouth shouting out something, presumably about the wares he has to offer. The sloping lines on either side of his head may represent his hands held up to make his voice carry. The Shouwen (说文) version on the right preserves these basic features, as does the modern version. Notice that in this case the right side of the character contributes only to its meaning, not at all to its sound. We now know both of the characters used in writing "Shuowen": 说文.

用 **yong4 aa 3571 用　use; need, expenses; eat, drink; hence, therefore**

Sears and the CCCC etymologists see in shell-bone figures such as the one on the left a bucket or tub. Since either was very much *used*, the figure came to mean, they argue, *use*. Wang thinks the object depicted may have been a been a bell, possibly of bamboo, and came to mean *use* by phonetic loan. There is remarkably little change from the shell-bone version on the left and the *Shuowen* version on the right.

懂 **dong3 heart 723 懂　understand, know**

This is a radical+phonetic character with a phonetic which contributes to the meaning. Understanding is a matter of the heart, so the heart radical (page 26) is natural. The right side is phonetic. The lower part, 重 zhong4, meaning *heavy,* is related etymologically to 东 (東). In an LST seal version on the left we see a man at the top presumably lifting a bundle of *heavy things.* 重 got combined with the grass radical to make 董 dong3, which must have been the name of an herb, but it was quickly borrowed phonetically to mean *direct, supervise, director*. Directors and supervisors need to *know and understand* what they are doing.

慢 **man4 heart 010 慢 slow, cold, unenthusiastic; slowly**

This is a radical + phonetic character with the heart radical on the left. Enthusiasm is certainly a matter of the heart, so a lack thereof must also be heart-related. The right side of 慢, 曼 man4, is a perfect phonetic, but it may also contribute to the meaning. Its own meaning is *drawn-out* as in *slow and long-drawn-out* – which fits nicely with the meaning of 慢. But 曼 can also mean *delicately made*. The hand at the bottom does the making or the drawing out; the top is phonetic 冒 mao4. Originally a picture of a hat pulled down around a man's forehead and eye – as in the *Shuowen* version on the left – it was phonetically borrowed to mean *brave, rash, incautious* . I don't think it is sound etymology, but when I see that cap all pulled down, I think it must be *cold* – and that helps me remember the meaning of 慢.

From the Shuowen version of 慢 on the top right we see that there has been virtually no change in this character over two millennia. There are no earlier versions and no LST examples.

只 (只, 隻) zhi3 mouth 34 只 but, only; (a classifier)

In the simplification of the 1950s, the traditional character 只 had loaded onto it, besides its own meanings, those of the homophone 隻. In traditional characters, 只 has the meaning of *but* and goes back only to the Shuowen version shown on the right. It is probably a picture of the idea of *but*. The mouth above has just said something, but now comes a separation, (八) a distinction and clarification.

 隻 shows a hand holding *one* bird and goes back to shell-bone versions. It is used as a classifier for one element of a pair (the classifier for pairs is 雙 shuang1) and for certain animals such as birds, dogs, cats, spiders, and bees and for boats and containers. A shell-bone example is on the far left; a bronze example is on the near left, and the Shuowen version on the right.

从 cong2 ab3434 从 follow, obey, participate; from

The LST seal version on the left shows two people, one following the other. Hence the meaning of *follow, obey*, Just how it came to mean *from* is less clear. Perhaps we can imagine that the two fellows must be coming *from* somewhere.

种 zhong3 grain 20 seed; kind, sort

For the meaning *seed* and the sound *zhong*, this is the perfect character. And the seed determines the kind or sort of plant which grows from it.

外 wai4 ab 35424 外 outside, foreign

The left side is a picture of the moon, while the right side is the crack in the bone or shell used in scapulimancy. We have already met the moon in 名 and the crack in 店. There seems to be no agreement on the etymology, so we may as well make up our own mnemonic: if the fortune telling was done by moonlight, it must have be *outside*.

俄 e2 man 364 俄 very soon, instantly, shortly, unexpectedly; Russia, Russian

This character is used to write foreign place names beginning with O, such as Oregon or Oklahoma. English speakers might expect one of the several nice characters pronounced *ru* to be used for Russia. But the Russian word for Russia is Rossiya, and there are no Chinese characters pronounced *ro* or *ra*. So the r was dropped totally, and the character 俄 was used. The character is of the radical-phonetic type. 我 wo3 is a fair phonetic and the man in the radical is presumably the one who does something unexpectedly or instantly.

韩国 Han2guo2 Korea

The Korean word for Korea is Hanguk.

韩 (韓) Han2 ab 7017 韩 one of the states of the Warring States period; Korea

The left side is phonetic, from the left side of gan4, meaning *dawn* and showing the sun rising. The right side is a picture of the woof of a loom and may indicate that the state of Han was known for weaving. The woof is the thread on the shuttle that goes back and forth in the weaving process. In the *Shuowen* character, top right, the top is the top of the loom, the vertical line is the warp, and the oval is the cloth being woven. Above the cloth is a foot going to the left and below the cloth is a foot going to the right, thus depicting the back and forth movement of the shuttle. All that is still fairly clear in the traditional but is pretty much lost in the simplified version.

字 zi4 roof 51 字 word, Chinese character

A child under a roof, phonetically borrowed to mean *word* or *character*. A bronze version is shown on the left; the Shuowen on the right.

报纸 bao4 zhi3 newspaper

报 (報) bao4 hand 52 报 inform, report; newspaper; repay

Sears reports no shell-bone versions of this character, but the CCCC gives two versions (shown on the left) which are critical to its interpretation. They show a kneeling figure with hands in handcuffs and, on the right, a floating hand, presumably that of the jailer. The original meaning was to sentence an offender, but to do so his crime had to be made known. Hence the meaning of "inform, report." The bronze version shown bottom left preserves the culprit, the

hand, and the complicated drawing of handcuffs. But, without the shell-bone version, one would never guess that it represents handcuffs because the culprit's hands are not in it; indeed, he has no hands. The *Shuowen* version, top right, preserves these elements, and the modern traditional remains close to it. The simplified character, with rather remarkable insight, replaces the complicated but unrecognizable drawing of handcuffs with just the *hand* radical.

纸 zhi3 silk 366 纸 **paper; classifier for papers, documents**

This is a radical+phonetic character. The silk radical (page 34) seems natural enough since silk can be used in paper or can be written on. The right side, 氏 shi4, is phonetic. There are dozens of shell-bone examples, such as the one on the top left. All show a man bent over and carrying something, maybe a bag or basket. It has been phonetically borrowed to mean *surname, mister*. The bronze version in the center on the left shows some relation to the original picture, but more commonly the many bronze examples look like the bottom example on the left, where the original sense is completely lost. The writers of the seal characters clearly had no idea what they were drawing. The *Shuowen* version on the right is typical; the bent man is barely recognizable, and his burden has become larger than he himself.

氏 is used as a phonetic in several characters pronounced *zhi* or *shi*, but none of them except 纸 are common.

杂志 za2 zhi4 **magazine**

杂 （襍,雜） za2 aa3651 杂 **to mix, mingle; mixed, miscellaneous**

This is an ideogram character. The etymology is fairly clear from the first traditional version. On the right is the character 集 ji4, a bird in a tree. We need to imagine, however, that there are many birds *assembled* in the tree, for the character means *assemble, gather, collect*. The element on the left is *dress* (see page 94). It is also used for various things of cloth. So the idea is to assemble various cloths, hence to mix, combine.

In the second traditional version, the tree has slipped out from under the bird and is under the cloths, which are no longer a standard radical but look like cloths hanging on a line. The simplification cut out the bird altogether and replaced the cloths with 九 jiu, perhaps intended to look like one cloth but meaning, as we know, the number 9. Perhaps we can just remember 杂 as a most *mixed up* character.

志 zhi4 sir 64 志 **aspiration, ideals; keep in mind, remember; annals, records**

The *Shuowen* version on the right shows a plant arising from a heart – a pretty good picture of an ideal or aspiration. Ideals need to be kept in mind, remembered. Things we want to remember we put in *annals, records*. The plant, however, turned into the sir radical.

So *magazines* are miscellaneous *mixed records*.

新闻 xin1 wen2 news

新 xin1 ax 414 新 new, recent; newly wed

 This is a phonetic loan character which originally meant *firewood*. In this meaning, it was an ideogram character showing a tree and an ax. The **ax radical** 斤 jin1 is a picture of a stone hatchet. The top and left side is the frame, the T is the stone. A shell-bone version, top left, shows the stone clearly. The bronze examples have already become more abstract, as shown on the right in an example very like the modern version.

 A shell-bone example of the ideogram meaning *firewood* is shown on the left; the fanciful Shuowen version is on the right. When it was phonetically borrowed to mean *new*, the character 薪 was invented by adding the grass radical to restore the drawing to its original meaning of *firewood*.

闻 wen2 gate 12 闻 hear, news, story, reputation; to smell.

An ear at the gate; what better picture for *hear, tell, news, story*!

 Yes, 耳 er3 is an ear, and in fact, the ear radical. Some shell-bone examples such as the one on the top left, look something like a human ear. The bronze examples, such as the lower figure on the left, become more abstract and decorative. The *Shuowen*, very abstract, version is on the right. A typical ear word is

聆 ling2 ear 344 聆 listen, hear

电视 dian4 shi4 television

视 (視) shi4 altar 253 视 see, look, inspect

This is a radical+phonetic character. The radicode system demands that we take the left side as the radical, but in this character it is actually the phonetic, the radical form of 示 shi4, a picture of an altar with a sacrifice on it. The right side – the eye on legs, the *see* radical – is the meaningful component. The Shuowen version is on the right.

Television is "electric seeing."

会话 hui4 hua4 conversation

Remember the *meet, assemble* part of the meaning of 会 and the *talk* part of the meaning of 话.

生词 **sheng1 ci2 new word**

词 **ci2 speech 510** 词 **word**

This is a radical+phonetic character. The speech radical clearly fits the meaning. 司 si1 is phonetic but contributes to the meaning. As we have seen, 公司 means "company, Inc." But recall the shell-bone version, repeated here on the left, showing a man pointing with his arm and barking out orders with his mouth. He is clearly using *words*. All elements have survived in 司.

语法 **yu3 fa3 grammar, "language law"**

句子 **ju4 zi3 sentence**

句 **ju4 wrap 0** 句 **sentence**

A sentence is a sort of wrapped up bundle of words coming out of a mouth. Since 句 by itself means *sentence,* why add the 子? Perhaps it is a sort of bisyllabism. There being a number of characters pronounced ju4 – the *Quick Guide* has 23 – perhaps the 子 was added as a kind of diminutive to distinguish this ju4 from all the others. So a 句子 is a little bundle from a mouth.

练习 lian4xi2 **exercise**

练 （練） **lian4 silk 615** 练 **white silk, to boil and scour raw silk to make it white; to practice, train**

The silk radical for the first meaning is natural. The phonetic exists as a character only in the traditional form 柬, is pronounced jian3, and means *letter, invitation,* but that must be a phonetic borrowing. Originally, very like 東, it meant a bundle of things tied up. How white silk or the process of making it came to mean practice I can only guess. Maybe the idea is that practice, like the boiling of the silk, improves the quality of the product. Recall 习 xi2 meaning *practice* from page 75. The *Shuowen* version of 练 is on the right.

练习 is practice + practice = exercise.

书法 **shu1 fa3 calligraphy, "book model"**

词典 **ci2 dian3 dictionary**

典 **dian3 aa 222 典 rule, law, book, standard work**

 In its shell-bone forms, this pictogram character show two hands holding something, presumably something with writing in vertical lines. The hands merged but the top stayed nearly the same. The *Shuowen* version is at right.

A 词典 is a *Wörterbuch,* a word book, a dictionary. The Chinese also have a 字典, a character book, which concentrates on individual characters rather than the detailed meaning of thousands of two- or three-character words.

写 (寫) **xie3 roof0 5 写 write**

The character is of the radical+phonetic type. The roof radical presumably just indicates that writing is usually done under a roof. The phonetic under the roof , 舄 xi4, today means *shoe, shoe sole* or *alkaline soil*. It is clearly not a picture of any of them, so in these meanings the character is a phonetic loan. Sears, however, gives also quite a different meaning which must be its original meaning: *magpie*! Wiktionary.org gives *magpie* in addition to the others. And *magpie* fits the early versions of the character, which are definitely bird-like. There are no shell-bone examples, but two of numerous bronze examples are shown on the left. The *Shuowen* version of 写 is shown on the right. As the character for *magpie*, 舄 has been largely replaced by 喜鹊 *happy magpie* in modern Chinese.

听 (聽) **ting1 mouth 3312 听 hear, listen; obey**

The modern simplified version, mouth+ax, must surely be one of the strangest representations of *listen* that one could imagine. Of course, it is not totally ridiculous because 厅 has the pronunciation *ting,* and maybe we should think of listening *to* the mouth, not *with* it. The shell-bone versions were all quite natural: an ear listening to one or more mouths, as shown on the top left. Bronze versions, such as the one on the bottom left, kept the same idea. There is no *Shuowen* version, but other seal-character versions, such as the one on the right, have dropped the mouth and added the phonetic we met in 德 de2 on page 107. There we saw that it meant *straight heart*. To truly listen, we need a straight heart, not one bent by our own objectives. The GHZ suggests that it has the sense of 意 yi4, *thought, idea, intention, meaning.* Now there is a nice idea! When we truly listen, we pick up the thoughts, ideas, intentions, and meaning of the speaker. Perhaps it is the speaker who appears in the lower left corner (of the seal character on the right) standing on earth 土. All of this survived into the modern traditional version.

翻译 fan1 yi4 translate

翻 fan1 ab374541 翻 flit about, cross, turn upside-down; translate

番 fan1 is a fairly common and reliable phonetic element as can be seen in this partial list of characters, all pronounced *fan,* in which it is the phonetic:

翻 幡 蕃 璠 藩 籓 燔 鐇 墦 轓 繙 蹯 膰 鷭.

There are no shell-bone examples. In the bronze characters, such as the one shown on the left, most sources see an animal track at the edge of field. Sears, however, sees rice grains above a winnowing or sorting pan. The *Shuowen* showed the version on the right, where the top part looks rather rice-like but it was interpreted as an animal track in a field. The CCCC authors adhere to the animal track theory and add that from the alternating motion of the feet, it came to mean "to alternate." It was restored to the "animal foot" meaning by adding the leg radical in 蹯. The ancient Han people were no more racially broad-minded than most peoples of the time and referred to minorities within their realm as 番 – "animal feet."

In our radical+phopnetic character, 翻, 番 is phonetic and the two wings, 羽 yu3 (meaning *feather*) are the meaning component for the basic meaning of "to flit about." From flitting about to turning upside-down is an easy step. From "to turn upside-down" to "to translate" is a transition easily understood by anyone who has done much translation.

译 （譯） yi4 speech 547 译 to translate

This is a radical+phonetic character. We met the lower part of the right side of the traditional version, 罩, in the character 報 on page 114, where it represented handcuffs. The full right side of the traditional is one of the basic *phonosemantic* elements identified by Lawrence J. Howell in his sinographs.kanjinetworks.com website. It shows an *eye* over *handcuffs.* Howell gives 罩 the meaning "to align and inspect prisoners" and then interprets a number of other characters (mostly pronounced *yi4*) as involving some form of aligning, in our case, aligning words in one language with words in another. This website is cited hereafter as Sinographs.

回答 hui2 da2 answer

回 hui2 wall 0 回 wind around; go back; answer

The *Shouwen* has two versions, one shown on the left and one on the right. The one on the left pictures the *wind around* meaning perfectly, and the other meanings derive from it. The version on the right, direct ancestor of the modern version, just simplified the picture. In traditional characters, the *wind around, circle* sense of this simplified character is represented by the character 迴, which just adds the **go** radical.

答 **da2 bamboo 3410** 答 **answer, respond; return, repay**

This character is not in the *Shuowen*, but there are several LST seal versions. The one closest to the modern character is shown on the left. The Wiktionary entry for 合 says that it shows two mouths speaking to one another, thus *answering and responding* to one another. The bamboo radical – which we meet for the first time here – may refer to writing on bamboo slips.

The Sinographs website will have none of this and instead offers: "fit/fasten a cover upon a bamboo vessel. 'Answer' in the sense of an answer corresponding to a question in the manner of a lid corresponding to a container." Take your choice.

Conversations Without Pinyin

你是中国人吗？　　是。

你也是中国人吗？　　我不是，我是日本人。

对不是。　　　没关系。

你是哪国人？　　我是中国人。

你太太呢？　　她是英国人。

你从哪儿来？　　我从法国来。

你是法国人吗？　　不是。我是德国人。

你是哪儿人？　　我是上海人。

你太太也是上海人吗？　　不是。她是广州人。

你会说广东话吗？　　我懂广东话，但是不会说。

你太太会说广东话吗？　　她会。

你太太会说英语吗？　　会。

你爸爸呢？　　他不会。

你妈妈呢？　　她会一点儿。

你会说几种语言？　　我会说四种语言。

哪四种？　　英语，法语，西班牙语，和一点儿中文。

请问，Mandarin 用中文怎么说？ Mandarin 用中文说普通话。

"四川话"　是什么意思？　　"四川话"的意思是 "Sichuan dialect."

谢谢。

不客气。

请问，中国银行在那儿？

对不起，我不懂你的话。清再说一遍。

你知道中国银行在那儿吗？　　知道。　　中国银行在中国城。

谢谢。

不谢。

请问，男厕所在那儿？　　在五楼。

谢谢。　　不客气。

香港人说什么话？　　香港人说广东话。

你会不会说广东话？　　我懂广东话但是我不会说。

In modern traditional characters:

你是中國人嗎？　　是。

你也是中國人嗎？　　我不是，我是日本人。

對不是。　　　沒關系。

你是哪國人?　　我是中國人。
你太太呢?　　她是英國人。

你從哪兒來?　　我從法國來。
你是法國人嗎?　　不是。我是德國人。

你是哪兒人?　　我是上海人。
你太太也是上海人嗎?　　不是。她是廣州人。
你會説廣東話嗎?　　我懂廣東話，但是不會説。
你太太會説廣東話嗎?　　她會。

你太太會説英語嗎?　　會。
你爸爸呢?　　他不會。
你媽媽呢?　　她會一點兒。

你會説幾種語言?　　我會説四種語言。
哪四種?　　英語，法語，西班牙語，和一點兒中文。
請問，Mandarin 用中文怎麼説? Mandarin 用中文説普通話。
"四川話"　是什麼意思?　　"四川話"的意思是 "Sichuan dialect."
謝謝。
不客氣。

請問，中國銀行在那兒?

對不起，我不懂你的話。清再說一遍。

你知道中國銀行在那兒嗎?　　知道。　　中國銀行在中國城。

謝謝。

不謝。

請問，男廁所在那兒?　　在五樓。

謝謝。　　不客氣。

香港人說什麼話?　　香港人說廣東話。

你會不會說廣東話?　　我懂廣東話但是我不會說。

And in seal characters:

你是中國人嗎?　　是。

你也是中國人嗎?　　我不是，我是日本人。

對不是。　　沒關系。

你是哪國人?　　我是中國人。

你怎怎呢?　　她是美國人。

你去哪兒來?　　我去法國來。

你是法國人嗎?　　不是。我是德國人。

你是哪兒人？　我是上海人。
你爸爸也是上海人嗎？　不是。他是廣州人。
你會說廣東話嗎？　我懂廣東話，但是不會說。
你爸爸會說廣東話嗎？　他會。

你媽媽會說英語嗎？　會。
你哥哥呢？　他不會。
你姐姐呢？　她會一點兒。

你會說幾種語言？　我會說四種語言。
哪四種？　英語，法語，西班牙語，和一點兒中文。
請問，Mandarin 用中文怎麼說？ Mandarin 用中文說普通話。
"四川話" 是什麼意思？　"四川話" 的意思是 "Sichuan dialect."
謝謝。　不客氣。

請問，中國銀行在哪兒？
對不起，我不懂你的話。請再說一遍。
你知道中國銀行在哪兒嗎？　知道。　中國銀行在中國城。
謝謝。　不謝。

請問，男廁所在哪兒？　在五樓。
謝謝。　不客氣。

香港人說什麼話？　香港人說廣東話。

你會不會說廣東話？　我懂廣東話但是我不會說。

Lesson 7. Money and Shopping

钱 **qian2 metal 643** 钱 **money**

This is a radical+phonetic character. The metal or gold radical is appropriate for *money*. The right

戋 side, 戋 jian1 is phonetic; in the *Shuowen* version (left) it shows two weapons and means *noise, conflict*. The similar *Shuowen* version of the entire character is on the right.

东西 **see page 109.**

百货公司 **bai3 huo4 gong1 si1 department store**

货 **huo4 shell 3263** 货 **goods, commodity; sell; money; idiot**

The shell radical in this radical+phonetic character fits any sort of monetary transaction. The top, 化 hua4, contributes to both sound and sense. It shows one man right-side-up and one up-side-down and means to *change, convert, transform*. Selling converts goods into money for the seller and money into goods for the buyer. A shell-bone version of the top is shown on the left. The *Shuowen* version of the whole character is on the right.

衣服 **yi1fu clothes, clothing**

服 **fu2 moon 52** 服 **serve, obey; clothes**

The numerous bronze versions, such as that on the left, show a boat, a seated man, and a hand. This pattern is preserved in the *Shuowen* version, shown on the right. The conversion of the boat to a moon (or meat) was simply an error. The GHZ says the character is an ideogram whose basic meaning is *to surrender, to give in*. That fits with the serve and obey meanings. But what exactly is depicted that would convey that idea? I think – and I have no authority for this notion save that it makes sense – that the man is a galley slave in the boat and the hand is that of the master, much as in the origin of 报 (page 114). What better picture of *serve and obey*? (Since I first wrote this, Wiktionnaire has adopted exactly the same explanation.) Most of the two-character words involving 服 are related to this sense. The puzzle then is how it came to mean *clothes*. Maybe the English expression *uniformed services* gives a clue. Or maybe we just have to appeal to phonetic borrowing.

毛衣 **mao2 yi1 sweater**

We met 毛 as *hair, fur, **feather**, down* on page 93 and 衣 on page 94.

大衣 **da4 yi1 coat**

裤子 **ku4 zi pants**

裤 **ku4 dress 413** 裤 **pants, trousers**

The dress radical in this radical+phonetic character is to be expected. The phonetic is the ideogram character ku4 库 （庫） which shows a shed with a cart under it and means *a warehouse or storehouse* – and certainly every warehouse needs a cart.

颜色 **yan2 se4 color**

颜 **yan2 head 414** 颜 **face, prestige; color, colorful**

颜 is a radical+phonetic character. The basic meaning is *face*. The head radical (see page 51) is natural for a character meaning *face*. It is on the right – its usual position – while on the left is the phonetic, 彦 （彦） yan4, meaning a man of talent, learning and virtue. The *Shuowen* version of 彦 is shown to the right. The man on top is clear; the "shed" may be a shelter under which the scholar sits and reads the lines of writing.

色 **se4 aa 3556** 色 **color; look, facial expression; scenery; feminine charm; lust, sexual passion**

The etymology is uncertain. The *Shuowen* version is shown on the right. It seems to show one person above another. The OECCD says that the fundamental meaning is *anger* and an angry facial expression; it views the upper person as beating the lower. The red face of the angry man leads to the *color* idea. With some justification, Sears sees copulation in the character and the sexual passion meaning as primary. 色情 se4 qing is *pornography*;色狼 se4 lang2 is *lecher* (狼 is *wolf*).

Notice how bisyllabism works in 颜色. 颜 has a number of meanings, one of which is *color*. 色 also has a number of meaning, one of which is *color*, so the meaning of 颜色 is the meaning shared by the two characters, namely *color*.

邮票 **you2 piao4 stamp**

We know 邮 from page 62.

票 **piao4 altarB 1** 票 **banknote, bill, ticket, certificate**

This appears to be a phonetic loan character having had the original meaning of *roaring fire*. In the *Shuowen* version on the right, the fire is visible below, while the top part is a remnant of 要 yao and functions as a phonetic. (Wiktionnaire sees the whole character as a picture of a fire spirit.)

美元 **mei3yuan2 American dollar**

元 **yuan2 see page Error: Reference source not found.**

人民币 **ren2 min2 bi4 Chinese money**

民 **min2 aa 5616 people, folk, residents, inhabitants**

The "authorities" offer a wide range of interpretations of the same set of antecedent forms. Wang and the CCCC authors look at the numerous bronze characters like that on the top left and see an eye socket with the eye plucked out with an awl and still impaled on the awl. Wang uses phonetic loan to get to the sense of "people." The CCCC authors say blinding was used on slaves to prevent them from running away or rebelling and that 民 was originally used only to refer to slaves, but then to all those ruled by the government. Wieger sees in forms such as the second on left a creeping plant with phonetic loan to mean *people*. Sears sees in the third figure on the left a woman with a line added to emphasize the womb area, whence "all people come." The *Shuowen* version is on the top right; it could be any of these or many other things.

币 （幣） **bi4 cloth 3** 币 **money, coin**

The top of the traditional radical+phonetic character 幣 is the phonetic 敝 bi4 which means *cloth*. It shows tattered cloth, presumably torn by the hand with the stick just right of it. The lower part of 幣 is just the *cloth radical* 巾 jin1. It is virtually unchanged from the shell-bone versions to the present. It may show cloth (the central vertical line) emerging from a loom (the frame). In *Science and Civilisation in China*, vol. V:9 p.19 it is mentioned that in Zhou dynasty times (1122 -221 BC) hemp cloth was used as a medium of exchange, the basic unit being about 11 meters long. The idea of cloth as money has survived in this character.

块 （塊）　kuai4 earth 3514 yuan; piece, lump, chunk; a piece of land.

This is a radical+phonetic character. In the meaning of *yuan* (the Chinese currency unit), it is slang, widely used in speech but not in price tags, where one always sees 元. The right side of the traditional is 鬼 gui1, meaning *ghost, stealthy, sinister.* A shell-bone example on the top left suggests a being of human form but with a frightening visage. The *Shuowen* form of 塊 is on the right. The *Shuowen* has two forms of 鬼; one looks exactly like the right side of the 块 character. The other, center left, adds an altar, a sign of the supernatural. Several LST seal examples, such as the one on the lower left, suggest that the little hook in the lower right of the character may be a wing.

While 鬼 is central to understanding the traditional and earlier versions of the character, it is irrelevant to the simplified character 块, where a whole different and unrelated phonetic has replaced it. As a character, 夬 has two pronunciations. One, guai4, meaning *resolute,* must have been the one the simplifiers had in mind when they used it to represent the kuai4 sound. It is the other, however, whose meaning explains the form. It is jue2, and so pronounced the character means a thumb ring used in playing stringed instruments such as the pipa. An LST seal character on the left shows it clearly. The hand is a right hand with the palm facing us, and the ring on the thumb is clear. The *Shuowen* version on the right is less clear but adequate once you know what you are looking at. Another jue character is 玦 which means a penannular jade ring.

毛　mao2 one tenth of a yuan

Remember that 毛 means *fur.* In early America, hides were money. Could the same have been true in China?

分　fen1 – the knife dividing something, we met on page 85.

买 （買）　mai3 aa 5443 买(net 0) buy, purchase; bribe

The idea back of the traditional form is clear: acquire things with money (the shell) and put them in a net (at the top) to take them home. The *Shuowen* form at right shows clearly the things in the net.

The simplification is rather strange. Generally 貝 simplifies to 贝. Where did 头 come from? Well, 頭 – meaning *head* and showing a human head on the right – was simplified to 头. We can only suppose that the simplifiers of 買 thought they were looking at a human head when they were in fact looking at a mollusk.

卖（賣） mai4 aa754 卖(sir 02) sell

The LST seal character on the left tells the story most clearly. The structure at the top is the character 出 chu, meaning *out;* we will deal with it when we meet it in its own right. The idea is to get the products (which have been brought to market in a sack or net) *out* in exchange for *money*, the shell. The simplifiers seem to have again taken a mollusk for a human head.

要 yao4 woman 1220 要 want; important; should

A phonetic loan character. Originally, this character meant the human waist as is suggested by the LST seal character version on the left. When it was phonetically borrowed for its current meaning, it was returned to its original meaning of *waist* or *kidney* in the character 腰 by adding the "moon" radical, which in this case (as in most cases) has nothing to do with the moon but rather with *meat* and here indicates human body. The *Shuowen* version is on the right. The woman radical appeared only in the transition to the modern version.

收 shou1 hit 26 收 receive, collect, harvest, accept, restrain, control.

Wiktionnaire presents a new etymology more plausible than earlier ones I have seen. According to it, the character is a pictograph; the hooked lines on the left of the *Shuowen* form on the right are entangled tendrils of plants. The hand with the tool on the right is cutting those plants *to collect, harvest and receive* their fruits. The hand is also *controlling* and *restraining* the plants.

能 neng2 ab 642 能 can, able, capable; ability energy

This character is a fine example of phonetic loan and character evolution. Bronze versions such as the one on the top left clearly show a bear. But since the word for *bear* and the word for the verb *can* had the same pronunciation, the picture of the bear got borrowed to mean *can*. Once the figure no longer meant primarily *bear*, it was natural to reshape it to fit typical character forms. In the *Shuowen* version, right, the feet are still attached to the body but are moving around to the right. In other seal character versions, such as the one on the lower left, the feet have become completely detached.

The drawing has been returned to its original meaning by adding the *fireB* radical below it to create the character 熊 xiong2 for *bear*. The scribes apparently preferred to think of bears as roasted.

130

可以 ke3 yi3 may

可 ke3 aa 150 可 may, can

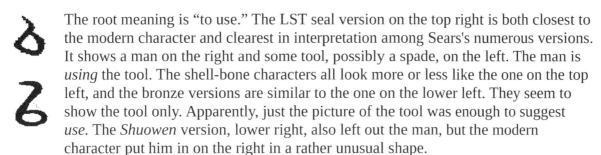

A phonetic loan character. The shell-bone versions show an ax handle and a mouth. It was phonetically borrowed to mean *may* and restored to the original meaning of the drawing by adding a tree radical (indicating things made of wood) to get 柯 ke1, ax handle. The mouth in even the earliest versions may have been used to distinguish the ax handle from similar drawings and may also indicate that even at that early stage it was functioning as a modal verb.

以 yi3 ab 6434 以 to use; with, by means of; according to; so as to; by; because

The root meaning is "to use." The LST seal version on the top right is both closest to the modern character and clearest in interpretation among Sears's numerous versions. It shows a man on the right and some tool, possibly a spade, on the left. The man is *using* the tool. The shell-bone characters all look more or less like the one on the top left, and the bronze versions are similar to the one on the lower left. They seem to show the tool only. Apparently, just the picture of the tool was enough to suggest *use*. The *Shuowen* version, lower right, also left out the man, but the modern character put him in on the right in a rather unusual shape.

The expression 可以 would seem to mean *[you] can use [it],* and by extension just *you may.*

换 huan4 hand 352 换 change, exchange

When goods are exchanged, they *change hands,* so the hand radical is appropriate. The phonetic, 奂 huan4, also means *exchange.* It is an ideogram character, and shows an exchange taking place. The earliest known versions are bronze and are all similar to the one shown on the left. The top is a door. At the door is a peddler bent over displaying his wares (the loops). Below are two hands eagerly reaching out for the wares. The meaning of the whole character is *exchange.* In the *Shuowen* version on the right, the man has rather strangely climbed up on top of the door, the goods have disappeared, but the hands are still eagerly reaching for them. In the modern version, the peddler is still on top, the goods and the door are combined, and the receiving hands have merged to form a sort of table. The meaning remains *to exchange.*

试 shi4 speech 641 试 try (in the sense of *test out*), test

The primary meaning is to test or examine in the sense of 口试, oral examination; hence the speech radical fits. 式 shi4 is phonetic; its basic meaning, in turn, is *form* or *pattern* such as a carpenter might work from. The little 工 in the lower left corner is a tool, often interpreted as a carpenter's square (though we saw that it is more likely a tamper), and serves as the meaningful radical in 式 shi4 while 弋 yi4 is the phonetic. How can something pronounced yi4 be the phonetic for something pronounced shi4? The answer, of course, is phonetic change. In Old Chinese, the ancestors of the two characters sounded similar but not identical, but they have grown apart. The character 弋 yi4 means *to shoot geese or ducks with a retrievable arrow*. The LST seal version on the left shows the story; the modern character is derived from the left side. The *Shuowen* version of 试 is on the top right.

告诉 gao4su tell

告 gao4 ox 0 告 accuse, tell, seek, ask foreigners

This is an ideogram. To accuse is to *gore w*ith the *mouth*. Hence, ox + mouth.

诉 su4 speech 331 诉 tell, relate, accuse, sue

This is a radical+phonetic character. The speech radical fits the meaning. The phonetic, 斥 chi1, means *open up, scout, repel, drive out, scold*. Its *Shuowen* form is shown at right. Sears suggests that the inside is an up-side-down man, leaving or being driven out. This inside is exactly the same as the *Shuowen* version of 屰 ni4, which means upside-down.

等 deng3 bamboo 715 等 wait; equal; class; rank

The etymology of this character is perhaps the most convoluted – not to say improbable – so far encountered. The top is the bamboo radical we met on page 120. On page 88 in connection with 时 we met the lower part as 寺 si4, meaning *temple*, which hardly seems a plausible phonetic for a character pronounced den3. What is going on?

First the radical. The OECCD says that the fundamental meaning of the character is *order*. Bamboo strips were used to write tags for putting things in order, so the bamboo radical is reasonable enough.

The Wiktionary authors say that 寺 originally represented a different word, also meaning *temple* but with quite a different pronunciation. It is the pronunciation of this word that is represented by 寺 in 等, which therefore is -- strange as seems with the current pronunciation of 寺 – a radical+phonetic character.

But how does "order" come to mean "wait" and the other meanings of 等? Now *order* can mean putting together things which are the *same* or *equal,* for example putting together all towels in one pile and all washcloths in another. Maintaining order in our lives requires *ranking*, doing the most important things first. Order in the check-out line in the grocery store means *waiting* patiently. *To wait* appears to have been the most recently acquired sense of 等, but it is now the most frequent.

觉得 jue2 de   feel, think

觉 （覺） jue2 see 44 觉 sense, feel, become aware

We met this character on page 99, where we noted noted its split personality. There it meant *sleep;* here it means *become aware, sense, feel,* meanings which fit better the form of the character. In the traditional, we see on top two hands stuffing sense impressions into the eye-on-legs below. Compare with 学 （學） .

得 de2 road 0115 得 to get, obtain, result in

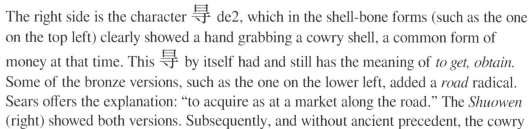

The right side is the character 㝵 de2, which in the shell-bone forms (such as the one on the top left) clearly showed a hand grabbing a cowry shell, a common form of money at that time. This 㝵 by itself had and still has the meaning of *to get, obtain.* Some of the bronze versions, such as the one on the lower left, added a *road* radical. Sears offers the explanation: "to acquire as at a market along the road." The *Shuowen* (right) showed both versions. Subsequently, and without ancient precedent, the cowry shell turned into a sun. So, as with so many characters, faced with the modern character, you have to visualize its ancient form to make sense of it.

便宜 pian2yi inexpensive, cheap

便 bian4 man 130 便 comfortable, convenient, simple; then, in that case; defecate, urinate

Although in the word 便宜 the character 便 is pronounced pian2, standing alone and in other combinations it is usually pronounced bian4 and basically means *comfortable, convenient.* Its etymology is connected to that meaning. Although the form makes one expect a radical+phonetic etymology, the GHZ calls it an ideogram. In the *Shuowen* version, shown on the right, we see a man on the left and on the bottom right a hand with a tool. In the top right there is what is probably a stove. The idea seems to be that the hand with a poker is stirring up the fire and makes the man *comfortable.*

宜 yi2 roof 251 宜 suitable, right, fitting, proper; should, ought to; of course

The character goes back to a few shell-bone versions, such as the one on the top left and numerous bronze versions such as the one on the bottom left. The *Shuowen* version is on the right. All of them show a house and something on it. Again, it is an ideogram – not surprising for a character meaning *suitable.* Sears suggests that the something on the house is the family plaque or crest. That fits well enough with the meaning *suitable, fitting.*

As for 便宜, it would seem to mean *well-priced, inexpensive,* and *cheap* only in this sense, not in the sense of *poor quality*.

长（長） chang2 aa 631 长 long; distance; strong point; forever

 This is a pictograph showing a man with **long** hair. Among the many shell-bone versions, one, upper left is very clear. It is, however, atypical. Most, like the middle left, are rather abstract. The bronze versions are even more abstract, and the long hair sometimes turns into something like a foot on the man's head; see lower left. The numerous LST seal characters show further abstraction but often keep the foot as well as some trace of the man but emphasize stylized long hair seemingly blown by a strong wind. A good example is at lower right. From this version to the modern traditional is a short step. The *Shuowen* version, top right, seems remote from most other versions. While the modern simplified shows some resemblance to the traditional, the essence – the long hair – is all but lost.

最 zui4 sun 127 最 most, best, first-rate, (superlative particle like English -est)

The bottom is the ideogram character 取 qu3, an ear and a hand. The modern meaning is simply *to take, get, obtain,* but one may imagine that originally it meant to grab livestock by the ear and lead it off, that is, *to steal* it. Etymologically, the top is not a sun but the top of 冃 mao, a cap. The GHZ says that 最 is an ideogram with the literal meaning *to steal a cap* and the basic meaning *to commit a crime*. That is now the meaning of the homophone 罪 zui4, and 最 is never used in that sense. I conclude that 最 is a phonetic loan, but there was no need to return it to its original meaning by adding a radical because 罪 replaced it in that meaning.

一共 yi2gong4 altogether, in total

共 gong4 aa 72134 共 share, together, Communist

We met this character on page 110 on the of the right side of 港 gang3 and noted that it meant *common, shared,* close to its sense in 一共 meaning *altogether*.

134

第 **di4 bamboo 57** 第 *makes a number ordinal (first, second, third ...)*

第 is a relatively new character not in the *Shuowen* or earlier sources. It is of the radical+phonetic type. Recall that 等, in addition to the meaning *wait*, also had the meaning of *order, rank*. There is thus some connection between bamboo and the idea of *order* and hence of *ordinal* numbers. Most of the lower part of the character is the phonetic: 弔 diao4, which means *to hang, suspend*. The *Shuowen* version is on the top right; it may show a man *hanging down* a fishing line. The fishing line idea is supported by several bronze forms, such as the one on the lower right, in which the line ends with a barb. In 第, a stroke has been added to 弔 in the lower left corner, perhaps just to give it stability.

张 (張) **zhang1 bow 631** 张 **to open, spread, expand; classifier for flat things like sheets of paper, paintings, beds, tables, mouths, faces and bows.**

This is our first meeting with the bow radical. As a character, it is 弓 gong1 and means *bow* as in *bow and arrow*. The shell-bone examples usually show the bowstring as well as the bow itself, as shown on the top left. Some of the bronze versions kept the bowstring, some dropped it, as on the lower left. The *Shuowen* version is on the top right. The phonetic in 张 is, of course, 长, which we have just had. As to why bow is the right radical for the character, think how the area between the bow and string *spreads* and *expands* as the string is drawn back.

条 (條) **tiao2 hit 51** 条 **twig, strip, bar, slip; classifier for long, thin things**

The basic meaning is *twig*, and thus it is a perfect classifier for long, thin things. There is no agreement about its etymology. GHZ says that it is radical-phonetic with the *tree* radical in the lower right corner of the traditional and 攸 you1 as the phonetic. But that is a strange place for the radical and the phonetic is remote. Sears seems to have looked at the LST seal version on the left – seen a man, a tree, and a river – and concluded that the man is taking soundings in the river with a *pole*. But no other versions show the river. The *Shuowen* version is on the top right. I imagine that I see a man on the left, with a *pole* or *branch* (the vertical line) cut from the tree (lower right) by the hand with a tool (top right). All that is preserved in the modern traditional. In the modern simplified all that is left is the tree and the hand with the tool. We have to supply the pole or branch or twig, which is the heart of the matter.

件 **jian4 man 741** 件 **(a classifier)**

件 is a classifier for articles which can be counted, such as pieces of clothing in the text – 这件衣服. The character is, of course, a picture of a man and an ox. Presumably, the character is an ideogram, and men and oxen are prime examples of things that can be counted.

当然 **dang1 ran2 of course**

当（當） **dang1 aa 2435** 当 **work as, serve as; run, manage;**

dang4: proper; equal, matching; regard as, serve as; simultaneous

In its modern traditional form, this is a radical+phonetic character; the radical is 田 field and the top part is phonetic. The GHZ says that the basic meaning is 与田互相对看, which seems to mean something like "to look at one another in the field," a situation with potential enough to lead to all the various meanings. The *Shuowen* version is on the right.

當

As for the phonetic value of the top, compare 常 chang2, 赏 shang3. 掌 zhang3, 党 dang3, 裳 chang2, 堂 tang2, and 棠 tang2. By itself, the top, 尚 shang2, now means *yet, still, even, is still; to esteem, to honor.* These are obviously phonetic loan meanings. The object pictured, as in the bronze version on the left, appears to be a house with a roof and window. Sears states that, with the pronunciation shang2, the character still has the meaning of *roof, house with a roof*. But it must be very rare; I have not found that meaning in other sources.

尚

然 **ran2 fireB 354** 然 yes, right, so

The top right corner shows the character 犬 quan4, meaning *dog*. A shell-bone version on the top left shows a recognizable dog. In the middle image on the left, note that the protrusion from the head to the left is the lower jaw, while that to the right is the ear. In the bronze version, lower left, the ear and the jaw have come to look more alike. In the *Shuowen* version, top right, the members can still be detected if you know what to look for. In the modern version, just remember that the dot in the upper right is the dog's ear, the left half of the 1 stroke is his lower jaw, the 3 stroke is his head and legs, and the 4 stroke is his back and tail – everything a dog needs.

犬

Now back to 然. It shows a piece of meat (top left) and a dog over a fire. Its original meaning was *to cook*. It was phonetically borrowed for the modern meanings and returned to something like its original meaning by adding the fire radical on the left, 燃, ran2, meaning *to ignite*. In China, as in many parts of the world, dog meat is a delicacy.

听说 ting1shuo1 it is said

听 see page 118. 说 see page 111.

要看 yao4kan4 it depends

不一定 bu2 yi2ding4 Not necessarily

定 ding4 roof 12 定 tranquil, fixed; to fix, to decide

 According to the GHZ, 定 is an ideogram with a basic meaning of *peace and tranquility*. The earliest examples are bronze characters such as the one on the left with a foot under a shelter. Perhaps the dot represents a stove at which the foot is warming itself – not a bad picture of tranquility. The very similar *Shuowen* version is on the right. In the expression 不一定，定 has the sense of *fixed*.

Here is the text of the conversations.

你去哪儿?
我去买东西。
你去哪儿买东西?
我去百货公司买东西。
你要买什么?
我要买衣服。
你知道哪个百货公司的东西最多?
第一百货公司的东西最多。

你们收不收美元?
对不起，我们不收美元。我们只
　　收人民币。
你能告诉我在哪儿能换美元吗?
你可以在银行换，也可以在饭店
　　换。+
谢谢。

不可气。

这儿能换美元吗?
能。你要换多少?
一美元今天能换多少人民币?
一美元今天能换七块人民币。
我换三百美元。
好。清等一下儿。
这是两千一百块人民币。
谢谢。

你买什么?
这件大衣多少钱?
两百五十块。
我能不能看看?
当然可以。

137

我能诗诗吗？
没问题。

请问，那条裤子多少钱？
一百块。
太贵了。　有没有便宜一点儿的？
有。　你看看这条。
谢谢。

听说上海的东西很贵。
不一定，要看什么店。　有的点
　东西贵，有的点东西很便宜。
什么点东西贵，什么店东西便宜？
大店的东西贵，小店的东西不太
　贵。

你们卖不卖邮票？

卖。　你要几张？
多少钱一张？
两毛一张。
我要十五张。一共多少钱？
一共三块。

这件毛衣怎么样？
很好看。
长不长？
我觉得不长。
颜色怎么样？
颜色也不错。多少钱？
一百二十块。
我觉得不太贵，你看吗？
我看也很好。

Here is the text in modern traditional characters.

你去哪兒？
我去買東西。
你去哪兒買東西？
我去百貨公司買東西。
你要買什麼？
我要買衣服。
你知道哪個百貨公司的東西最多？
第一百貨公司的東西最多。

你們收不收美元？
對不起，我們不收美元。我們隻收
　人民幣。
你能告訴我在哪兒能換美元嗎？
你可以在銀行換，也可以在飯店換。

謝謝。
不可氣。

這兒能換美元嗎？
能。你要換多少？
一美元今天能換多少人民幣？
一美元今天能換七塊人民幣。
我換三百美元。
好。清等一下兒。
這是兩千一百塊人民幣。
謝謝。

你買什麼？
這件大衣多少錢？

138

兩百五十塊。
我能不能看看?
當然可以。
我能詩詩嗎?
沒問題。

請問，那條褲子多少錢?
一百塊。
太貴了。 有沒有便宜一點兒的?
有。 你看看這條。
謝謝。

聽說上海的東西很貴。
不一定，要看什麼店。 有的點東
　西貴，有的點東西很便宜。
什麼點東西貴，什麼店東西便宜?
大店的東西貴，小店的東西不太貴。

你們賣不賣郵票?
　賣。 你要幾張?
多少錢一張?
兩毛一張。
我要十五張。一共多少錢?
一共三塊。

這件毛衣怎麼樣?
很好看。
長不長?
我覺得不長。
顏色怎麼樣?
顏色也不錯。多少錢?
一百二十塊。
我覺得不太貴，你看嗎?
我看也很好。

And here it is in the *Shuowen*-style font:

你買什麼？
這件大衣多少錢？
兩百五十塊。
我能不能看看？
當然可以。
我能試試嗎？
沒問題。

請問，那條裙子多少錢？
一百塊。
太貴了。 有沒有便宜一點兒
的？
有。 你看看這條。
謝謝。

聽說上機的東西很貴。
不一定，要看什麼地。 有的
點東西貴，有的點東西很便
宜。
什麼點東西貴，什麼地東西便宜
宜？

大地的東西貴，小地的東西不
太貴。
你們賣不賣鞋興？
賣。 你要幾雙？
多少錢一雙？
兩毛一雙。
我要十五雙。一共多少錢？
一共三塊。
這件毛衣怎麼樣？
很好看。
貴不貴？
我覺得不貴。
顏色怎麼樣？
顏色也不錯。多少錢？
一百二十塊。
我覺得不太貴，你看呢？
我看也很好。

Lesson 8. Food and Eating

米饭　　**mi3 fan4　(cooked) rice**

米　　　**mi3　rice** 米 **rice**

 This is a pictograph, a picture of a stalk of rice. In the shell-bone version on the left, the dots are the kernels of rice, while the cross in the center is the stalk and leaves, some of which often bend over in the middle so that their upper half lies in a horizontal position, as suggested by the cross bar. The *Shuowen* version, right, is virtually identical to the modern character. As a radical, rice may appear on the left as in 粘, or on the top as in 类 or on the bottom as in 粱.

面包　　**mian4 bao1 bread, bun**

包　　**bao1 wrap 5** 包 **wrap, package, bag; bun; include; take full responsibility for.**

This is another pictograph. The only known shell-bone version, top left, seems to show an embryo *wrapped* in its mother's womb. This interpretation is reinforced by several LST seal characters such as the one on the lower left. The *Shuowen* version, right, is also compatible with this idea.

As for how 面包 came to mean *bun* or *bread*, recall from page 51 that 面 basically means *flat.* Now *flat wrap* hardly suggests *bread.* But perhaps the 面 is a sort of abbreviation for 面条, *noodles,* so 面包 is sort of *noodles wrapped up,* which is a fair description of the buns that are the basic bread of China.

菜　　**cai4 grass 3447** 菜 **dish, vegetable**

This is *dish* as in "This dish is delicious," not as in "wash dishes." At first glance, the bottom looks like 米. But look carefully; the four strokes just below the grass radical are a hand picking the plant at the bottom of the character. That is clear in the *Shuowen* version on the right. That plant will soon become a *dish*.

The radicode may require a comment. The grass radical is clear, as is the 3 stroke just below it. Below that are three strokes, from left to right a 4, 4, and 3. While in some fonts the 3 may be slightly higher, it is not necessarily so, but the 4 is definitely to the left, so it is coded first. The component rule cuts off this component after three strokes. The final 7 is from the "tree" at the bottom.

白菜 bai2cai4 is known in the American market by the Cantonese pronunciation of its Chinese name: bok choi.

烤鸭　**kao3 ya1　roast duck**

烤　**kao3 fire 7311 烤 bake, to warm or dry by a fire; to roast; to toast**

This is a radical+phonetic character. The fire radical is natural. The phonetic 考 kao3 shows an old man with long hair leaning on a cane. as seem in the bronze version on the left and the *Shuowen* version on the right.　It formerly meant *deceased ancestor* and *to depend.*. Currently, however, presumably by phonetic loan, it has come to mean a test or examination.

鸭 （鴨）　**ya1 bird 07 鴨 duck**

This is a radical+phonetic character. The radical is bird,鸟 （鳥）　niao3. The early versions, such as the shell-bone example on the top left look very bird-like. Even the LST example on the lower left is unmistakably a bird. The *Shuowen* version, on the right, however, has undergone a most surprising metamorphosis. Its head has been chopped off and placed over its back. In the modern traditional, it has strangely become a four-footed bird looking very like a horse （馬）. The simplification kept the first three strokes of this Pegasus-like creature, added an eye, and merged the four feet into one.

The phonetic in 鴨 is 甲 jia3. It is the character we have translated as *shell* in *shell-bone* （甲 骨）.　 It is thought to represent a turtle shell, and looks somewhat like one in some bronze versions such as the one on the left. Presumably the vertical line protruding from the bottom is the turtle's tail.

海鲜　**hai3 xian1　seafood**

鲜 （鮮）　**xian1 fish 4317 鮮 delicious, delicacies**

This is an ideogram, a picture of a fish and sheep. (In the radicode system, the fish counts as the radical, but etymologically it is not a radical in this character.) The fish is a compressed version of the fish character 鱼 （魚） yu2 which has a rich history back to shell-bone versions such as the top left example. The numerous bronze examples are even more elaborate and very fishy, as for example the lower left figure. Then almost all of the seal characters seem to loose the fish idea. The *Shuowen* version, right, is typical. The fins are gone; the mouth has become a man; the edges of the tail fins no longer come together in a point but are parallel. In the modern traditional, the tail fins look like the horse's feet. But all the same, it is somehow recognizable and a welcome friend when you see it on a menu.

We met 羊 yang, a picture of a sheep, as a phonetic on page 27.

In this ideogram character, 鲜, we must ask What do *fish* and *sheep* have in common? The answer: they are both *delicious*. So 海鲜陽 are *sea delicacies* or seafood.

菜单　　cai4 dan1　menu (for 单, see page 56)

汤 (湯)　tang1 water 533 汤 soup

 This is a radical+phonetic character. The water radical clearly goes well with *soup*. The right side, the phonetic, goes back to shell-bone versions such as shown on the top left. Above is the sun, and below is probably a sundial. (This interpretation is offered by Sears and fits better than any other I have seen.) The two examples on the lower left are typical of numerous bronze versions. We can think of the top line as the rod of the sundial which casts a shadow, while the curving line below it is the surface on which the shadow is cast. The parallel lines are the scale marked on the sundial. (They are often interpreted as the sun's rays, but since they are separated from the sun by line, that seems improbable.) The right side by itself, 易, meant *sunshine* in Old Chinese and is an alternative form of 陽 yang2, the traditional form of the yang of yin1-yang2, 阴阳 in simplified characters. (Note the nice opposition of moon and sun in these simplified characters not present in the traditional 陰陽.) 易 appears in several characters pronounced *yang*, but this is the only one in common use pronounced *tang*. It can be felt as appropriate because the sun suggests that the soup is warm. The *Shuowen* character is on the right.

西兰花　xi1 lan2 hua1　broccoli

花　hua1 grass 3261 花 flower; flower-shaped; multi-colored; mixed. not pure; smallpox

This is another radical+phonetic character. The grass radical, which is used for most herbs and wildflowers, fits. The bottom, 化, hua4, is the phonetic. It itself is an ideogram character; it shows one man right-side-up and another upside-down – a clever way to convey its meaning, which is *to change, to transform.*

牛肉　**niu2 rou4 beef**

肉　**rou4 aa 32534** 肉 **meat (pork if not otherwise indicated)**

This is a picture of ribs or chops. The *Shuowen* version is on the right.

素材　**su4 cai2 vegetable dish**

素　**su4 silkB 711** 素 **white silk fabric; plain; vegetable dish**

This is an ideogram. The earliest examples are bronze, one of which is shown top left. One of the LST seal versions, lower left, makes the idea clearer. On the bottom is plainly silk, and on the top is plainly a plant. One is, so to speak, the noun and the other the adjective; but they can change roles. First, take the silk as the noun. Then the plant, as it opens its blossoms to the sun, represents purity. The silk is plain, white. Conversely, if the plant is the noun, the plain white silk indicates purity; the vegetable dish is prepared without meat. The *Shuowen* version is on the right.

材 **cai2 tree 513** 材 **timber; material (raw material and study material) ; talent, ability; coffin**

This is a radical+phonetic character. The tree radical fits the basic meaning *timber*. 才 cai2 functions as the phonetic. 才 is thought to be a phonetic loan character depicting a seed sprouting; a shell-bone version of 才 is shown on the left. The *Shuowen* version of 材 is on the right. (Yes, we met 才 on page 57 where it had a totally different origin.)

白酒　**bai2 jiu3　liquor**

白　**bai2 white** 白 **white**

The character is a picture of a bobbin wrapped with cotton thread, which is, of course, *white*. A shell-bone version is on the left, the *Shuowen* verion on the right.
The GHZ classifies 白 as a pictogram.

酒　**jiu3 water 13601** 酒 **wine or any alcoholic beverage.**

A picture of an amphora or wine jug with the water radical sometimes added to indicate its liquid contents. The images are, left to right, shell-

144

bone, bronze and *Shuowen*. (This character does not fit any of the five standard types. The GHZ says it is radical+phonetic character, but 酉 you3 is clearly not phonetic. This is really a radical+radical character.)

红酒   hong2jiu3   wine

红   hong2 silk 121 红   red

This is a radical+phonetic character. The silk radical is used for several characters that are names of colors. Besides 红 red, there are: 绿 green, 绛 crimson, 绯 red, 缥 pale green, 缇 reddish orange, 缁 black. 工 gong1, the tamper, (page 40) is here used as a phonetic.

啤酒   pi2jiu3   beer

啤   pi2 mouth 303 啤 beer

This character has no meaning of its own but is used to write the *pi* sound in borrowed foreign words, in this case, probably the pi of Russian пиво, *pivo*, meaning *beer*. The right side of 啤, 卑 bei4, shows armor over a left hand, and basically means *inferior*. Its *Shuowen* version is on the right. The addition of the mouth in 啤 indicates, in this case, that the character conveys only sound.

瓶   ping2   ab 4311 瓶   jug, bottle

This is a radical+phonetic character with 瓦 wa3 as the radical. Though not used in the radicode system, it is in fact one of the 214 traditional radicals and is used for things made of clay. It depicts a clay roofing tile, as is a little more plausible from the *Shuowen* version on the left. The phonetic is 并 bing4 which we met on page 110. The *Shuowen* version of 瓶 is on the right.

帐单   zhang4 dan1   check, bill

帐   zhang4 cloth 63 帐 curtain, canopy; account

This is a radical+phonetic character. The radical is 巾 jin1, cloth, page 128; the phonetic is 长 chang2, which we met on page 134. As to how 帐 came to mean *account*, it was by use to refer to a *sheet* in a ledger.

消费   **xiao3 fei4   tip**

First, how does 消费 manage to mean *tip*? Recall that *tip* fundamentally means money to allow the server to *tip* a bottle, that is, to have a drink. Think of the German word for tip: *Trinkgeld – drink money* or French *pourboire – for drink*. One meaning of 消 is *to drink* and one meaning of 费 is *expense*. So there it is, 消费 = *drink expense* = *Trinkgeld* = *pourboire* = *tip*.

消   **xiao4 water 243 消 to melt away, disappear, vanish; to drink**

This is a radical+phonetic character. The water radical fits both the *melt away* and the *to drink* meanings. The exact phonetic is 肖 xiao4; it means to *resemble* and has an upside-down version of 小 at the top as a phonetic element while the lower part, the meat radical, refers to the faces or bodies which resemble one another. In the *Shuowen* version of 肖 on the left, the 小 phonetic on the top is still right-side-up, as also in the Shuowen version of 消 on the right.

费   **fei4 shell 32 费 expense, fee; spend, consume**

In this radical+phonetic character, the shell radical indicates, as usual, something related to money. 弗 fu2 is the phonetic. One of many very similar shell-bone versions is shown on the left. Wang believes that it depicts arrow shafts tied together so they will not warp. Its current meaning is *not,* but that is a phonetic loan. The *Shuowen* 费 is on the right.

味道   **wei4 dao4   flavor, taste**

味   **wei4 mouth 7134 味 taste, flavor; savor; smell, aroma; interest, delight; ponder**

The mouth radical in this radical+phonetic character clearly fits the meaning. 未 wei4 is an exact phonetic. It shows a tree with new branches at the top, thus pointing to the future, and meaning *not yet.* A shell-bone example is on the left and the *Shuowen* version on the right.

味 is the first character of one of the most important words for me in Chinese restaurants: 味精 wei4 jing1 = MSG = monosodium glutamate = headache. 精 jing1 means *fine, exquisite.*

146

次 **ci4 ice 3534 次 second, inferior; time (occurrence – as in "the third *time*")**

This is our first example of the *ice* radical. It appears in a number of characters referring to something cold. But etymologically, our character has nothing to do with ice or cold or with the ice radical. Our character is, in fact, all one picture, a picture of a sneeze! The shell-bone versions (top left) show a man sneezing. In the bronze characters (lower left), the sneeze has become really dramatic. The *Shuowen* version is top right. In its present senses, 次 is a phonetic loan character. (The modern word for sneeze is 喷嚏 pen1ti4, with no relation to 次 save the phonetic similarity of ci4 and ti4.)

月宫 **Yue4 gong1 Moon Palace**

宫 **gong1 roof 00 宫 palace**

A pictograph of a large building with several floors. A shell-bone version is on the left; strangely, it was overlooked in the *Shuowen*.

青岛 **Qing1 Dao3 (a brand of beer)**

青 **qing1 meat 711 青 green**

See 清 page 56.

岛 **dao3 mount 3554 岛 island**

This is a pictograph showing a bird flying over a mountain, presumably a rocky off-shore island with many sea birds. The radical is *mount* rather than *bird*, because the bird is incomplete; it has no feet. The character is, however, listed under both radicals in the *Quick Guide.*

好像 **hao3 xiang4 seem**

像 **xiang4 man 3503 像 to be like, to resemble; like, such as; a portrait or likeness**

This is a radical+phonetic character. The *man* radical fits since the character is frequently used to express resemblance among people. The exact phonetic, 象 xiang4, is a picture of an elephant. It may mean either *elephant*, or – more commonly – as a phoenetic loan, *shape, form, symbol, symbolize,* and thus in our character contributes to the meaning. Some of the shell-bone examples, such as the top left, look very like elephants, as do the bronze and LST seal versions on the bottom on each side. But the

Shuowen version, top right, has undergone a curious transformation. The loops on either side of the neck appear to be ears, and they survive in the rectangle near the top of the modern character. Although there have been no wild elephants in China since the 14th century BC, their existence there earlier is well attested.

 he1 mouth 01356 喝 **to drink**

 This is a radical+phonetic character. Pronounced he4, the same character means *to shout loudly*. The mouth radical fits both meanings. The right side is phonetic; it is the character 曷 he2, meaning *how? why? or when?* in classical Chinese. An LST seal version is shown on the left and the *Shuowen* version on the right. Since it is hard to draw a picture of "how?" one may well suspect that we are dealing with a phonetic loan, and indeed Wiktionnaire says that 曷 originally meant to menace or threaten and shows a beggar below and a mouth above threatening him to drive him away.

 zuo4 earth 343 坐 **to sit**

This is a pictograph showing to people sitting on – or about to sit on – the ground. The *Shuowen* version is on the right.

 gei3 silk 341 给 **give**

Recall from 答 that 合 ge3 shows two mouths speaking to one another. Here this picture serves as the phonetic component of a radical+phonetic character. Perhaps the silk radical is used because silks make such good presents.

欢迎 **huan1 ying2 welcome!**

We met 欢 on page 33.

迎 **ying2 go 365** 给 **welcome, greet, move forward**

The meaning of this radical+phonetic character is to welcome someone coming from a long journey, hence the *go* radical fits. The 卬 yang3 is the phonetic. It means a high dignitary and shows him on the left with a man kneeling before him on the right. The *Shuowen* character is on the right.

酸 suan1 wine 64 酸 sour, acid, fermented

In this radical+phonetic character, the radical fits fine but the phonetic is remote. The wine radical refers to the fermentation. On the right is the *Shuowen* version. (The 酸辣汤 in the text is a *hot and sour soup*, not a sweet and sour soup as translated in the text.) 酸奶 suan1 nai1 "sour milk" is really yogurt and has become very popular in China. The phonetic 夋 qun1was a common phonetic in Old Chinese but is now an extremely rare character said to mean *to walk or dawdle*, and appearing among characters in general use only in this character and in 逡 qun1 meaning *to shrink from.*

辣 la4 club 703 辣 hot, peppery, spicy

The club radical 辛 xin1 shows some sort of instrument of torture. Sears calls it a chisel; Wang calls it a sword. It is called *club* in the radicode system. As a modern character, it means *hard, laborious, suffering* and *peppery hot in taste*. The character 辣 does not appear in the *Shuowen* or earlier sources, probably because most of the hot, peppery plants are nightshades from the New World. 束 shu4 is probably not phonetic but is an abbreviation of 刺 with the knife radical and suggesting *sharp*. Thus 辣 is an ideogram conveying the idea of a *sharp and punishing* taste.

还 (還,還) hai2 go 132 还 additionally, still, yet; even more; also, too; unexpected

huan2: to return

 This common character is more than a little puzzling. The *go* radical, the extended foot, makes sense for a character meaning *return, come back*. Clearly, 不 bu4 is not functioning as a phonetic in the simplified character. It was probably taken from the bottom of the non-radical part of the traditional character 還. As an independent character, 睘 qiong2 means *to look in fright,* but is very rare. A bronze version is shown on the upper left. The eye at the top is the radical and the rest is phonetic. It probably shows the top of a coat and evolved into something like the bottom of 衣 yi1 meaning clothes. On the top right is the Shuowen version of 还.

极了 ji2 le extremely

极 （極） ji2 tree 534 极 pole; extreme, extremely

This is a radical+phonetic character. The tree radical makes perfect sense for a character meaning *pole*. Now think of the other sense of pole, as in north pole or polar opposites, and the meaning *extreme* becomes clear. The right side of the traditional character is an exact phonetic 亟 ji2 meaning *urgently, pressingly*. Shell-bone versions (top left) show a man literally being *pressed* between two plates. Some bronze versions add a hand with a stick threatening the poor man and a mouth harassing him – center left. One of the LST seal versions shows the wretch reduced to a quivering heart directly attacked by the hand with the stick. The *Shuowen* version, top right, has the basics, as does the modern traditional character. While 及 might be a plausible simplification of 亟, it is not. Rather it is an independent character going back to shell-bone times and showing a man being grabbed by a hand, as shown on the lower right. It means *to reach, to come up to, in time for*. It is also pronounced ji2 and is used as a phonetic in a number of characters. The simplifications of the 1950s substituted it for the more complicated phonetic of 極.

了 le aa 5 了 (a particle used after to verb to indicate completion of an action.)

The character is a picture of a child wrapped in swaddling clothes so that neither arms nor legs are visible. The *Shuowen* version is on the right. Presumably it is a phonetic loan character, because the meaning has nothing to do with what is depicted.

位 wei4 man 414 位 place, position, status; honorific classifier for people

This is an ideogram. 立 li2 goes back to numerous shell-bone examples such as the one on the left. It means to *stand, found, build, erect*, and other praiseworthy actions. It is not phonetic in 位 but rather points to the dignity of the people it "classifies." The man on the left first appears in the *Shuowen* version (right); earlier versions had only the dignified fellow on the right.

过 （過） guo4 go 514 过 to pass through (see text for usage)

The *go* radical fits the "pass through" sense. The phonetic in the traditional, 咼, is a picture of a bone plus a mouth and is usually pronounced gua3, so it is a fairly close phonetic. Perhaps it does not look like a bone to you, and the shell-bone version (top left) may look even less like a bone. But the Chinese wiktionary shows us what is being depicted (lower left). By the time of the *Shuowen* example, upper right, the picture seems lost and pure design has taken charge. In the modern simplified, the "phonetic" is 寸 cun4, meaning *inch*. Since that makes no sense sound-wise, perhaps the 寸 was intended as a visual simplification of of 咼.

猪 zhu1   dog 731 猪 **pig, pork**

This is our first character with the **dog radical**. It appears in the names of various four-legged animals such as – besides 猪 – 猴 hou2 monkey, 狐 hu2 fox, 狼 lang2 wolf, 狮 shi1 lion and in characters for various dog-like qualities or actions such as 狰 zheng1 ferocious and 狺 yin2 bark, snarl, growl – "dog speech".

The phonetic in 猪 is 者 zhe3 – meaning *those who, he who*. It is most likely a phonetic loan character. There are many bronze and seal versions roughly similar to the elegant Shouwen version shown on the right, but no one knows what it depicts.

羊 yang2 aa 4317 羊 **sheep**

See page 27.

鸡 (雞) ji1 bird 54 鸡 **chicken**

Like 肉, 羊, 鸭 and 鱼, 鸡 is essential for dealing with menus. The simplified character was derived from the traditional by replacing the *fowl* radical on the right by the *bird* radical and drastically simplifying the phonetic, 奚 xi1. This 奚 is a phonetic loan character now meaning *who* but showing a person wearing a queue or pigtail. The person is at the bottom, the pigtail is in the middle, and the hand that plaited the pigtail is at the top. A shell-bone and a bronze example are shown on the left; the *Shuowen* version of the entire 鸡 character is on the right.

茶 cha2 grass 347 **tea**

This distinctive character does not appear to be one of the standard types. Rather, above it has a radical, but below a picture that is not a phonetic.

Prior to the appearance of the *Classic of Tea* in the 8th century (Tang dynasty), there was no sharp distinction between 茶 cha1 (tea) and 荼 tu2 (a bitter-tasting plant). The *Shuowen* shows only the the form on the right, which is closer to 荼, but among the LST seal versions are the characters shown on the left, which are closer to 茶. Although the tea plant, *Camellia sinensis*, is a hardy evergreen shrub, the grass radical is understandable. The part below the grass radical appears to be an open mouth over a plant, a suggestive image for tea.

鸡蛋（雞蛋） ji1dan4 (hen's) egg

蛋 dan4 worm 52 蛋 egg

The worm radical presumably comes from the worm-like appearance of the early stages of the embryo when it develops in the egg. The top of the character is 疋 pi3, now meaning a roll of cloth. Possibly it suggests roundness; possibly it was once phonetic, though now it certainly is not. Strangely, 蛋 is not listed in the GHZ. Egg drop soup is really "egg flower soup", and we know how to write it: 蛋花汤.

饺子 jiao3 zi dumpling

饺 jiao3 eat 41 饺 dumpling

This is a radical+phonetic character. The *eat* radical fits, as does the 交 jiao1 phonetic except for the tone. 交 means *to cross, intersect* and is a picture of a man crossing his legs, as is clear in the bronze version on the left. 饺 is not found in the *Shuowen* or earlier sources.

水果 shui3 guo3 fruit

水 shui3 waterB 水 water

This is a picture of water flowing in a stream. On the left is a shell-bone version; near right is the *Shuowen* version, and far right, an LST version which appears to be on the way to becoming the modern version.

果 guo3 field 734 果 fruit

See 课 on page 93.

甜点（點） tian2dian3 "sweet spot", dessert

甜 tian2 tongue 67 甜 sweet, honeyed, pleasing

This is an ideogram. We met the tongue character on page 111 in the character 话. The right side is 甘 gan1. The *Shuowen* version of 甘, on the left, shows a mouth with something in it. Since as a character by itself means *sweet*, we may assume that that something is sweet. The Shuowen version of 甜 is on the right. Note that the sides got reversed in the transition to the modern character. Probably someone thought that 舌 was the radical and should be on the left.

碗 **wan3 stone 4453 碗 bowl, bowl-like**

This is a radical+phonetic character. Since bowls can be made of stone, the radical fits well enough. The right side, 宛 wan3, is an exact and reliable phonetic; it appears in eight characters in the *Quick Guide*, all pronounced *wan*: 宛, 碗, 畹, 菀, 惋, 琬, 婉 and 腕.

宛 wan3 itself now means *winding, tortuous,* a meaning derived from its original meaning which is the source of the picture. Under a roof we see the moon and a crumpled up man. It is night, but he is uncomfortable and can't sleep soundly. The character originally meant *to toss and turn in bed*, which is exactly the meaning of the expression 宛转 wan3zhuan3.

盘子　**pan2 zi plate**

盘（盤）　**pan2 boat 252** 盘 **plate, tray; coil, twist**

The 盘 character consists of two radicals, the boat radical on top and the bowl radical on the bottom. The rules of the radicode system require the character to be listed under the top radical, the boat, but the meaning of the character is related to the bottom radical, the **bowl radical** 皿 min3. (In the traditional character, the radicode rules put the character under the bowl radical, because the boat does not occupy the whole of the top.) The bowl character has a rich history. A shell-bone example is shown top left, followed by a bold bronze version and a graceful LST seal version. The *Shuowen* form is top right, as usual. It is mostly base and handles, but would still hold a little something. The modern version is all base and handles and holds nothing, but it is easy to draw.

The 盘 character makes sense only in its traditional form, 盤, for whereas 舟 is pronounced zhou1 and cannot possibly be a phonetic for a character pronounced pan2. 般 is pronounced ban1 and is a fair phonetic approximation of pan2. The usual use of 般 is as a phonetic loan character meaning *way, like, sort, kind*; but it also retains its etymological meaning of *to carry or move*. It shows a boat on the left and a hand with a stick on the right. The hand is presumably loading or guiding or propelling the boat. The character goes back to shell-bone examples, as shown on the top left. There are numerous bronze versions, such as shown lower left. The *Shuowen* version is top right.

筷子　**kuai4 zi chopsticks**

筷　**kuai4 bamboo 244** 筷 **chopsticks**

筷 is a radical+phonetic character. The bamboo radical fits, since chopsticks are traditionally made of bamboo. 快 kuai4 – meaning *glad, quick, fast* – is an exact phonetic. It somehow also seems appropriate: chopsticks make me *glad* because with them I can eat *fast*. In 快, the heart radical fits the *glad* meaning. 夬 guai4 we met on page 129.

刀　**dao1 aa 53** 刀 **knife**

See page 85.

cha1 aa 544 叉 to cross, intersect; prick; fork

An LST seal version of this ideogram, left, shows two hands with interlaced fingers, a nice picture of "to cross, intersect." When two things – such as my leg and a blackberry bush – intersect, one is likely to stab or *prick* the other. A tool we use to prick something in order to lift and move it is called "a prick" in Chinese but "a fork" in English. The Chinese emphasizes the sharp points; the English, the separated tines. In the *Shuowen* version of this character (top right), the hand on the left has been reduced to a single finger. In the modern version, that finger is reduced to a dot and the hand on the right collapsed to a 又.

餐巾 **can1 jin1 napkin**

A napkin is an "eat cloth."

糖 **tang2 rice 4132 糖 sugar**

This is a radical+phonetic character, where the rice radical stands in for the sugar cane – and indeed looks as much like sugar cane as it does like rice. Since refined sugar did not come into China until about the 7th century, it is not surprising that the character does not appear in the *Shuowen*.

The phonetic, 唐 tang2, has a long history unrelated to sugar. It is the name of the Tang dynasty (618 - 907), with a basic meaning of *to boast, brag, speak outrageously*. It also is a radical+phonetic character, with the bragging mouth at the bottom being the radical and the rest being phonetic. This phonetic is thought to be a much-transformed picture of a 庚 geng1, a flail, a device used in separating grain from chaff. One of many similar shell-bone versions is on the left. The *Shuowen* version of 庚 is at the top right and that of 唐 just below it. The flail is still visible in the center, but hands have been added to work it. (Maybe someone saw hands in the sides of the shell-bone flail.) In the modern versions of both characters the top of the flail has combined with the left hand to make a shed, and in 庚 the handle of the flail has split apart at the bottom. (Phoneticists believe that in shell-bone times, the pronunciation of the two characters was closer than now.) Be sure to remember all that the next time you need to ask for some 糖 for your 茶.

盐 （鹽） **yan2 bowl 71 盐 salt**

The correct etymology of 盐 is too complex to be of any use in remembering the character, so I will give you my own mnemonic: the *earth* in the *bowl* on the table is *salt*. But why the fortuneteller's crack 卜? It is there so that, if you spill the salt, you won't forget to throw a pinch of it over your left shoulder.

Do you really want to know the correct etymology? It will only get you as far as the traditional; and as you can see, there is a big jump to the simplified. But all right then. 鹽 is a radical+phonetic character. The thing in the top right corner is a box of salt and is the meaning component. The rest of the character is phonetic taken from the character 監 jian1, meaning *to supervise, watch, inspect, jail*. Its *Shuowen* version is at top right. The component in the top left is the eye of the supervisor looking down. The bent figure on the right may be the one being watched. Across the bottom is a bowl, and we can see that there is something in the bowl. From other characters, we know that that something is blood, presumably the blood of those who step out of line and get caught. A bronze version with all these elements is shown on the left. On the right is a bone-shell example with the large eye of the supervisor above, the kneeling body of the supervised below, and the blood in the bowl on the left.

For the simplifiers of the 1950s to replace the elaborate salt box with the earth radical is easily understood. But to replace the eye with the fortuneteller's crack seems strange.

电影（電影） **dian4 ying3 movie**

影 **ying3 sun 41033** 影 **shadow**

This is a radical+phonetic character, but the radical is the right-hand side which is not one of the radicals in the radicode system. Remember that under the radicode rules, if no radical occupies a whole side, but there is one in the upper left corner, it claims the character. So here sun is the radical in this system. The whole left side of 影 is 景 jing1 and it is the phonetic element. It means *scenery, view, situation*. The sun is above, and below is the 京 of 北京 serving as a phonetic within the larger phonetic. The three lines on the right are a radical in the traditional 214-radical system. Here they appear to represent the rays of the sun, which, falling upon the scenery, cast *shadows*.

 In the traditional black-and-white movie shown from film, what the viewer sees on the screen is the shadow cast by the image on the film. The movie is thus a 电影, an electric shadow.

Here is the text of the conversations.

你们饿不饿？

我有点儿饿。

我很饿。

我们去吃中国菜，怎么样？

当然好！我们去哪儿吃？

去中国城，好不好？

好。你知道中国城哪家餐馆好吗？

月宫好像不错。

月宫的什么菜有明？

月宫的烤鸭和海鲜最有名。

几位？
三位。
清这儿坐。
这是菜单
谢谢。

你们要什么菜？
我们要一个酸辣汤，一个西
　　兰花牛肉　和一个烤鸭。
还要什么？
我们还要一个素菜。
你们要喝点儿什么？
你们有什么？
我们有白酒红酒和啤酒。
你们有没有青岛啤酒？
有，要几瓶？
我们要五瓶。
你们要米饭还是要面条？
我要米饭。

我要面条。
我都不要。能不能给我面包？
当然可以。

你吃过北京烤鸭吗？
没有。这是第一次。
味道怎么样？
味道好极了。
你有没有喝过青岛啤酒？
喝过。
你觉得怎么样？
青岛啤酒很好喝。

你最喜欢吃中国的什么菜？
我最喜欢吃四川菜。
听说四川菜很辣。
对，但是很好吃。

我们的菜怎么样？
很好吃。

谢谢。　这是帐单。

一共多少钱？

一共四十五块。

这是四十五块。

这是小费。

谢谢。欢迎再来。

Here it is in modern traditional characters.

你們餓不餓？

我有點兒餓。

我很餓。

我們去吃中國菜，怎麼樣？

當然好！我們去哪兒吃？

去中國城，好不好？

好。你知道中國城哪家餐館　好嗎？

月宮好像不錯。

月宮的什麼菜有明？

月宮的烤鴨和海鮮最有名。

幾位？

三位。

清這兒坐。

這是菜單

謝謝。

你們要什麼菜？

我們要一個酸辣湯，一個西　蘭花牛肉 和一個烤鴨。

還要什麼？

我們還要一個素菜。

你們要喝點兒什麼？

你們有什麼？

我們有白酒紅酒和啤酒。

你們有沒有青島啤酒？

有, 要幾瓶？

我們要五瓶。

你們要米飯還是要面條？

我要米飯。

我要面條。

我都不要。能不能給我面包？

當然可以。

你吃過北京烤鴨嗎？

沒有。這是第一次。

味道怎麼樣？

158

味道好極了。

你有沒有喝過青島啤酒?

喝過。

你覺得怎麼樣?

青島啤酒很好喝。

你最喜歡吃中國的什麼菜?

我最喜歡吃四川菜。

聽說四川菜很辣。

對，但是很好吃。

我們的菜怎麼樣?

很好吃。

謝謝。　這是帳單。

一共多少錢?

一共四十五塊。

這是四十五塊。

這是小費。

謝謝。歡迎再來。

And here it is in the *Shuowen*-like font.

你們餓不餓?

我有點兒餓。

我很餓。

我們去吃中國菜，怎麼樣?

當然好！我們去哪兒吃?

去中國城，好不好?

好。你知道中國城哪家餐
館好嗎?

Ｐ宮好像不錯。

Ｐ宮的什麼菜有名?

Ｐ宮的烤鴨味海鮮很有名。

幾位?

三位。

請這兒坐。

這是菜單

謝謝。

你們要什麼菜?

我們要一個酸辣湯，一個
宮爆牛肉　　　　　味

一個烤鴨。

還要什麼?

我們還要一個菜。
你們要喝點兒什麼?
你們有什麼?
我們有白酒紅酒啤酒。
你們有沒有青島啤酒?
有,要幾瓶?
我們要五瓶。
你們要米飯還是要麵條?
我要米飯。
我要麵條。
我還不要。能不能給我菜單?
當然可以。

你吃過北京烤鴨嗎?
沒有。這是第一次。
味道怎麼樣?
味道好極了。

你有沒有喝過青島啤酒?
喝過。
你覺得怎麼樣?
青島啤酒很好喝。
你們喜歡吃中國的什麼菜?
我們喜歡吃四川菜。
聽說四川菜很辣。
對,但是很好吃。
我們的菜怎麼樣?
很好吃。
謝謝。這是帳單。
一共多少錢?
一共四十五塊。
這是四十五塊。
這是小費。
謝謝。歡迎再來。

Lesson 9: Travel

路   **lu4 leg 354 路 road, way; region, district; class**

 This radical+phonetic character holds no exciting secret. The leg radical loosely fits the sense; we use our *legs* to walk along *roads*. The phonetic 各 ge4 goes back to many shell-bone examples such as shown on the left. They show a foot entering a cave or house. 各 now is a phonetic loan character meaning *each, every, various.* It is used as a phonetic in characters pronounced ge, he, ka, ke, la, le, lao, lo, lu, lü, and luo.

钟 （鐘）   **zhong1 metal 10 钟   bell, clock, time**

In this radical+phonetic character, the metal radical goes well with the *bell* sense. The 中 phonetic in the simplified version is exact and certainly simple.

圣诞节 （聖誕節）   **Sheng4 dan4 jie2 Christmas**

圣 （聖）   **sheng4 earth 54 圣 holy, sacred; saint, sage**

The simplified version is literally "radically" different from the traditional. It shows a hand (又 you4) above earth (土 tu3). Neither element is in the traditional, and neither works well as radical or phonetic. Wiktionary says it is an "unorthodox variant of 聖 found in Ming dynasty orthographic dictionaries." Does it perhaps show the divine hand above the earth? Or does it suggest "to work the earth" and thus perhaps to gain sanctification by work, *ora et labora?*

In the traditional, however, we have an ear and a mouth above a king, 王. We met 王 wang2 as a surname in Lesson 1, and I promised to explain it when we met it with meaning. It turns out that 聖 is as close as we will get to 王 with its meaning, which is simply *king.* A shell-bone version, top left, depicts an ax head, presumably as an indication of the king's power and authority. There are many known shell-bone examples, all looking more or less like this one, which, however, is especially well executed. It was presumably intended as an indication of the king's power. Lower left is a bronze version. The *Shuowen* had two versions. One, top right, is essentially the modern character; the other, lower right, retained the curved edge of the ax head.

The traditional form of 聖 is a radical+phonetic character with the ear as the radical and the character 呈 cheng2 as the phonetic. But 呈 also contributes to the sense. It means to present a petition; we see a king, 王, and the mouth of the petitioner. 聖 thus shows an ear listening to the petition. The GHZ says that the fundamental meaning of 聖 is 听觉灵敏 which means something like "sensitive listening".

灵 ling2 in this phrase is an interesting character; it means both *quick and clever* and also a *spirit*, especially of a dead person. Thus 聖 seems to involve attentive listening to the spiritual world, the work of a saint. My own personal mnemonic for 聖 is the king whose ear listens to the praying mouth.

诞 （誕） dan4 speech 543 诞 to be born, birthday; boast, wildly arrogant, absurd, fantastic

The usual expression for birthday is 生日. This is a radical+phonetic character with the basic meaning of *to boast*. Perhaps on your birthday you are allowed to boast a bit; after all, you have managed to live another year. The speech radical fits the *boast* idea, and 延 yan2 is a reasonable phonetic. The left side of 延 (ab 5432) is a rather rare version of the road radical – the *Quick Guide* has three characters with it – while walking down the road is a foot which, however, is about to trip on an obstacle – the 3 stroke at the top of the foot. (The *Shuowen* version of 延 is shown upper right.) We may perhaps imagine that this mishap will *extend* and *prolong* the trip, exactly the meaning of 延.

节 （節） jie2 grass 52 节 node, joint, section, period, festival, knot (speed of a ship)

The basic meaning is a node on a bamboo cane – the point where the leaves attach – or a section of cane from one node to the next. Because festivals divide the year into periods just as nodes divide the cane, it is natural to speak of them as the "nodes" of the year. The traditional character, 節, very appropriately uses the bamboo radical. The *Shuowen* picture is on the right.

The lower part of the traditional character is phonetic, ji2 即. As a character, it is a phonetic loan meaning *promptly, now, immediately.* It shows, however, a man sitting down about to eat. The man is on the right, the food is on the left. A clear bone-shell example is at top leftt. Below it is a suggestive bronze version, and the rather strange *Shuowen* version is top right. The phonetic is, of course, highly appropriate because most festivals are associated with eating.

The simplifiers changed the radical from bamboo to grass – thus loosing the nodes idea – and took away the man's food.

地铁 di4 tie3 subway

This is an important expression for getting around Chinese cities. Since about 1995, China has experienced a boom in urban rapid transit construction; soon close to a hundred cities will have mass rapid transit systems.

地 **di4 earth 265** 地 **earth, ground; place; insight; mind; background**

The earth radical certainly fits. We met the phonetic 也 on page 28 where it was pronounced ye3 by itself and served as a phonetic in 他 and 她, both pronounced ta1. In 池, 驰, and 胣 it indicates a chi sound. In no other common character is it pronounced di as here.

铁 （鐵,銕） **tie3 metal 3311** 铁 **iron, hard, determined**

This is a radical+phonetic character with the metal radical. The Shuowen version of the first of the traditional forms – apparently the standard one – is on the right.

www.shuowen.org

The phonetic of the traditional appears to be a character having the *lance* radical, the pronunciation zhi1, the meaning "sharp cutting" and appearing in the *Shuowen* as shown on the left, but not in any computer font to which I have access.[4] The phonetic in the simplified version, 失 shi1, is in any event not derived from the phonetic of the standard 鐵 but apparently by simplifying the phonetic of a traditional variant, 銕.

As a simplification of this phonetic, 失 shi1 was chosen. It is a common character meaning *to loose, miss, fail, mistake*. It does not contribute to the meaning and its sound is rather remote from *tie*. One may wonder why the simplifiers did not choose a character pronounced more like *tie*. It seems, however, that they did not have good candidates. There are no simple characters pronounced *tie*, so they went with 失, which is at least clear and simple. Its *Shuowen* version is on the left; it seems to show a five-fingered hand dropping, *loosing* something on the lower right. 铁路 "iron road" is a railway.

自行车 **zi4 xing2 che1 bicycle**

自 **zi4 nose** 自 **nose, self**

A human nose seen from the front with a pronounced bridge and nostrils. It is used to mean *self*, so a bicycle is a "self go cart" – meaning self-powered. Top left is a shell-bone version 自, below it, a bronze version, and the *Shuowen* is on the right.

---

4   Sears mentions the character, which however appears as a blank rectangle. Searching Sears's website for that rectangle brings up the answer shown on the right. Unicode standard: U+229DC
Searching the Internet for that rectangle brought up the appropriate passage from www.shuowen.org.

旅馆 lü3 guan3 hotel

旅 lü3 square 31364 旅 travel; troops, forces; together

This is our first character with the *square* radical, 方. If you want to explain to someone the logic of Chinese characters, just show him 圆 meaning *circle* and 方 meaning *square*! Of course, it isn't all that bad. A fairly typical shell-bone ancestor of 方 -- there are scores of known examples – is shown upper left. It appears to be a sort of carpenter's square, an instrument for laying out square corners and 45 degree angles. In the bronze examples, the lower part of the square is always curved, as shown center left. Most of the LST seal versions have become fantastic figures of no possible use to a carpenter, but one, lower left, was drawn by a scribe who knew what he was depicting. The *Shuowen* version is top right, and below it a seal version produced by a scribe aware of the contrast between the by-then conventional version and the meaning. 0

Few if any of the other characters under the *square* radical in the *Quick Guide* or other dictionary have anything to do with the concept *square*. Most of them have a form seen in these characters: 施, 族, 旖, 旆, 旄, 旅, 旌, 旒, 旋, 旃, 旗, and 旆. Note that the top of the right side of each of them is the same. Etymologically, the square radical plus those two strokes on the top right form a unit which might be called the *flag* radical – though it is not used as a radical in either the traditional or radicode system. These characters all go back to pictures with a flag flying, as seen in the shell-bone example of 旅 top leftt. In some of the bronze versions, the flag has become almost a sheltering tent, as on lower left. In the *Shuowen* version of our character 旅, top right, as in a number of the LST seal characters, the flag has broken loose from the flag pole, and the pole has come to look like the *square* radical. From this version to 旅 is a fairly long but understandable step.

Note that the early versions of this character show the *troops and forces* mentioned in its meaning. Also, the *together* idea is clear from the picture. To get the *travel* idea from the picture, we have to imagine that the troops are on the march but have camped for the night. Then 旅馆 fits *hotel* very nicely.

164

天堂 **tian1 tang2 paradise**

堂 **tang2 roof3 071** 堂**principal room of a house; court; courtroom; the kinship of cousins of the same generation.**

The rules of the radicode system make roof3 the radical, but etymologically 土 tu3, the earth radical, is the radical while 尚 chang2 is the phonetic. A bronze version of 堂 is on the top left, its Shuowen version on the right. 尚 is a house with a roof and a window, so it contributes to both meaning and sound. Its *Shuowen* version is shown lower left.

苏州 **Suzhou (a city)**

苏 （蘇,穌） **su1 grass 3544** 苏 **perilla; Suzhou; to revive, regain consciousness**

This is the *su* of both **Su**zhou city and Jiang**su** province. The traditional form shows fish and grain on the bottom, products for which the province likes to be known, while the top is the grass radical to go with perilla, an herb in the mint family, important in the cuisine of Korea, Japan, Thailand and Vietnam. The people of Jiangsu Province like the traditional form and its association with grain and fish. I had assumed that this association was the origin of the character. But the GHZ says no, 蘇 is a radical+phonetic character with the grass radical and 穌 su1 as phonetic. Now in Chinese 穌 means "to come to, to regain consciousness, to revive." How can fish + grain = revive? My usual sources were not helpful. While puzzling over this, I happened to notice that in Japanese the same character means "to gather, collect." Sometimes characters keep old meanings in Japanese that have gone out of use in Chinese. So could that be the clue? If 穌 is an ideogram, we must ask What do fish and grain have in common? They both must both be gathered, collected. And when we have lost consciousness, what must we do to revive and regain consciousness? Collect ourselves, of course. I have no authority for this speculation, but it makes sense.

穌, by the way, remains an independent character among the simplified characters, despite having had all of its meaning officially subsumed under 苏.

Except for the radical, the simplified version, 苏, defies sensible interpretation. 办 is pronounced ban4 and means "handle, do, act; found; punish". It thus contributes to neither sound nor sense in 苏.

州 **we met on page 108.**

骑 (騎) qi2 **horse 324** 骑 **ride**

This is a radical+phonetic character. The horse radical clearly fits the meaning. The right side is an exact phonetic, 奇 qi2, originally also meaning to ride a horse but now phonetically borrowed to mean *strange, queer, rare.* The bottom of 奇, however, is not a horse but 可 ke3 (page 131) as a phonetic (within the phonetic).

玩 wan2 **jade 1136** 玩 **play**

This is our first character with the jade radical. As a full character it is 玉 which we met and discussed on page 31. The jade radical occurs mostly in characters relating to jade or other fine stone or stone-like materials such as coral or pearl, but it also appears in a few characters for nice things. 理 li3 means *reason, logic, science.* Interestingly, the character for *play,* 玩 wan2, has the same radical (with 元 yuan as phonetic) and 玩儿 wanr2 means *toy.*

想 xiang3 **heartB 7340** 想 **think, hope, want; guess, consider; remember, miss**

This is a radical+phonetic character. The heart radical fits the *hope, want, remember,* and *miss* senses well. As for the *think* sense: "As he thinketh in his heart, so is he." Proverbs 23.7. 相 xiang3, meaning *to observe, look at,* is an exact phonetic. It shows an eye *looking* at a tree, perhaps even *considering* or *guessing* its value.

找 zhao3 **hand 6413** 找 **look for, find, give back; make change**

Wiktionary says this character appeared only in the Ming dynasty and that its etymology is uncertain. It has a 扌 hand radical on the left and the 戈 ge1 lance on the right. The hand radical might fit the meanings, but 戈 ge1 is nowhere close to phonetic. The GHZ says it is an ideogram with its meaning derived from the combination of the two sides, and there is a popular mnemonic that says it shows a hand searching for a lance. But this is just a modern mnemonic, not an etymology. A shell-bone version of 戈 is shown top left, and below it a bronze example. The *Shuowen* version is at top right. The hand guard has become much exaggerated.

可能 ke3 neng2 maybe

差不多 cha4 bu duo1 approximately, about

The literal, character-by-character translation of this expression would be "fall-short not much". We need to study the first character.

差 cha1 aa 431121 差 fault, differ from, fall short

We have gotten get this far without the characters for left and right. They are: 左 zuo3 left, and 右 you4, right, and are both have nice folk etymologies which will serve for now. 右 is a hand and a mouth; we eat with our **right** hand. 左 is a hand with a carpenter's square, which is held with the **left** hand while marking with the right.

The *Shuowen* version of 差 is shown on the right. We see what is plainly a left hand holding something. That something appears to be the top part of the *Shuowen* version of 垂, shown lower right. 垂 means to hang down, to let fall. Thus 差 suggests *like a drooping left hand,* a vivid image for *fall short, be at fault, be useless.*

常 chang2 roof3 0 常 often

In the sense of *often,* 常 is a phonetic loan character. Originally it and 裳 had the same meaning, namely, the traditional Chinese lower garment (see CCCC page 375). Both 裳 and 常 have 尚 chang2, which we met earlier in this , as a phonetic element. 常 has *cloth* as a radical, while 裳 has *dress* as its radical. In modern usage, 常 has, by phonetic borrowing, come to mean *often,* while 裳 has kept the original meaning.

上 shang4 aa 211 上 up, 下 xia4 aa 124 下 down

These are indicatives, with the position of the short line relative to the long horizontal line showing the intended direction.

- - - Selected characters from the supplementary words and expressions - - -

出租汽车 chu1 zu1 qi4 che1 taxi

A taxi is an out-hire-gas-cart. Usually the cabs have TAXI written on them, so if you ask for a "taxi" (pronounced as if it were pinyin, not English) you will be understood.

chu1 aa 26262 出 **out, go out; exceed; issue; attend; leave; produce; arise; happen. FR 28.**

This is an ideogram. Numerous shell-bone images, such as the one on the top left, show a foot going out of a house. Bronze versions, such as the one on the lower left, have become more abstract but follow the then-current conventional representation of a foot. The Shuowen character, top right, is barely recognizable as either descendant of what had been or ancestor of what was to come – which was better predicted by the LST character on the lower right. 出 is frequently seen in signs reading 出口 chu1 kou3, literally *out mouth*, but meaning *exit*.

租 **zu1 grain 251** 租 **to rent, hire, charter, rent out**

租 is a radical+phonetic character with a basic meaning of a rent paid in grain. 且 we met on page 20, where we noted that it often functions as a phonetic with pronunciation *zu*.

街 **jie1 road 717** 街 **street, country fair, market**

Remember that the road radical has two sides and something may come between them, in this case, earth above earth, packed earth. That is a pretty good description of a basic unpaved street.

护照 **hu4 zhao4 passport**

护（護） **hu4 hand 4531** 护 **protect, guard, aid**

The simplified character is obviously unrelated to the traditional. In the simplified, a hand is on the left and a door on the right. The hand is guarding and protecting the door. I use a mnemonic: you need your *passport* in your *hand* to get through the *door* at customs.

照 **zhao4 fireB 015** 照 **shine, illuminate, reflect; photograph**

This is a radical+phonetic character. There are actually two radicals, a fire at the bottom and the sun on the top left. Both relate to the "shine, illuminate" meaning. On the top right is the phonetic 召 zhao4. By itself, it is a radical+phonetic character

meaning *to call together* and composed of the mouth radical and a knife 刀 dao as the phonetic. A nice bronze example is on the top left; in it a hand carrying a light replaces the sun and fire1. As for the *photograph* meaning, recall that in its Greek roots a photograph is *light-writing*. This meaning explains why 照 is used in the expression for passport.

Your passport is your "guardian photograph". (The bureaucrat who thought that up deserves a gold star for official double talk! The photo doesn't guard you; you have to constantly guard the photo!)

签证 qian1 zheng4 visa

签 （籤） qian1 bamboo 3414 签 bamboo slip, sticker or label

This radical+phonetic character is not in the *Shuowen* or earlier sources. The part below the bamboo radical is 佥 qian1 meaning *unanimous, all together*.

证(証) zheng4 speech 12211 证 prove, demonstrate; evidence

The speech radical fits. 正 zheng4, the phonetic, is an old friend from page 22.

The visa in your passport is the *sticker* that *proves* you have permission to enter. Chinese visas, by the way, are not stamped onto the passport page but are full-page stickers.

行李 xing2 li3 luggage

李 li3 tree 51 李 plum, plum tree

The child under the tree is surely enjoying fallen plums. But why "traveling plum" or "traveling plum tree" means "luggage" seems to be a well-guarded secret. I have read that the expression goes back over 2000 years, so maybe no one knows exactly where it came from.

近 jin4 go 3312 近 close, near

This is a radical+phonetic character. The go radical fits a word about distance. The phonetic is the ax radical, 斤 jin1,

Here are the conversations, which are getting longer.

你在哪儿工作?

我在中国银行工作。

你每天怎么去上班?

我每天坐地铁去上班。

你太太每天也坐地铁去上班吗?

她不坐地铁，她坐汽车。

上还有地铁吗?

有。

从南京路坐地铁到火车站要多少时间?

差不多五分钟。

上海有几路地铁?

上海有十五路地铁。

设个周末你去哪儿?

我和我太太去华盛顿。

你们去华盛顿做什么?

我们去玩.

你们怎么去?

我们开车去。

从纽约开车到华盛顿要几个小时?

差不多要四个小时。

你家离学校远不远?

不太远。坐汽车只要十五分钟。

你每天怎么去上学?

我有时骑自行车去有时走去。

你骑自行车要多少时间?

骑自行车要十五分钟。

走呢?

走要三十分钟。

你今年在哪儿过圣诞节?

我去加州。

你去加州的什么地方?

我去洛杉矶。

你怎么去?

我想坐飞机去，可是飞机票很贵，我可能坐火车去。

你去洛杉矶住那儿?

我住旅馆。

旅馆好找不好找?

好找。洛杉矶有很多旅馆。

你去过中国吗?

去过。

你去过几次?

我去过两次。

你去过中国的什么地方?

我去过中国的北京，上海，苏州，和杭州。

你最喜欢的什么地方?

我最喜欢苏州和杭州。你知道吗? 中国人常说"上有天堂，下有苏杭。"

Here are the conversatio++++++ns in modern traditional characters.

你在哪兒工作?
我在中國銀行工作。
你每天怎麼去上班?
我每天坐地鐵去上班。
你太太每天也坐地鐵去上班嗎?
她不坐地鐵，她坐汽車。

上還有地鐵嗎?
有。
從南京路坐地鐵到火車站要多
　　少時間?
差不多五分鐘。
上海有幾路地鐵?

上海有十五路地鐵。

設個周末你去哪兒?
我和我太太去華盛頓。
你們去華盛頓做什麼?
我們去玩.
你們怎麼去?
我們開車去。
從紐 約開車到華盛頓要幾個小
　時?
差不多要四個小時。
你家離學校遠不遠?
不太遠。坐汽車隻要十五分鐘。
你每天怎麼去上學?
我有時騎自行車去有時走去。
你騎自行車要多少時間?
騎自行車要十五分鐘。
走呢?
走要三十分鐘。

你今年在哪兒過聖誕節?
我去加州。

你去加州的什麼地方?
我去洛杉磯。
你怎麼去?
我想坐飛機去，可是飛機票很
　貴，我可能坐火車去。
你去洛杉磯住那兒?
我住旅館。
旅館好找不好找?
好找。洛杉磯有很多旅館。

你去過中國嗎?
去過。
你去過幾次?
我去過兩次。
你去過中國的什麼地方?
我去過中國的北京，上海，蘇
　州，和杭州。
你最喜歡的什麼地方?
我最喜歡蘇州和杭州。你知道
　嗎? 中國人常説"上有天堂，
　下有蘇杭。"

And here they are in the *Shuowen* font.

你在哪兒工作?
我在中國銀行工作。
你怎麼去上班?
我怎麼坐地鐵去上班。

你怎麼今天也坐地鐵去上班
嗎?
她不坐地鐵，她坐汽車。
上還有地鐵嗎?

171

有。

从南京路坐地铁到火车站要多少时间?

差不多五分钟。

上海有几条地铁?

上海有十五条地铁。

这个周末你去哪儿?

我跟我爸爸去拉斯维加斯。

你们去拉斯维加斯做什么?

我们去玩.

你们怎么去?

我们开车去。

从纽约开车到拉斯维加斯要几个小时?

差不多要四个小时。

你家离学校远不远?

不太远。坐汽车只要十五分钟。

你每天怎么去上学?

我有时骑自行车去有时走去。

你骑自行车要多少时间?

骑自行车要十五分钟。

走吗?

走要三十分钟。

你今天想去哪儿玩啊?

我去加州。

你去加州的什么地方?

我去洛杉矶。

你怎么去?

我想坐飞机去,可是飞机要很贵,我可能坐火车去。

你去洛杉矶住哪儿?

我住旅馆。

旅馆好找不好找?

好找。洛杉矶有很多旅馆。

你去过中国吗?

去过。

你去过几次?

我去过两次。

你去过中国的什么地方?

我去过中国的北京,上海,苏州,杭州。

你最喜歡的什麼地方？

我最喜歡蘇州和杭州。你知道嗎？中國人常說"上有天堂，下有蘇杭。"

Lesson 10: Weather

雨 **yu3 rain** 雨 **rain**

  Many of the questions asked of the shell-bone diviners were about weather, so it is not surprising that there are many, many examples of the rain character. A typical one is shown top left. There are a few bronze versions, but all seem to enclose the rain in downspouts (lower left), a practice continued in the *Shuowen* (top right) and modern versions.

雪 **xue3 rain 522** 雪 **snow**

 There is considerable variety in the shell-bone versions but the example on the left catches the essence: rain that can be held in the hand or wiped away with the hand. There are no bronze versions. An LST seal version which appears to be the direct ancestor of the modern character is shown left center. The creator of another version, bottom right, must have used branches when sweeping away snow. This idea was picked up by Xu Shen in the *Shuowen*, top right, but was not carried into the modern version.

风 （風） **feng1 aa 367** 风 **wind; air out; winnow; style, view; news**

   A shell-bone inscription used a wind-borne insect, top far left, to represent *wind*. A bronze version, middle left, has become even more fantastic. In the next step, a picture of a sail, shown in a bronze version lower left, was combined with the insect to get a Qin dynasty version of 風 on a bamboo strip shown lower right. The insect has been greatly simplified and is close to the modern 虫. At this point, we have a typical ideogram character: wind-blown insect + sail = wind. To get the modern traditional character from this Qin version, we need only detach the bottom of the sail from the rest of the sail and slide it down to rest on the top of the insect. The Shuowen version, top right, seems to be a digression from this path, though the two elements – sail and insect are still detectable if you know what to look for. (The images for this character are from Wiktionnaire.)

季节 **ji4 jie2 season**

季节 is bisyllabism. 季 by itself means *season*, while 节, as we know (page 162), can mean *period*.

季 ji4 grain 51 季 season

Nothing is more associated with the seasons than the planting, growing and harvesting of *grain*. It is the perfect radical for the character. The child, 子 zi3, is phonetic.

冬天 dong1 tian1 winter

冬 was discussed on page 63, 天 on page 87.

夏天 xia4 tian1 summer

夏 xia4 aa 1303 夏 summer

It is commonly said that this character shows a man walking. That is plausible for the *Shuowen* version (right) and other seal character versions. But look at the shell-bone versions below. They and all the other numerous shell-bone versions given by Sears look like insects to me. And what is more typical of summer than insects? While 夏 has come a long way from any of these, I think I can still see the antennae in the horizontal line at the top, then the neck, then the scaly body and then the tail at the bottom. For me, 夏 is an insect; I can almost hear it buzzing!

秋天 qiu1 tian1 autumn, fall

秋 qiu1 grain 343 秋 autumn

Grain plus fire! What a beautiful ideogram to represent autumn when the wheat stalks turn red and the field looks as if it were afire! Indeed, in ancient Greek, *pyros* meant both *wheat* and *fire*. (From the *fire* meaning comes our word *pyrotechnics*, and from the *wheat* meaning comes *pyramid*, for when the Greeks got to Egypt, the shape of the mighty structures in the desert reminded them of the little wheat cakes they called pyramids.)

春天 chun1 tian1 spring

175

春 chun1 sun 311 春 spring

In the shell-bone characters, the antecedents of 春 have two forms. One (top left) shows just a tender plant springing up. The other, lower left, seems to suggest a seedling in a planting pot. By the time of the *Shuowen*, top right, a sun had been added, the plant reduced to the stereotyped grass radical at the top and a large phonetic, lower right, added. This phonetic is the *Shuowen* version of 屯 tun2, meaning *to sprout* and a clear enough picture of a seed sending leaves up and and a root down. It is another appropriate phonetic. The transition from the *Shuowen* to the modern form was drastic. The sun was the only meaningful component to survive in recognizable form; the rest is replaced by a sort of abstract combination of the phonetic and grass radical. Note that this character, despite its understandable evolution, now defies categorization into any one of the five standard types.

度 du4 shed 612 度 degree; pass time

This is a radical+phonetic character. The etymological radical is the hand, bottom right, while the phonetic is 庶 shu4, without the fire across the bottom. 庶 means *numerous* and shows twenty (people) huddled together in a shed warmed by a fire. (廿 man4 is two 十, so 20.) The hand radical way refer to a handbreadth. It is a fundamental traditional measure in China as elsewhere. Or the hand may be thought of as measuring. The degree is a unit of measurement, especially of angles and temperature. The Shuowen version is on the right.

伞 san3 top 743 伞 umbrella, parachute

A modern pictograph, not in the *Shuowen*, but that is no surprise and no problem!

海滩 hai3 tan1 beach

This is a radical+phonetic character. The water radical fits. 难 nan2, the phonetic, means *difficult*. The traditional form of 难 is 難 coming from the *Shuowen* version on the top right. The right side of the *Shuowen* character is definitely a bird, and the left side definitely has an earth radical at the bottom. What the upper part of the left side represents is not totally clear.

Sears interprets it as 黃 huang2, meaning *yellow*. The *Shuowen* version of 黃 is shown on the lower right, so the match is good though less than perfect. But on the assumption that the left side means *yellow earth*, Sears believes that the idea is that on infertile, yellow earth – loess – birds find it *difficult* to find food. Whether or not that is

176

historically correct, it worked as a mnemonic – until the left side got simplified beyond any possible usefulness. As for 黃 huang2, yellow, it is a phonetic loan character returned to its original meaning of a jade pendant by adding the jade radical in 璜 huang2. The shell-bone versions of 黃 show a man wearing a jade pendant, as in the upper image on the left. Bronze versions often added an upward-turned, laughing mouth, as in the lower image on the left. Who wouldn't be happy and laughing with a big jade pendant like that!

带 **dai4 cloth 722** 带 **belt, tape; bear, carry**

This is a pictograph showing a belt across the top holding up a skirt below. The *Shuowen* version is on the right. There are no known examples before the seal characters, which are all quite similar to the *Shuowen* version.

度假 **du4 jia4 spend vacation**

假 **jia4 man 521** 假 **falsehood, fake, false, borrow, make use of; vacation**

The radical is the man who tells the falsehood. 叚 jia3 is phonetic but also means *false*. An LST version is on the right. It shows a hand with a stone knife on the right and an animal on the left. The hand is thought to be skinning the animal. The skin becomes a *false* body. The extension to mean vacation may at first seem strange, but remember that *vacation* derives from *vacate* and *vacant,* an idea not unlike the empty skin of the the animal.

滑雪 **hua4 xue3 ski ("slide snow")**

滑 **hua4 water 255** 滑 **slip, slide, glide**

This is a radical+phonetic character. The water radical suggests a slick and slippery surface. 骨 gu3, an approximate phonetic, is a picture of a bone, top, and chop of meat, bottom. (It means *bone, skelton, framwork, character and spirit.*) Its *Shuowen* version is at right. The shell-bone versions of 骨, such as the one on the left, show a bovine scapula with the diviner's crack 卜 and mouth 口. The evolution from the Shuowen, right, to the modern is standard.

溜冰 **liu4 bing1 ice skate**

溜 **liu4 water 364** 溜 **slide, smooth; sneak off**

Another radical+phonetic character. The water radical indicates both the slickness of a wet surface and and the smoothness of the surface of a lake. 留 liu2 is the phonetic; as a character, it means *to stay, remain, take, keep.* Below is the field radical, 田 tian2; above is 卯 mao3, the fourth terrestrial stem, also indicating the period from 5 A.M. to 7 A.M., thus the period of sunrise. On the left are shown, top, a shell bone version, and bottom, a very similar bronze version of 卯. They show the sun below the horizon and then above the horizon, thus the time of sunrise. The transformation of the right side of 卯 into 刀 seems to be just the error of a scribe who didn't get the picture. As to why 留 should mean *stay,* I can offer only a mnemonic: *stay* in the *field* all night, and you can see the *sunrise.*

冰 **bing1 ice 554** 冰 **ice**

An ideogram. The combination of the ice radical with the water character means *ice.*

阴 **yin1 place 3511** 阴 **the yin of yin-yang; moon, feminine, negative, shade, overcast, hidden**

Yin-yang is 阴阳, the place of the moon and the place of the sun. Remember that in Chinese yin sounds like the *een* of *green.* The silent y is a pinyin spelling convention.

大 **da1 aa 314** 大 **big**

See page 31.

为什么 **wei4 shen2 me why**

为 （為） **wei4 force 44** 为 **do, act, act as, become, be, make, take.**

The force radical first appeared on page 47. I often translate this frequent character to myself as just *is.* It is a phonetic loan character.

The shell-bone versions, such as the one on the top left, show a hand leading or feeding an elephant. That idea is still discernible in the bronze version lower left. There is no *Shuowen* version, but some or the LST seal characters – such as the one on the right – preserve the idea. Even in the modern traditional we can clearly see the feet of the elephant, its back and tail, and – it seems to me – his trunk and a big ear. There is even some remnant of the hand at the top. Maybe in the simplified we can still see the back and tail of the elephant (the 5 stroke), his head and trunk (the 3 stroke), one foot, and the leading hand (top left).

 bi1 ab 616 比 **than, compare, compete**

An ideogram. From the shell-bone versions (left) to the *Shuowen* (right), the character is just two men side by side presumably competing or being compared.

- - - - selected characters from the supplementary words and expressions - - - - -

 nuan2 sun 3441 暖 **warm, warm up; genial**

A radical+phonetic character. The sun radical requires no comment, save that it is new. The Shuowen version, right, had the fire radical. The phonetic is 爰 yuan2, a phonetic loan character meaning *therefore*. It is picture of two hands holding onto a stick, as can be seen in shell-bone version on the top left or the *Shuowen* version lower left. Presumably, the upper hand is using the stick to rescue the other person, for, returned to its original meaning by the addition of the hand radical in 援 yuan2, it means *lead by the hand, help*.

空调 **kong1 tiao2 air conditioning**

This is our first character with the cave radical, 穴, which appears only on the top of characters, as in the case of 空. It often indicates something hollow or empty. In 空, 工 gong is phonetic. In 空调, 空 means simply *air*.

调 **tiao2 speech 357** 调 **tune, melody; accent; mix, move, adjust, transfer**

This is a radical + phonetic character. The speech radical comes from the *tune, melody and accent* meanings; but the use in 空调 is in the *mix, move, adjust* sense.

 周 zhou1 is phonetic; its meanings include *cycle, circle, periphery* and *week*. It is an ideogram. Numerous shell-bone characters, all very similar to the one on the top left, seem to show a planted field, 田, and thus to suggest the annual *cycle* of planting and harvesting as well as the periphery of the field. Most bronze versions add a mouth below the field, as on the lower left. Precisely why the mouth was added is not clear to me. Was it maybe to show that the planted field is a metaphor for something else? The *Shuowen* version, top right, and most of the LST seal versions, such as the one on the lower right, extend the sides of the field down to include the mouth. In the the modern version, the field at first seems to have

179

disappeared completely, but if you stretch the lines of the 土 just a little, the field will miraculously reappear!

云（雲） **yun2 aa1164 云 cloud**

云

Sears has no examples before the LST seal characters. One of these, shown on the top left, is a simple picture of a cloud. This picture, however, was phonetically borrowed to represent the homophone 云 yun2, meaning *to say, to speak*. It was then restored to its original meaning by adding the rain radical above it, as in the *Shuowen* version on the right. These two characters then evolved into 云 (meaning *say*) and 雲 (meaning *cloud*). The simplifiers of the 1950s reduced 雲 back to 云. So 云 now means both *say* and *cloud*.

雷 **lei2 rain 07** 雷 **thunder**

See page 34

闪电 **shan3 dian4 lightning (bisyllabism: lightning lightning)**

闪 （閃） **shan3 gate 34 闪 lightning, flash, sparkle; twist, sprain**

The picture shows a man at the gate. It originally meant, according to Sears, to suddenly enter – as lightning can.

凉（涼） **liang2 ice 410 凉 cool**

A radical + phonetic character with 京 jing as the phonetic and the ice radical. The traditional radical was water, which was cool enough in the old days, but the simplifiers saved a stroke by changing to the ice radical, no doubt a cool move.

Text of Conversations

今天天气怎么样？

今天是晴天，但是很冷。

见天多少度？

今天 28 度。

你知道明天天气怎么样吗？

听说有雨。

大雨还是小雨？

可能是大雨你最好带伞。

谢谢。

你们哪儿昨天下雨了吗？

下了。

昨天的雨大不大?

不太大。

昨天有没有下 雪?

没有。

北京冬天的天气怎么样?

北京冬天很冷，常常有大风。

北京冬天常常下雪吗?

对，常常下雪。

北京什么季节最好?

北京秋天最好，不冷也不热。

广州夏天热不热?

广州夏天非常热。

有多热?

广州夏天常常有 40 度。

美国人夏天一般做什么?

美国人夏天常常去度假。

他们一般去哪儿度假?

有的人出国旅行，有的人去海滩。

今天冷还是昨天冷?

今天比昨天冷。

今天的风大还是昨天的风大?

昨天的风大。

你喜欢热天还是冷天?

我喜欢冷天。

为什么?

冷天可以去滑雪，还可以去溜冰。

Here it is in modern traditional characters.

今天天氣怎麼樣?
今天是晴天，但是很冷。
見天多少度?
今天 28 度。
你知道明天天氣怎麼樣嗎?
聽說有雨。
大雨還是小雨?
可能是大雨你最好帶傘。
謝謝。

你們哪兒昨天下雨了嗎?
下了。
昨天的雨大不大?
不太大。
昨天有沒有下 雪?
沒有。

北京冬天的天氣怎麼樣?
北京冬天很冷，常常有大風。
北京冬天常常下雪嗎?
對，常常下雪。

北京什麼季節最好?
北京秋天最好，不冷也不熱。

廣州夏天熱不熱?
廣州夏天非常熱。
有多熱?
廣州夏天常常有 40 度。

美國人夏天一般做什麼?
美國人夏天常常去度假。
他們一般去哪兒度假?
有的人出國旅行，有的人去海灘。

今天冷還是昨天冷?
今天比昨天冷。
今天的風大還是昨天的風大?
昨天的風大。
你喜歡熱天還是冷天?
我喜歡冷天。
為什麼?
冷天可以去滑雪，還可以去溜冰。

Here it is in the *Shuowen* font.

今天天氣怎麼樣？
今天是晴天，但是很冷。
現在多少度？
今天28度。
你知道明天天氣怎麼樣嗎？
聽說有雨。
大雨還是小雨？
可能是大雨你最好帶傘。
謝謝。

你們聽見昨天下雨了嗎？
下了。
昨天的雨大不大？
不太大。
昨天有沒有下雪？
沒有。

北京冬天的天氣怎麼樣？
北京冬天很冷，常常有大風。
北京冬天常常下雪嗎？
對，常常下雪。

北京什麼季節最舒服？
北京秋天最舒服，不冷也不熱。
廣州夏天熱不熱？
廣州夏天非常熱。
有多熱？
廣州夏天常常有40度。

美國人夏天一般做什麼？
美國人夏天常常去度假。
他們一般去哪兒度假？
有的人出國旅行，有的人去爬山。

今天冷還是昨天冷？
今天比昨天冷。
今天的風大還是昨天的風大？
昨天的風大。
你喜歡熱天還是冷天？
我喜歡冷天。
為什麼？
冷天可以去滑雪，還可以去溜冰。

Intermediate Chinese

Lesson 1. Past and Present

最近 **zui4jin4 recently, shortly, these days**

最 **zui4 sun 127 most, best, first-rate, (superlative particle like English -est)(BC Lesson 7)**

近 **jin4 go 3312 close, near (BC Lesson 9)**

事 **shi4 aa 5105 matter, thing (to do), affair, business; do, work on (BC Lesson 2)**

新娘 **xin1 niang2 bride**

娘 (嬢) **niang2 woman 456; mother, woman, young woman. FR 881.**

This is a radical+phonetic character. In the simplified character, the phonetic looks confusingly similar to that of 很 hen3, but the 4 stroke at the top completely changes the sound and meaning. This phonetic in the simplified character is not derived from the phonetic of the traditional form. Instead, the simplifiers took as a phonetic a rhyming character, 良 liang2. 良 by itself is a fairly frequent character – in the second 500 in frequency – and means *good, fine*. In this meaning, however, it is a phonetic loan character. The shell-bone and bronze versions on the left show a prehistoric dwelling with porches, as seen from above. The *Shuowen* version is on the top right. 良 has been returned to something like its original meaning by adding the shed radical in 廊 lang2, meaning *porch, veranda*. It appears as the phonetic in such characters as 粮, 悢, 駺, 踉, and 蜋, all pronounced *liang* and in even more characters pronounced *lang* such as 狼, 浪, 琅, 阆, and 郎.

祝贺 **zhu4he4 congratulate, congratulations**

祝 **zhu4 altar 036 to express good wishes; an incantation, spell. FR 1651.**

A pictogram showing a man on the right and an altar on the left. The man's mouth is repeated above his head to emphasize that he is saying something. From the context it is clear that it is a benediction, an incantation of good wishes. A shell-bone example is on the top left. Some bronze versions remained close to this simple picture, but in some – such as the one on the lower left – the well-wisher has become a genii. The *Shuowen* (top right) and other seal character versions enlarge the altar but go back to the man with the emphasized mouth. The modern character remains close to this idea.

贺 (賀) he4 shell 350 congratulate. FR 1696.

A radical+phonetic character, but there seems to be a mix-up in the phonetic.

The phonetic, 加 jia1 (meaning *plus, add*) appears in a number of characters

pronounced jia such as 加,架驾 and 茄. Ours is the only character with this "phonetic" pronounced *he* or anything similar. All of the characters pronounced *jia*, when traced back to the *Shuowen*, have a *plow* and mouth as the phonetic, as in 茄 shown upper left. The earliest version of our character found by Sears is the bronze character on the lower left. It shows not a plow but a *hand* and mouth as phonetic. The *Shuowen* version of our character is shown in the upper right. The hand has been drawn with the fingers pointing down, and in this position was apparently mistaken for a plow in the creation of the modern character. It seems doubtful that our character ever had a pronunciation close to that of the *jia* characters.

The cowrie shell radical suggests that the congratulations were often accompanied with a gift of money.

The 加 combination also turns up in 咖 meaning *coffee* when pronounced ka1 and *curry powder* when pronounced ga1.

新郎 xin1lang2 bridegroom

郎 lang2 placeR 456 A form of address for a young man. FR 1457.

We have just discussed 良 liang2. Here our phonetic is missing one stroke on the lower right corner, but it is clearly the same character, The reason for the placeR radical is not clear; perhaps it indicates that the form of address implied that the young man had some connection with a place, such as "von" indicates in German or "de" indicates in French.

打算 da3 suan4 – plan

打 da3 hand 15 hit, strike. FR 223.

As in 打算, 打 often combines with other verbs to create new verbs. The hand radical fits the meaning. 丁 ding is phonetic. It is a picture of a nail, phonetically borrowed for a number of meanings but returned to the meaning of *nail* by adding the metal radical, thus 钉(釘) ding1. Most characters with 丁 as phonetic are pronounced *ding*. The en.Wiktionary.org website advances an unusual explanation of why this one is not: "By the early Ming period, the character had been borrowed for another word with the same meaning but a different pronunciation, without the nasal ending."

算 **suan4 bamboo 01137 calculate, reckon; plan; regard as; let it pass; at long last. FR 403**

There seem to be no examples before the *Shuowen* version shown on the right. There are clearly two hands at the bottom and the bamboo radical at the top. The object in between is probably an abacus, but it could be counting rods, used in China before the abacus came into wide use. The bamboo radical fits perfectly for counting rods; the frame with a horizontal bar inside fits the abacus.

结婚 **jie2hun1 get married**

结 **jie2 silk 710 tie,weave; knot; assemble; congeal; settle, conclude; give a guarantee. FR 236.**

The use of 结 in 结婚 is very reminiscent of the colloquial expression "tie the knot" to mean "marry". 结 is a radical+phonetic character; the silk radical clearly fits the first meanings. The phonetic, 吉 ji2, meaning "lucky" and composed of the "sir" radical over a mouth, is more than a little erotic.

婚 **hun1 woman 366 to marry, married. FR 942.**

A radical+phonetic character. The woman radical clearly fits. The exact phonetic, 昏 hun1, means dusk, dim, dark, confused. While the sun radical fits the "dusk" meaning, the top, 氏 shi4, can hardly be phonetic. It shows a man bowing deeply with his arms stretched out behind him. Its evolution is shown from shell-bone (top left) through bronze (bottom left) to Shuowen (top right). The compound of sun and bowing man, however, goes back to shell-bone characters (lower right). Maybe the man is bowing to the sun as it sets, or maybe the sun itself is bowing out as night falls during dusk.

就 **jiu4 ab 41034** 就 **approach, undertake; right away; only; with regard to, to go with. FR 27.**

This ideogram is not found back of the *Shuowen* version on the right. The French *Wiktionaire* tells us that it shows the open-mouthed amazement of the simple fellow on the right when he *approaches* the tall building on the left. The *approach* meaning is original.

会 hui4 **top 115** 会 **can, know how to, be able to; repeat; meet, assemble; city; pay for; moment, opportunity.** (BC Lesson 6.) **FR 29.**

收到 **shou1 dao4 to receive**

收 **shou1 hit 26** 收 **receive, collect, harvest, accept, restrain, control.** (See BC Lesson 7) **FR 351.**

到 **dao4 knife 164 arrive, reach, go to, leave for. FR 22.**

The *Shuowen* form (right) shows the idea clearly. On the left is a fisher bird diving and *arriving* at the water, the horizontal line at the bottom. The right side is the knife radical, and indeed our first example of this important radical. Here however, though it counts as the radical under the rules of the radicode system, is really the phonetic. It is the combining form of 刀 dao1, a knife, an exact phonetic except for tone.

请帖 **qing3tie3 invitation letter or card**

帖 **tie3 cloth 210 an invitation card. FR 2191.**

The invitation is probably to be thought of as written on silk, hence the cloth radical. 占 zhan, the diviner's crack in the shell or bone, is the phonetic. It was apparently an inexact phonetic so that the sound of 帖 and 占 evolved differently. But 占 was also used as a phonetic in several other characters now pronounced tie, such as , 贴咕, 怗, 鉆 and 跕. The Shuowen version of 帖 is on the right.

到时 **dao4shi2 at that (future) time**

到 **dao4 (see above in this lesson)**

时 **See BC Lesson 5**

参加 **can1jia1 participate (in), join, take part (in)**

参(參) **can1 aa 643143 join, take part in. FR 507.**

pronounced shen1, 参 means ginseng and a constellation of the zodiac.

This phonetic loan character is a picture of a person either wearing a fancy headdress or receiving the influences of a constellation, perhaps the three-star belt of Orion. The *Shuowen* version is on the right. The three parallel lines are phonetic 彡 shan1, a component of the pictograph 须 xu1 showing hair beside a head and meaning *beard.* 彡 is phonetic in several characters pronounced *shan* such as 衫 , 杉, and 髟.

188

加 jia1 force 0 add; carry out an action. FR 166.

According to Wiktionnaire, the character is probably a simplification of 駕 jia1 which means to drive a horse-drawn coach. The driver uses both his strength 力 on the reins and whip and his voice 口 to control the horse 馬. There are several other explanations and no decisive evidence.

婚礼 hun1 li3 wedding

礼 (禮) li3 altar 6 ceremony, rite, courtesy. FR 926.

The altar radical fits the meaning. The phonetic in the simplified defies explanation. It is not a character by itself, nor does it appear in other simplified characters pronounced li, nor is there a shortage of simple characters pronounced *li*, e. g. 力 and 立. How the simplifiers came up with 礼 remains a mystery unless the right side is just L for Li. The traditional phonetic is quite clear. It shows a drum below and a bowl with strings of jade above and means to perform a ceremony at an altar. A shell-bone version is on the left; the *Shuowen*, on the right. In fact, 豊 is an earlier version of 禮 itself, to which the altar radical was later added. Moreover, the simplifiers were not consistent: 澧 a river and 醴 a sweet wine were not simplified.

以后 yi3hou4 after, later, in the future

后 (後) hou4 a3310 behind, future; ruler, king, queen. FR 48.

In the simplification, this character was merged with the homophone character of which the traditional as well as the simplified was 后. In traditional characters, 后 means *ruler, king, queen*. In simplified characters, it adds to those meanings those of the traditional character 後, namely *behind, future*. A bronze version of 後 is shown on the left and the *Shuowen* version is on the right. It is an ideogram character composed of 彳, 幺 and 夂. The first two we know: the road and the silk radicals. The third is a downward-pointing foot. The silk radical – often referring to any kind of string or rope – may indicate that the line across the foot means that the foot is tied to something, perhaps to the other foot. The combination means *go slowly,* as one would if hobbled. If one *goes slowly* on a *road* one may fall *behind.*

Since this is our first encounter with the downward pointing, bound foot, it is perhaps the place to mention a point stressed by the Wiktionary authors. In the traditional characters, the three character components 夂 sui1, 夂 zhi3 and 夂 pu1 are distinguished. 夂 sui1, being a foot, is usually written as the bottom component of a character while 夂 zhi3 is often written as the top component and 夊 is often written as the right component. Traditionally, 夊 sui1 is written with the final 乀 stroke slightly protruding above 夂 . In simplified characters, 夊 seems to have merged with 夂 . I could find no font which made 後 with 夊 on the bottom right. 夊 is a variant of 攴 pu1 and of 文 wen2,

以前 **yi3qian2 before, previously, in the past**

蜜月 **mi4yue4 honey moon**

蜜 **mi4 roof 4364 honey; sweet. FR 2014.**

A radical+phonetic character. Although under the rules of the radicode system, the radical is *roof*, etymologically the radical is "worm" on the bottom. This radical often indicates something to do with insects -- in this case, the bee that makes the honey. The top half, 宓 mi4 is an exact phonetic. It means *tranquil, quiet*. It is, in turn, a radical+phonetic character. The roof radical is reminiscent of the same radical in 安 which has a similar meaning. The phonetic in 宓 is 必 bi4 Despite the similarity to 心 xin1 (heart) , there is no etymological connection between the two characters. 必 means *surely,*

 must and appears to be a phonetic loan from a character showing a halberd dividing something. A bronze version is on the left, and the *Shuowen* version on the right. From the *Shuowen* to the modern is a big step, but there is a stroke-to-stroke correspondence as you can easily work out.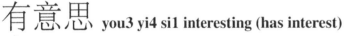

有意思 **you3 yi4 si1 interesting (has interest)**

意 **yi4 stand 014 meaning, idea, thought, wish; expect, anticipate; a little bit, trace; Italy. FR 104.**

 This is an ideogram character. The top of the bronze version on the left shows a tongue sticking out of a mouth (the circle) and represents speaking. At the bottom is something which by the *Shuowen* version, right, had developed into a heart. What is it that originates in the heart and leads to speaking? Thoughts, ideas, wishes, of course, for the ancient Chinese, like the American Indians, knew that thought begins in our hearts, not our brains. The LST seal characters remained faithful to this idea, and then in the
transition to the modern, the tongue came out of the mouth and turned into *stand*, 立 li4, while the mouth became a sun, 日 ri4. The beautiful idea was lost, and the character became nonsense, unless, of course, you know its story.

思 **si1 field 46 think, consider, remember; thinking, idea. FR 298.**

An early modern version 恖 remained truer to the *Shuowen* (on the right) which shows the brain above and the heart below and has the gloss "When one thinks, the vital spirit of the heart rises to the brain." Sadly, the brain has turned into a field; we can hope it is a fertile field.

这样 **zhe4yang4 so, like this**

Frequency ranks: 这 11, 样 88.

半岛 **ban4dao3 peninsula**

半 **ban4 aa7431 half, in the middle, very little. FR 513**

半 To cut in half(八) the carcass of a bull (牛). A bronze version is on the left; the *Shuowen* is on the right.

回 **hui2 wall 0 return, go back, turn around, wind around, answser; classifier for times. FR 172.**

The bronze version on the left expresses clearly the turn-around, wind-around idea. By the *Shuowen*, the spiral had fallen into two pieces, which then got squared off.

风景 **feng1jing3 scenery**

景 **jing3 sun 41053 bright; scenery, view, situation, scene; admire. FR 814.**

景 is a radical+phonetic character. We immediately recognize the phonetic from 京 in 北京 Beijing, and the sun radical fits nicely. We need the *sun* to *admire* the *view* of the *scenery*.

除了 **chu2le besides, in addition to**

除 **chu2 place 3415 besides; eliminate, except; divide; steps. FR 864.**

While there is considerable difference of opinion among the the experts, both Sears and the GHZ see a flight of palace steps, with the palace on the right and the steps on the left. Thus, among the current meanings, "steps" is original and the others presumably phonetic borrowings. The *Shuowen* version is on the right.

澳门 **Ao4men2 Macao**

澳 **ao4 water 3257 bay, harbor; Australia. FR 1627**

(Curiously, there is a problem with all of my serif fonts for this character. For example, the Free Sans gives 澳 but the Free Serif gives 澳. Note the extra 3 stroke above the grain radical on the top right. This seems to be an alternate form, but the extra stroke makes no sense but may originate from the bent top of the central vertical stroke of the *Shuowen* version shown below.)

This is a radical+phonetic character, and the water radical is clearly appropriate. The phonetic 奥 ao4 is exact. It was originally an ideogram meaning southwest and now phonetically borrowed to mean *profound, hard to understand*. The *Shuowen* version is on the right. Hands pick up a sheaf of grain and place it in a room as a memorial gift. Since it was the practice to place this gift in the southwest corner of the room, the glyph originally meant *southwest*. In the subsequent evolution of the character, the hands fell out of the house, merged together and turned into 大. But the character has nothing to do with *big*.

私 **si1 grain 64 private, personal; secret, illegal; secretly, privately. FR 1023.**

厶 si1 by itself means "private" and was used in older writings; the addition of the grain radical gave the sense of "my share of the grain," hence "private". The *Shuowen* version of 厶 is on the right. The French Wiktionnaire says that it shows a bowl. What is in my bowl is my own *private* property. Léon Wieger sees a silk worm curled up in its cocoon, which is a pretty good picture of "private". The *Shuowen* says that it means "treacherous, evil" – meanings that are perhaps back of the modern meanings of *illegal, secret*. Folk etymology sees in 厶 a nose, and certainly everybody's nose is his own *private* property.

介意 **jie4 yi4 mind (as in "I don't mind if you do.")**

举行 **ju3xing2 hold**

举 (舉) **ju3 aa44371 lift, act, deed; start, choose, cite. FR 586.**

On the upper left is a bronze version; on the right, the *Shuowen* version. The basic meaning is *to lift*. It is a radical+phonetic character with the hand at the bottom center being the radical and the rest being the character 與 yu3 as phonetic. Now simplified to 与, 與 means *with, and, get along with* and is among the 100 most frequent characters. And what is the origin of 與? A bronze version is shown on the lower left. The hands are *getting along with* one another. The thing in the middle is phonetic, but what is it? On the lower right is shown a bronze version of 牙 ya2, meaning *tooth* and showing interlocking upper and lower teeth. (Think of the lines as showing just the front edge and bottom of the upper tooth and back edge and top of the lower tooth.) From this image we can recognize what is in the middle of the top of the bronze version of 與. It is *tooth* 牙 ya2, serving as the phonetic. (In the lower center of this particular bronze version is a mouth to help us recognize the teeth above. This mouth is not in other bronze versions nor in modern versions.) Note, by the way, that 與 is a very appropriate phonetic for 舉; the four hands in it seem to be helping the one at the bottom to *lift*.

192

职员 zhi2yuan2 clerk, staff member, office worker; manage, direct; because of

职 (職) zhi2 ear 043 duty, position, job, post. FR 616.

This is a radical+phonetic character. The right side of the traditional character is the now extremely rare character 戠 zhi2, of which, however there are scores of shell-bone examples, such as the one on the top left. A lance or battle axe is on the right and a tongue sticking out of a mouth on the left. The meaning is thought to be a *sentry*, who stands guard with his lance but is always ready to shout and give the alarm. A bronze version is in the middle on the left. There is something in his mouth – maybe a whistle. The sentry's ear is perhaps his most important asset, so by the time of the Shuowen (top right) an ear had been added on the left. In the transition to the modern traditional, the lance cut off the sentry's tongue from his mouth. A sentry has a post, a duty, job and position, and now it is his lance, mouth and ear that represent all of these. Because 戠 zhi2 by itself is a (rare) character meaning *sentry*, 職 is considered a radical+phonetic character, but to my mind the whole thing is a nice ideogram.

The phonetic of the simplified character, 只, is not derived from that of the traditional. Rather it is a character pronounced zhi3 and shown on the right in its *Shuowen* form and on the left in an LST version. It meant "but" and shows a mouth above and a picture of "separation" below. The mouth indicates a speech particle as we saw in 吗 , and "separation" is a pretty good description of what *but* does in a sentence.

员 (員) yuan2 mouth 2534 person engaged in some work; member; classifier for generals. FR 200.

This is a phonetic loan character returned to it original meaning of *round* by the addition of the wall radical in 圆 yuan2. Surprisingly, in its origin it has nothing to do with cowrie shells or mouths but is rather an ideogram with a *round* kettle on a tripod, as shown in the shell-bone version on the upper left. The circle above the kettle emphasizes its roundness. All of the bronze versions were careful to keep the round circle above the sometimes fantastical kettles on two-legged "tripods", as in the version on the lower left. It is easy to see why Xu Shen thought he saw a cowrie shell in such versions and came up with the version on the top right for the *Shuowen*. It unambiguously shows a mouth over a cowrie shell, elements which survive in the modern versions.

Conversations

A: 玛莉, 你最近怎么样?
B: 坐下, 我要告诉你一件事.

A: 什么事?
B: 我快结婚了.

A: 你要当新娘了? 太好了. 祝贺你! 新郎是谁?
B: 是大卫.

A: 你是什么时候认识他的?
B: 我失去年认识他的.

A: 你实在哪儿认识他的?
B: 我实在北京认识他的. 当时我们都在北京学中文.

A: 你们是在什么学校学的中文?
B: 我们是在北京大学学的中文.

A:你们打算什么时候?
B: 下个月三号. 你很快就会收到我们的请帖. 到时你一定要来参加我们的婚礼.

A: 我一定来. 婚礼以后你们要去哪儿度在蜜月?
B: 我们要去香港.

A: 你们以前去过香港吗?
B: 没有, 这是第一次.听说香港是个很有意思的地方.

A: 你回来以后告诉我是不是这样.
B:一定.

* * * * *

A: 玛莉, 你们是什么时候从 香港挥泪的?
B: 我们是上星期回来的.

A: 你们在香港玩儿了几天?
B: 我们在香港玩儿了一个星期.

A: 香港怎么样?
B: 香港很好玩儿,风景也很美.

A: 你们在香港的时候, 住在哪儿?
B: 我们住在半岛饭店.

A: 除了香港, 你们还去了哪儿?
B: 我们还去了澳门.

A: 是吗? 你们怎么去澳门的? 是不是做飞机去的?
B: 我们不是坐飞机去的,我们是坐船去的.

A: 从香港坐船到澳门要多长时间?
B: 澳门离香港很近坐船只要一个小时.

* * * * *

A:王先生, 我想问你一件私事. 不知道你会不会介意?
B: 你问把.

A: 你有没有结婚?
B: 我结了.

A: 你是什么时候结的婚?

B: 我是三年前结的. 你呢, 李先生? 你有没有结婚?
A: 还没有.
B: 有奴朋友吗?

A: 有. 他和我在一个单位.
B: 你们准备什么时候结婚?

A:现在还不知道. 可能两年以后吧.

In modern traditional characters:

A: 瑪莉, 你最近怎麼樣?
B: 坐下, 我要告訴你一件事.

A: 什麼事?
B: 我快結婚了.

A: 你要當新娘了? 太好了. 祝賀你! 新郎是誰?
B: 是大衛.

A: 你是什麼時候認識他的?
B: 我失去年認識他的.

A: 你實在哪兒認識他的?
B: 我實在北京認識他的. 當時我們都在北京學中文.

A: 你們是在什麼學校學的中文?

A: 瑪莉, 你們是什麼時候從 香港揮淚的?
B: 我們是上星期回來的.

A: 你們在香港玩兒了幾天?
B: 我們在香港玩兒了一個星期.

A: 香港怎麼樣?

B: 我們是在北京大學學的中文.

A:你們打算什麼時候?
B: 下個月三號. 你很快就會收到我們的請帖.
　　到時你一定要來參加我們的婚禮.

A: 我一定來. 婚禮以後你們要去哪兒度在蜜月?
B: 我們要去香港.

A: 你們以前去過香港嗎?
B: 沒有, 這是第一次.聽説香港是個很有意思的地方.

A: 你回來以後告訴我是不是這樣.
B:一定.

＊　　＊　　＊　　＊　　＊

B: 香港很好玩兒,風景也很美.

A: 你們在香港的時候, 住在哪兒?
B: 我們住在半島飯店.

A: 除了香港, 你們還去了哪兒?
B: 我們還去了澳門.

195

A: 是嗎? 你們怎麼去澳門的? 是不是做飛機去的?

B: 我們不是坐飛機去的,我們是坐船去的.

A: 從香港坐船到澳門要多長時間?

B: 澳門離香港很近坐船只要一個小時.

* * * * *

A:王先生, 我想問你一件私事. 不知道你會不會介意?

B: 你問把.

A: 你有沒有結婚?

B: 我結了.

A: 你是什麼時候結的婚?

B: 我是三年前結的. 你呢, 李先生? 你有沒有結婚?

A: 還沒有.

B: 有奴朋友嗎?

A: 有. 他和我在一個單位.

B: 你們准備什麼時候結婚?

A:現在還不知道. 可能兩年以後吧.

And in the Shuowen font

A: 玛莉，你最近怎么样？
B: 圣下，我要告诉你一件事。

A: 什么事？
B: 我快结婚了。

A: 你要当新娘了？太好了。祝贺你！新郎是谁？
B: 是大卫。

A: 你是什么时候认识他的？
B: 我去年认识他的。

A: 你在哪儿认识他的？
B: 我在北京认识他的。当时我们都在北京学中文。

A: 你们是在什么学校学的中文？
B: 我们是在北京大学学的中文。

A: 你们打算什么时候？
B: 下个月三号。你想会收到我们的请帖。到时你一定要来参加我们的婚礼。

A: 我一定来。婚礼以后你们要去哪儿度蜜月？
B: 我们要去香港。

A: 你们以前去过香港吗？
B: 没有，这是第一次。听说香港是个很有意思的地方。

A: 你回来以后告诉我是不是这样。
B: 一定。

      *   *   *   *   *

A: 玛莉，你们是什么时候从香港回来的？
B: 我们是上星期回来的。

A: 你们在香港玩儿了几天？
B: 我们在香港玩儿了一个星期。

A: 香港怎么样？
B: 香港很好玩儿，风景也很美。

A：你们住宾馆的时候，住在哪儿？
B：我们住在半岛饭店。

A：除了宾馆，你们还去了哪儿？
B：我们还去了澳门。

A：是吗？你们怎么去澳门的？是不是坐飞机去的？
B：我们不是坐飞机去的，我们是坐船去的。

A：从香港坐船到澳门要多长时间？
B：澳门离香港很近，坐船只要一个小时。

        *   *   *   *   *

A：王先生，我想问你一件私事。不知道你会不会介意？
B：你问吧。

A：你结没结婚？
B：我结了。

A：你是什么时候结的婚？
B：我是三年前结的。你呢，李先生？你结没结婚？
A：还没结。
B：有女朋友吗？

A：有。她呀我在一个单位。
B：你们准备什么时候结婚？

A：现在还不知道。可能两年以后吧。

Lesson 2. Chinese and English

在 **zai4** *progressive aspect marker* See BC Lesson 3.

得 **de** *verb complement marker* See BC Lesson 7.

还(還,還) **hai2 fairly, passably.** See BC Lesson 8

可以 **ke3yi1. See** BC Lesson 7

已经 **yi3jing1 already**

已 **yi3 aa561 stop, cease; already; too; thereafter, afterwards. FR 117.**

This frequent character is of recent origin; it is not in the *Shuowen* or any earlier sources. It was derived from 巳 si4 to distinguish these common meanings from the rather specialized meanings of 巳 – the sixth of the twelve earthly branches and therefore also the time between 9 a.m. and 11 a.m. 巳, in turn, is a phonetic loan character. It is a picture of a human embryo. The *Shuowen* version is upper right. That it is an embryo is made clear by the *Shuowen* version of 包, lower right. 包 bao1 is now a phonetic loan character meaning *to wrap up, include,* or *a bun.* But it has been restored to something like its original sense by adding the "moon" radical which as usual is more nearly the "meat" or "flesh" radical in meaning. Thus 胞 bao1 means the womb or placenta.

经 **jing1 warp**

See BC Lesson 2

真 **zhen1 aa7253 真 real, true, genuine; really, truly; clear, obvious; nature. FR 204.**

(In the radicode, note that the component rule has been applied. After three strokes from the top component, the 3 came from the bottom.)

There are several bronze versions known, such as the one on the left, The *Shuowen* is on the right. Both Sears and Wang advance unconvincing explanations, so I turned to the GHZ where I read that the etymology is not known clearly and none was offered. I won't trouble you with speculations.

哪里 **na3li3 (Polite answer to a compliment. Where? What on earth are you talking about?)**

哪 BC Lesson 3

里 was discussed in connection with 理 in BC Lesson 2.

流利 **liu2li4 fluent**

流 **liu2 water 416 flow, spread, circulate; stream, current; class, grade; exile. FR 396**

This is a radical+phonetic character, The water radical is clearly appropriate. According to the English Wiktionary, the phonetic, 㐬 is a pictogram of a newborn baby, shown upside down. The upper portion is an inverted 子. The three lower lines may represent amniotic fluid. It appears in several other characters pronounced liu, such as 硫, 琉, and 旒.

利 **li4 grain 25 利 gain, profit, advantage, benefit; sharp. FR 155.**

An ideogram. The grain that has been harvested with the knife is *gain, profit*. And the knife that can cut the grain stalks must be *sharp*.

语法 **yu2fa3 grammar (language law)**

Both characters are in BC.

难 (難) **nan2 fowl 54 difficult FR 295**

难 was discussed in connection with 滩 (tan1, beach) in lesson 10 of BC.

一些 **yi4xie1 somewhat, a little**

些 **xie1 foot 631 some, several, a few. FR 86**

The GHZ says the etymology is not clear, and other sources say nothing. The character appears in the *Shuowen* but not in earlier sources. The top is the character 此 ci meaning *this* or *these;* the bottom is the number two. So one could read it as "these two" and two is *some* but only a *few*. As for 此, it shows a foot on the left and a man on the right. The foot, 止 zhi³ means *stop*. So the character could be interpreted as *where the man stops*, or *here*. And what is *here* is *this* or *these*. This interpretation is advanced by

English Wiktionary, but is clearly just modern speculation. Still, it may help remember the character and is not contradicted by what is known of its history.

汉字 han4zi4 Chinese character

汉(漢) Han4 water 54; the Han Dynasty (206 B.C. - 220 A.D.) FR 711

The Han Dynasty, the second dynasty, was so important in the formation of the Chinese culture that the language 汉语 (Han Yu), the characters with which it is written, 汉字, and the ethnic group which speaks it still bear the Han name. (In the West, the names of the language (Chinese) and of the country (China) come from the name of short-lived preceding dynasty, the Qin.) The Han name comes from the name of a river, hence the water radical. The phonetic is the same as the left side of 难(難) nan2 earlier in this lesson and in 滩 (灘) tan1 in BC Lesson 10, where the etymology was explained. But note that whereas 難 nan2 is an ideogram, with the bird combining with the yellow earth to yield *difficult*, and in 滩 tan1 the whole of the 难 character is used as the phonetic, in 漢 it seems someone took a look at 難 and said "That weird thing on the left must have the sound *nan*; I'll use just it to write Han as 漢."

练习 lian4xi2 practice

练 (練) lian4 silk 615 (silk 704) white silk; boil and scour raw silk to make it soft and white; practice, train, exercise; skilled, experienced. FR 1005.

This is a radical+phonetic character. The silk radical clearly fits the original meaning. The phonetic is 柬 jian3, now meaning *card, note, letter*. The *Shuowen* version of 柬 is on the right. It means to *open* something, or perhaps better said, something that has to be opened. The top and bottom of the *Shuowen* version can be read as hands pulling in opposite directions to open the *something* in the middle. Since the something opened was frequently a letter or note, the character came to mean *letter, note, card*. The frequency rank of 柬 is 3047.

习 xi2 practice. See BC lesson 4.

办法 ban4fa3 way, means, method

办 See BC Lesson 3 (handle, do, act)

法 See BC Lesson 6 (law)

短期 duan3qi1 short term

短 duan3 arrow 10 short; lack, fault

短 is a radical+phonetic character with 矢 shi3, arrow, as the radical and 豆 dou4 as the phonetic. We met 矢 in BC Lesson 1 in connection with the character 医. But what does an arrow have to with *short*? Sears suggests: the spear is long; the arrow is short.

The phonetic, 豆 dou4, goes back to shell-bone versions such as that on the top left. It is a picture of a stemmed vessel. Bronze versions and the very similar *Shuowen* version, right, add a line above the vessel to represent what is in it. Since that was likely to be beans, the character came to mean beans and especially soy. 豆腐 dou⁴fu, bean curd, has actually become an English word in the guise of its Japanese corruption, tofu.

期 qi1 See BC Lesson 5. Remember 星期 ?

班 ban1 jade 3317 class, team, squad (of public transport) regular, scheduled. FR 884.

This is an ideogram character. The basic idea is a unit that is sub**division** of a larger whole, and it is the "division" idea that the character depicts. It shows a piece of jade being cut in half by a knife. Remember the knife in 分 from BC Lesson 5? And jade from 现 in the same lesson?

如果 ru2guo4 if, in case, in the event that

如 ru2 woman 0 according to, in compliance with; like, as if; if, in case; for instance, such as. FR 67.

 The character is an ideogram composed of a woman and a mouth. There are numerous shell-bone versions similar to the one on top left. There is no agreement among the authorities as to its original meaning. The GHZ, the English Wiktionary and the Chinese Wiktionary hold that the woman is obeying an order from the mouth of a man and that the character originally meant to obey, follow, comply. The French will have none of this. The Wiktionnaire authors write (in my free translation) "The character shows a woman who is speaking. The original meaning of "feminine speech" is not entirely clear, especially since the character has taken on a generally grammatical sense, which must, however, be derived from its original meaning. The principal classical non-grammatical senses are "to make similar" and "to have the intention to" which suggest a root meaning of presenting things orally "with intention" that is, "according to" and "in compliance with" the way one wants them to be understood. Retrospectively then, the ideogram would seem to evoke the capacity attributed to woman to convince by her discourse. The fundamental meaning is therefore to present matters favorably (to one's self), perhaps even to hoodwink (*embobiner*)."

In short, is the woman obeying the mouth of the man or using her own mouth to make him comply with her wishes?

果 **guo4 tree 07 fruit; result; decisive, determined; really, as expected. FR 165.**

We met 果 in BC Lesson 5 as the phonetic in 课 ke4 and noted that it shows a tree bearing fruit and means *fruit* both literally and figuratively.

As to how 如果 came to mean *if*, try "**in case** it came to **fruition** that ..."

应该 **ying1gai1 should, ought to.**

应(應) **ying1 shed 44 should, ought to; answer, promise. FR 144/**

This frequent character seems to puzzle the experts on etymology; neither the GHZ nor Sears nor Wang nor wiktionary in any language has any explanation of its evolution, though Sears and some others show examples going back to bronze versions. So I will make bold to advance my own theory.

應 is a radical+phonetic character with the heart radical as befits befits a character meaning *should, ought*. All the rest is phonetic. This phonetic has been given its original meaning by adding a bird radical

in 鹰(鷹), ying1, meaning *falcon, eagle,* or other bird of prey.

 A typical bronze version of 应 is shown on the left. The bird is very clear. The big, vaguely Y-like thing on the left is a man. And what is the dot between the bird and the man? It is in 18 of the 19 images that Sears has collected, so it is not accidental but essential. I see in the bird a falcon; in the man, a falconer with outstretched arm for the falcon to ride upon, and in the dot, the essential hood for the falcon.

The *Shuowen* version of 鹰 is on the left. The falconer was not recognized as a man and is on his way to becoming a shed, while the dot representing the hood has moved up beside the upper bird and become a man. The *Shuowen* version of

应 (應) has undergone a parallel development and is on the right.

Of all this, the only recognizable element left in the simplified 应 is the once proud falconer who has turned into a shed.

Even if you can't remember all that every time you see 应, just remember that you *ought* to.

该(該) **gai1 speech 416 ought, should, will probably; that, the above-mentioned. FR 319.**

This is a radical+phonetic character. The speech radical probably merely means that this is an auxiliary verb. The phonetic, 亥 hai4, is the 12th and last of the earthly branches. It has no other meaning and was seemingly invented for the purpose. (The 10 "stems" and 12 "branches" form a way of marking or naming years in a 60 year cycle. You may wish to read about it on the Internet.)

城市 cheng2shi4 city

城 cheng2 earth 641 city wall. FR 413.

A radical+phonetic character. Since a city wall was either mostly or entirely made of earth, the earth radical fits. The phonetic 成 cheng2, meaning *completed, accomplished,* shows a halberd and a nail, as seen in the bronze version on the left. Experts differ on the deeper analysis of this character, so I will just note that it is a very appropriate phonetic since the city wall must be defended to be effective.

市 see BC Lesson 2

进步 jin4bu4 progress

进(進) jin4 go 371 enter, advance; receive, buy; hand in, submit. FR 81.

A radical+phonetic character. The *go* radical fits the *advance, enter* meanings. The phonetic of the simplified is 井 jing3, a well. Some early versions such as the bronze version on the left have a dot in the center to make clear that we are looking down the well. Today wells are drilled and are circular; in former times, they were dug and were typically square or rectangular. The *Shuowen* (right) and earlier versions relate to the modern traditional character with a bird 隹 zhui1. It is an ideogram. Wiktionary says that a bird can only go forwards, not backwards, so go + bird = forwards.

步 bu4 foot 233 step, pace, stage (in a march or process). FR 349.

This one is easy! The GHZ calls it an ideogram, but it is almost a pictogram. The shell-bone versions, left, show two footprints, and a 步 is the distance between them. Some versions, such as the lower one, add a road that the footprint maker walked along. A bronze version, lower right, made the footprints quite unmistakable, but the *Shuowen*, top right, returned to its usual symbolism for footprints, from which the modern character derives.

The word *pace* in the above definition is perhaps not quite correct. A *pace*, from Latin *passus* (as in *mille passus*, 1000 paces = 1 mile) is strictly speaking the distance form one footprint to the next footprint of the *same* foot, whereas these pictures show the distance to the footprint of the *other* foot.

差 **cha4 aa 43112 differ from; fault, not good enough, poor; fall short. FR 732.**

  It should be said just as a warning that this character has four different pronunciations with four different meanings. It goes back to bronze forms such as those on the left. These show a stalk of grain, wheat or rice, above a hand and a tool or a mouth. The hand is rubbing the stalk or about to flail it with the tool to separate the grain from the chaff. Hence, the original meaning was *separation*. But separation or *differing* was likely to lead to *error* and *fault*, and thus to *poor quality* and *falling short*. The *Shuowen* version is on the right.

够（夠）**gou4 ab350 enough, sufficient, adequate; to reach for**

This character went through a strange reversal of sides in the simplification. It is a radical + phonetic character. 多 duo, meaning *many* is the radical; we met it in BC Lesson 4. 句 ju4, which we met in BC Lesson 6, is the phonetic. In the traditional, the radical was on the left in the more usual place; why the simplifiers moved it to the right seems inexplicable. 多 is not a radical in either the radicode system or in the traditional 214 radical system. But that does not mean that it cannot serve as a radical – a root meaning element – in some characters.

机会 **ji1hui4 opportunity**

机 **ji1 tree 36   machine (See BC Lesson 3)**

会（會）   **hui4 top 115 can, know how to, be able to; repeat; meet, assemble; city; pay for; moment, opportunity (See BC Lesson 6)**

练 **lian4 practice (See BC Lesson 6)**

口语 **kou3yu3 spoken language**

Both characters are very familiar.

帮助 **bang1zhu4 help**

A good example of bisylabism; 帮 means *help* and 助 means *help*.

帮 (幫) **bang1 cloth 31152   help, assist; outer leaf (as of cabbage); group (of people), band, gang**

205

Let us begin with the top, 邦 bang1, meaning a village, city or state. A shell-bone example is on the top left. The field 田 at the bottom seems to indicate just an area, not necessarily a cultivated field. Indeed, the tree growing in it indicates that it is a settlement; outside the villages, most land is cultivated and the cultivated fields have no trees. This image does not appear among the bronze characters. Instead, the tree moves to the left and the town is depicted by a circle and a sitting citizen, as shown lower left. The *Shuowen* version is on the right.

In BC Lesson 3, in connection with 哪, we noted "In the transition from seal characters to modern characters, the character for town, 邑, became 邑 yi4, but the radical – always on the right – uniformly turned into the β-like figure which appears on the right in 那."

In 帮 (幫, 幫), the 邦 bang1 is phonetic, but what is the bottom? Sears and some of the Wiktionary authors think it depicts the top part of a shoe or sandal . Since there are no known bronze or seal versions, and no *Shuowen* version, we must rely on the several LST versions. One of these – the clearest for our purpose – is shown on the left. The bottom half shows some object and hands on either side. The idea is that the hands are *helping* the object to do whatever it does or that the object helps to do something, something that may have to do with lifting, as the hands seem to be doing. The object is somewhat reminiscent of the Egyptian ankh, left, which depicts a sandal strap. In 幫, the two hands have slid up and merged with the loop of the sandal strap, but the two side straps have become clear. To repeat, the idea seems to be that the straps of the sandal *help* to hold it on. Not the most convincing etymology, I'll agree. But it will have to do until someone has a better idea.

助 zhu4 force 2511 help, aid, assist

The GHZ says that 助 is a radical+phonetic character. The *force* radical, which also represents strength, fits the meaning well, for strength is often necessary to help and assist. The left side, 且 qie3, is an interesting character but a phonetic so remote that it is hard to believe that the GHZ is correct in calling it a phonetic. Indeed the French Wiktionnaire – which has a fine article on 且 – says that it is a semantic element. It depicts a cabinet in which devotional sacrifices are placed. Thus 助 would mean *devote strength* to someone, and that is a fine way to say *help* them.

跟 gen1 leg 561 heel; follow; with

The leg radical is natural for a character meaning *heel*. The phonetic is familiar from 很 hen3, Remember 我很好. As to the *follow* and *with* meanings, did you ever teach your dog to *heel* when walking *with* you?

Text of the Conversations

A: 马丁, 听说你在学中文.

B: 对, 我很喜欢中文.

A: 你学了多长时间了?

B: 我学了一年多了.

A: 你学的怎么样?

B: 我想我学得还可以. 我现在已经能认识五百个字, 会写三百个子了.

A: 真不错. 你说中文说得也很好.

B: 哪里. 我说中文说得还不太流利.

A: 你觉得中文难不难?

B: 有的地方难,有的地方不难. 语法和发音不难, 但是写字难一些.

A: 你每天写汉字吗?

B:我想每天写, 但是有时工作忙,没有时间练习.

A: 你觉得什么是学中文的最好的办法?

B: 我觉得最好的办法是去中国学. 你想去吗?

A: 当然象. 可是我在工作, 不能在中国住很长时间.

B: 你可以夏天去. 中国的很多学校有短期中文班.

A: 我如果去中国学中文, 你想我应该去哪个城市?

B: 我想你最好去北京. 北京人都说普通话.

* * * * *

A: 小王, 你的英语最近有很大的进步.

B:谢谢. 我的英语还很差.

A: 你学英语学了几年了?

B: 我学英语已经学了两年多了. 但是我想我的英语还不够好.

A: 你为什么要学英语?

B: 我想以后去英国上学. 懂英语工作机会也会多一些.

A:你觉得学英语什么最难?

B:我觉得说最难. 我没有机会练口语.

A: 我可以帮助你. 你跟我练英语,你如果有时间也可以帮助我练习中文.

B:这是一个好主意.

In modern traditional characters:

A: 馬丁, 聽説你在學中文.

B: 對, 我很喜歡中文.

A: 你學了多長時間了?

B: 我學了一年多了.

A: 你學的怎麼樣?

B: 我想我學得還可以. 我現在已經能認識五百個字,會寫三百個子了.

A: 真不錯. 你説中文説得也很好.

B: 哪裏. 我説中文説得還不太流利.

207

A: 你覺得中文難不難?

B: 有的地方難,有的地方不難. 語法和發音不難, 但是寫字難一些.

A: 你每天寫漢字嗎?

B: 我想每天寫, 但是有時工作忙,沒有時間練習.

A: 你覺得什麼是學中文的最好的辦法?

B: 我覺得最好的辦法是去中國學. 你想去嗎?

A: 當然象. 可是我在工作, 不能在中國住很長時間.

B: 你可以夏天去. 中國的很多學校有短期中文班.

A: 我如果去中國學中文, 你想我應該去哪個城市?

B: 我想你最好去北京. 北京人都說普通話.

   * * * * *

A: 小王, 你的英語最近有很大的進步.

B: 謝謝. 我的英語還很差.

A: 你學英語學了幾年了?

B: 我學英語已經學了兩年多了. 但是我想我的英語還不夠好.

A: 你為什麼要學英語?

B: 我想以後去英國上學. 懂英語工作機會也會多一些.

A: 你覺得學英語什麼最難?

B: 我覺得說最難. 我沒有機會練口語.

A: 我可以幫助你. 你跟我練英語, 你如果有時間也可以幫助我練習中文.

B: 這是一個好主意.

And here are the conversations in the Shuowen font, so you won't forget where the characters came from.

A: 玛丽, 听说你在学中文.

B: 对, 我很喜欢中文.

A: 你学了多长时间了?

B: 我学了一年多了.

A: 你学的怎么样?

B: 我想我学得还可以. 我现在已经认识五百个字, 会写三百个字了.

A: 真不错. 你说中文说得也很好.

B: 哪里. 我说中文说得还不太流利.

A: 你觉得中文难不难?

B: 有的地方难, 有的地方不难. 语法和发音不难, 但是汉字难一些.

A: 你考不考虑字呢?

B: 我想考虑字, 但是有时工作忙, 没有时间练习.

A: 你觉得什么是学中文的最好的办法?

B: 我觉得最好的办法是在中国学. 你想去吗?

A: 当然想. 可是我在工作, 不能在中国住很长时间.

B: 你可以暑假去. 中国的很多学校有短期中文班.

A: 我如果在中国学中文, 你想我应该去哪个城市?

B: 我想你最好去北京. 北京人都说普通话.

* * * * *

A: 小王, 你的英语最近有很大的进步.

B: 谢谢. 我的英语还很差.

A: 你学英语学了几年了?

B: 我学英语已经学了两年多了. 但是我想我的英语还不够好.

A: 你为什么要学英语?

B: 我想以后去英国上学. 懂英语工作机会也会多一些.

A: 你觉得学英语什么最难?

B: 我觉得说最难. 我没有机会练口语.

A: 我可以帮助你. 你跟我练英语, 你如果有时间也可以帮助我练习中文.

B: 这是一个好主意.

209

Lesson 3. Calling and Answering

喂 **wei2 or wei4 mouth 0716 hello! (telephone greeting); to feed (a baby or animal) FR 1988**

 This is a radical+phonetic character, and the mouth radical fits both meanings. 畏 wei4 is phonetic. It means *fear, dread*. One of several very similar shell-bone versions is on the top left. It is thought to be a ghost with an uplifted club such as would strike *fear* into anyone. In the bronze versions, lower left, the ghost has put down the club, which some believe to be the forefoot of a tiger with a claw showing – even more fearful than the club. In the Showen version, top right, the ghost's head has become detached, while his body and the club or tiger foot has become quite foot-like. Maybe that is a claw over on the lower right.

开会 **kai1hui4 attend a meeting**

开 **kai1 to open, start, begin, liberate, exploit, expand, develop. See BC Lesson 5.**

给 **gei3 silk 341** 给 **give. See BC Lesson 8.**

留 **liu2 field 36 to leave (a message); to leave behind; to stay, remain; to accept, take; reserve, keep.**

This character was discussed as the phonetic in 溜 in BC Chapter 10.

号码 **hao1 ma1 telephone number**

号 **hao1 number See BC Lesson 5.**

码 **ma1 stone 551 a scale or other measuring instrument; a sign indicating a number or numeral**

A radical+phonetic character. The stone radical presumably points to stone weights for use with a balance. In the forum in Pompeii there is a stone with holes hollowed out to serve as a standard measure of volumes. Doubtless there were also stone standards of length. The phonetic is, of course, 马 ma1, horse.

让 (讓) rang4 speech 211 ask, invite; let, permit; yield; avoid. FR 339

This is a radical+phonetic character. The speech radical fits the "ask, invite" meanings. The phonetic of the simplified character is obviously not derived from that of the traditional but is a rhyming character 上 shang. There are about 12 characters in general use pronounced *rang*; all the others use the phonetic of the traditional form of this character and were not simplified. That phonetic,

襄 xiang1, means *to help, aid, assist*. A bronze version is shown on the left. The explanation by the French Wiktionnaire is that it shows people working together, *helping* one another to make a garment. The frame is the garment; the circles are mouths talking to one another; the hand is doing the work, and the ⊥-like thing is perhaps a stitching awl for making holes in the leather garment for sewing it together. Well, *peut être*.

接 jie1 hand 4146 connect, join; pick up (a telephone); catch; receive; meet, welcome. FR 247.

A radical+phonetic character. The hand radical fits the basic meanings such as *pick up, catch, receive.*

The phonetic is 妾 qie4. The shell-bone versions, such as the one on the top left, show a woman with a headdress, presumably not unlike that of the Qing dynasty empress shown on the far left. (Picture from Wiktionnaire). The *Shuowen* version, right, complicated the headdress beyond recognition, and indeed it was not recognized as a headdress in the transition to the modern version which shows a 立. This was read as an abbreviation of 辛 xin1, thought to be a tool for marking criminals, slaves, and servants. Thus the woman with the regal headdress became a servant, a concubine, which is the current meaning of 妾. 接 is the only character pronounced either jie or qie which uses 妾 as the phonetic.

手机 shou3 ji1 a cell phone

Literally, a "hand machine". We know both characters.

关掉 guan1 diao4 turn off (an electric device)

关, meaning *close, shut,* we met in BC Lesson 5.

掉 diao4 hand 2101 fall; drop, lose; exchange; turn. FR 849.

 This is a radical+phonetic character. The hand radical fits most of the meanings well enough, especially if we note that the "turn" meaning is as in "turn on" or "turn off". The "phonetic" is 卓 zhuo2 meaning *tall, erect, outstanding;* it appears in no other character pronounced *diao* but in several other characters with various pronunciations. It, in turn, has the phonetic zao3 早 which we met in BC Lesson 5. The *Shuowen* version of 卓 on the left shows that the top two strokes are a man, not the diviner's crack. Presumably it is this man who is *tall and erect*, though he looks rather bent over. Maybe he is so tall he had to bend over to get into the character. The *Shuowen* version of 掉 is on the top right.

只是 zhi3 shi4 merely, only, just

We met 只 (but) in Lesson 1 of IC, and of course 是 is very familiar.

聊 liao2 ear 36 chat, kill time; merely, just a little, rely on. FR 1932.

This is a radical+phonetic character. The ear radical clear fits the *chat* sense, which seems to be the original sense. We met the phonetic 卯 mao3 in the discussion of 溜 liu4 in Lesson 10 of BC.

对(對) dui4 inch 54 to, for regarding. FR 33.

We met 对 in the expression 对不起 in BC Lesson 5. Here we add to its meanings.

方便 fang1bian4 convenient, convenience

方 fang1 square; square; direction, side, party; upright, honest; way, plan; only when, just, fair; square meter. FR 60.

We met the square radical, as in 旅, in BC Lesson 9. This is, however, our first encounter with 方 as a character. It's origin from the carpenter's tool is the same as for the radical.

便 bian4 man 130 便 comfortable, convenient, simple; then, in that case; (as a euphemism) defecate, urinate. FR 271. See BC Lesson 7.

送 song4 go 43131 deliver, take someone somewhere; make a present of; see off. FR 656.

This looks like a radical+phonetic character but isn't. It is an ideogram and might seem to mean *go through the closed gate.* In fact, it has nothing to do with 关 either in meaning or sound. An earlier version of the character was 遂 which preserves the structure of the *Shuowen* version on the right. It combines the *go* radical with a picture of two hands carrying fire. Now when do hands carry fire? In years gone by, they often did with the fire was in the form of glowing embers. In the days before the invention of matches (in 1844) carrying glowing coals was an effective way to start a new fire from one already burning. So the combination of *go* with glowing *coals* suggests that the coals are being *sent* to someone who needs them. Some scribe must have mistaken the hands carrying fire for 关. And so the sensible but unusual component was replaced by a nonsensical but usual component.

炒饭 chao3fan4 fried rice

炒 chao3 fire 2343 fry, stir fry, sauté. FR 2590.

A radical+phonetic character. The fire radical fits nicely. The phonetic, 少 shao3, means few, late, little, lack, lost.

饭 (飯) fan4 eat 3354 饭 cooked rice or other grain; a meal. FR 935.

See BC, Lesson 3.

Text of Conversations

A: 喂!
B: 您找谁?

A: 我找你们的经经理, 他在不在?
B: 请等一下儿. 我去看看. ...对不起, 他在开会.
你过一会儿打来.好吗?

A: 我能不能给他留个话?
B: 当然可以. 您贵姓?

A: 我姓张, 我叫张明.
B: 您的电话号码是多少?

A: 我的号码是 212-734-8659
B: 请问, 您要留神么话?

A: 你们的经理回来后,请他给我打电话.
B: 好, 张先生. 我一定让他给您回话.
* * *

A: 我做体晚上给你打电话, 没有人接. 你去哪儿了?
B: 我那儿也没去. 你是几点给我打的电话?

A: 我是八点给你打得电话.
B: 我的手机那个时候关掉了. 对不起,

你找我有事吗?

A: 没有大事, 只是想和你聊聊.
B: 你星期六能来我这儿坐坐吗?

A: 可以, 星期六什么时间对你方便?
B: 我一天都在加. 你什么时间来都可以.
* * *

A: 中国餐馆吗?
B: 是, 这是中国餐馆.

A: 你们送不送饭?
B: 送, 你要什么饭?

A: 请给我送一个炒饭和一个豆腐.
B: 什么时候要送到?

A: 请在七点送到.
B: 没问题. 请告诉我您的地址

A: 我的地址是公园路在 530 号.
B: 你的电话号码是多少?

A: 我的电话号码是 754-3698.
B: 好, 一会儿见.

A: 谢谢.

A: 喂!
B: 您找誰?

A: 我找你們的經經理, 他在不在?
B: 請等一下兒. 我去看看....對不起, 他在開會.
你過一會兒打來.好嗎?

A: 我能不能給他留個話?
B: 當然可以. 您貴姓?

A: 我姓張, 我叫張明.
B: 您的電話號碼是多少?

A: 我的號碼是 212-734-8659
B: 請問, 您要留神麼話?

A: 你們的經理回來後,請他給我打電話.
B: 好, 張先生. 我一定讓他給您回話.
* * *

A: 我做體晚上給你打電話, 沒有人接. 你去哪
兒了?
B: 我那兒也沒去. 你是幾點給我打的電話?

A: 我是八點給你打得電話.
B: 我的手機那個時候關掉了. 對不起, 你找我有
事嗎?
A: 喂!

A: 沒有大事, 只是想和你聊聊.
B: 你星期六能來我這兒坐坐嗎?

A: 可以, 星期六什麼時間對你方便?
B: 我一天都在加. 你什麼時間來都可以.
* * *

A: 中國餐館嗎?
B: 是, 這是中國餐館.

A: 你們送不送飯?
B: 送, 你要什麼飯?

A: 請給我送一個炒飯和一個豆腐.
B: 什麼時候要送到?

A: 請在七點送到.
B: 沒問題. 請告訴我您的地址

A: 我的地址是公園路在 530 號.
B: 你的電話號碼是多少?

A: 我的電話號碼是 754-3698.
B: 好, 一會兒見.

A: 謝謝.

So that Xu Shen can learn to use the telephone, here are the conversations in his characters.

214

A: 中國餐館嗎？
B: 是，這是中國餐館.

A: 你們送不送飯？
B: 送，你要什麼飯？

A: 請給我送一個烤鴨和一個豆腐.
B: 什麼時候要送？

A: 請在六點送到.
B: 沒問題. 請告訴我您的地址

A: 我的地址是公園路 530 號.
B: 你的電話號碼是多少？

A: 我的電話號碼是 754-3698.
B: 好，一會見見.

A: 謝謝.

Lesson 4. Here and There

词典 **ci2 dian3 dictionary**

See BC Lesson 6.

书架 **shu1 jia4 bookshelf**

书 (書) **shu1 book. FR 282.**

See BC Lesson 1

架 **jia4 tree 350 shelf, rack stand; to prop up; classifier for plane surfaces**

This is a radical+phonetic character with the tree radical – a radical that fits shelves, racks, and stands made of wood – and 加 jia1 as phonetic. 加 is an ideogram showing an arm and a mouth and meaning "to put in, to add." The arm is presumably putting something into the mouth. 加 also means "add" in the arithmetic sense, and has a high frequency rank, 166. On the top left is a bronze version of 加; and below it, the Shuowen version. There is no Shuowen, LST or earlier version of 架.

椅子 **yi3 zi chair**

椅 **yi3 tree 3141 chair. FR 1663**

This is a radical+phonetic with the very natural tree or wood radical for a character meaning chair. The phonetic 奇 qi2 is a fairly common character, FR 563, meaning *strange, odd, weird, wonderful, fantastic, remarkable.* Its *Shuowen* version is on the
left. Sears says that it originally meant *to ride a horse*, but that is hard to believe since there is nothing suggestive of a horse in any of the early versions he presents. Wiktionnaire interprets the upward curving line as breath suddenly stopped (by the horizontal line), and the whole picture as a representation of a breath-stopping surprise to the man above, whose arms, legs and open mouth show that he can scarcely believe his eyes. The *Shuowen* version of 椅 is in its usual place on the right.

刀 **dao1 knife**

See the character 分 in BC Lesson 5.

叉子 **cha1 zi fork**

叉 **cha1 aa 544 to cross, intersect; prick; fork, pitchfork. FR 2231**

See BC Lesson 8.

盘子 **pan2 zi plate, tray**

盘 (盤) **pan2 boat 252: tray, plate; coil, twist; check, market quote; build with bricks.**
FR 1049.

This is a radical+phonetic character with the bowl radical, 皿 min3, and 般 ban1 as phonetic in the traditional character. *Bowl* works well enough as the radical for a character meaning *plate*. The problem is in the phonetic. Clearly 舟 zhou1 in the simplified character gives no clue of the sound, but the phonetic in the traditional character, 般 ban1, works well enough. Today, 般 is a phonetic loan character meaning *sort, kind, class, similar to*. But, as is often the case, the drawing has been returned to its original meaning by adding a radical, in this case the hand radical to get the character 搬 ban1. The original meaning seems to have been to move something by boat – or to move the boat – and today it means to move something big, to move one's household, and – as slang – to rake in boatloads of money! The *Shuowen* version of 盘 is on the top right and and of 般 on the lower right.

书包 **shu1 bao1 book bag**

门 (門) **men2 gate (radical) door, gate. FR 185**

包 **bao1 wrap 5** 包 **wrap, package, bag; bun; include; take full responsibility for. FR 454.**

沙发 **sha1fa1 sofa**

沙 **sha1 – water 234 sand, granule; hoarse, raspy FR 848.**

This character was discussed under 少 shao in BC Lesson 4.

发 (發) **fa1 aa3645 send forth, fire, shoot; develop. FR 47**

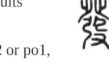

This is a radical+phonetic character with the bow radical 弓 gong1 that suits beautifully a character that means "to shoot forth". All the rest, 癹 ba2 or po1,

is phonetic. This phonetic is an extremely rare character that did not even get into the frequency list. It is said to mean "to level out or remove grass with one's feet." A shell-bone version is on the top left, and the *Shuowen* version on the lower left. Note in the upper figure that the right foot is plainly on the left side and vice-versa. The man who left those footprints must have been swinging his feet back and forth leveling out the ground. In the *Shuowen* version, we seem to see the man down on his hands and knees. In the *Shuowen* version of 發, the man and the hand have moved over to the right to make room for the bow on the left, and there they remained until 1956. Then the bow completely disappeared. I think I still see the hand in the lower right and maybe part of a foot in the upper left. What do you see?

Despite the devastation, the resulting character makes a rather pleasing design, and I have noticed that calligraphers enjoy writing it.

韩国 Han2guo2 (South) Korea

韩 (韓) Han2

The appearance of a second Han in addition to the one we already know, 汉 (漢) Han4, is bound to be confusing.

This Han, 韩 (韓), was one of the Warring States of the period (475 – 221 BC). It was the smallest of the states and lay directly in path of attack of the aggressive Qin against the states of the north China plain. Han withstood heavy attack for some years, but was eventually

Source: Wikipedia, Wikimedia Commons

overcome. The Qin Dynasty (221 – 206 BC) survived through only one emperor, and was followed by the long-lived but only loosely organized Han 汉(漢) Dynasty (206 BC – 220 AD) which took its name from the Han River, a tributary of the Yangtze. The Han River is shown on the above map just

218

inside the Qin area on its eastern side and just south of the Han (韩 or 韓) area, which is shaded quite dark on the map. The official name of South Korea in Chinese is 韓国. Apparently the Koreans chose it for themselves, possibly because they liked the similarity in sound between "han" and "khan" meaning "powerful" in Mongolian-Turkic languages. But they chose to write it with the character (韓) once used by long ago by a valiant little state rather than with the character still used for the national language of China and the ethnicity of its most numerous people (漢). [1]

The meaning of 韩 (韓) – other than serving as the name of countries – is a fence or wall surrounding a well, a puteal. It is a radical+phonetic character. The radical is on the right, 韋 an old form of the character 围(圍) wei2, meaning *to surround* and is perfect for the puteal of a well . Within 圍, the phonetic is 韋 wei2, which means the *woof* of woven cloth, and shows the fabric as a rectangle in the middle, while the shuttle that flies back and forth is represented by the little feet on the top and bottom going in opposite directions. This is a a little tricky; the *radical* in 韓 is 圍, but it is represented by just its *phonetic* part. On the left side of 韓 is its *phonetic,* which is the phonetic of several characters such as 倝 pronounced *gan*. This particular character, 倝, however, reveals what the picture shows, for it means *sunrise.* Once we know that, and look at its *Shuowen* form on the left, we immediately see on the left the sun with upward reaching rays rising above a marker or sundial.

国家 guo2jia1 country

From BC, recall that 家 jia1, the pig-under-the-roof, means family.

蒙古 Meng2gu3 Mongolia

Since these characters are being used just for their sound, not their meaning, we will skip their origins.

---

1 A chapter from the history of the conflict between Han and Qin as told by China's first historian, Sima Qian, is such a good story I must share it.

"But Han heard that Qin was fond of embarking on enterprises, so with the intention of causing its energies to be dissipated and in order to prevent it from making an attack to the east, it accordingly dispatched a water engineer named Zheng Guo to give controversial advice to Qin by making it excavate a canal from the Jing River west of Mount Zhong as far as Hukou, from where it was to go east along the Northern Mountains and flow into the Luo. It would be more than 300 li long, and the intention would be to use it to irrigate the fields. When it was half completed the true purpose was realized, and Qin intended to kill Zheng Guo, but Zheng Guo said: 'At first I was acting in order to cause dissension, but when the canal is completed it will surely be a benefit to Qin.' Qin thought this was true, so in the end had the progress on the canal continued. When the canal did make further progress, it was used to cause the stagnant waters to flow, and irrigate the salty land over an area of more than 40,000 qing, so that the harvest totalled one zhong per mou. Thereupon the area within the passes was turned into fertile but uncultivated land, and there were no calamitous years, and thus Qin became rich and strong, and in the end unified the feudal states. Because of this it was called the Zheng Guo Canal."

Han's scheme back-fired and made Qin so strong that it could defeat Han and all the other states and unify China.

俄国 E2guo2 Russia

俄 now almost exclusively means Russia or Russian. The original meaning is *suddenly, very soon*. We see in the the character a man on the left and 我 wo3 on the right. One may wonder why the missionaries, who picked such nice names for America 美国, England 英国, France 法国 and Germany 德国, could not have found something better for Russia. But they did not have any good choices. For example, Ruguo is sure to sound a lot like ru2guo3 (如果) which means *if,* and *if* is not a nice name for a country. And 肉国, Rouguo, sounds fine but means Pork Country, and is probably no better. 热国 Reguo also sounds all right but means Hot Country, which would be a bit comical. So 俄国 is not such a bad choice.

部 bu4 placeR 4140 part, section; ministry, unit; classifier for books or machines

This is a radical+phonetic character. If we think of the character as meaning a part or section of city, the placeR radical is appropriate. The left side, the phonetic 音 pou3, means "to spit out" and shows a mouth spitting out something, which in the Shuowen version (right), is so much bigger than the mouth that I suspect we are missing something.

学期 xue2qi1 semester

期 qi1　　moon 7213 期　a scheduled time, issue number of a publication; hope; expect.

See BC Lesson 5.

把 ba3 (direct object shifting preposition. See the IC textbook p. 87-88) FR 110.

 把 is a radical+phonetic character. Besides the grammatical function explained in the text, it has many meanings including: *hold, grasp; control, monopolize; guard, watch; handle (of a cart or bicycle)*. The appropriateness of the hand radical is clear. 巴 is a common phonetic in characters pronounced *ba,* but in this case it has just been restored to its original meaning by adding the hand radical. A shell-bone example of 巴 is shown on the top left. It pictures a kneeling figure *grasping.* By the *Shuowen* version, lower left, the figure has curled up and is grasping to his bosom whatever he is holding.

教室 jiao4shi4 classroom

教　jiao1 to teach; jiao4 education, religion. See BC, Lesson 3.

室　shi4 roof 164 室 room See BC, Lesson 3.

重新 chong2xin1 again, anew

重 **chong2 repeat, duplicate.**

Pronounced zhong4, the same character means heavy or weight, and the character's origin is connected with that meaning. The Shuowen version is on the right. At the bottom, we see the earth symbol, 土, and at the top a man bent over seeming to be trying to lift the thing below him. And the thing is just the generic sack of things, the *dong* shown on the left, that been phonetically borrowed to represent east: 東.

布置 **bu4zhi4 arrange (furniture); decorate**

布 **bu4 cloth 31 布 cloth; spread, publish**

This is a just what it appears to be, a pictogram of a hand holding a cloth. Maybe the hand is using the cloth to spread something.

置 **zhi4 net 7251 置 place, put; set up; buy.**

This is our first encounter with the net radical, the long, divided rectangle on top. In some characters, it indeed represents a net. In others, and in particular this one, it was originally an eye. The radicode system cannot make the distinction because it cannot be seen just by looking at the characterl

Since 直 zhi2 is a good phonetic, and the net radical on top could easily be refer to catching with the net of money – that is, buying – one might well suppose that this is a simple radical+phonetic character. The experts, however, maintain that it isn't. The GHZ says it is an ideogram, and Wiktionnaire explains its evolution.

First, let us look at the story of 直 zhi2, which means *straight, just, upright, straightforward, vertical.* A shell-bone example is on the top left, which shows an eye looking *straight up, vertically.* A bronze version, bottom left, added a curved line on the left of uncertain purpose. It was preserved in the *Shuowen* version, on the right, and became the long line across the bottom of the modern character.

Now return to 置. The net refers to a prisoner held captive in the net, and 直 represents justice. The prisoner is being brought to justice. Thus, he will be *put in his place*, either free or in jail. As to the *buy* meaning, perhaps it comes from acquiring something, *netting* it, *justly*, not by theft.

先 **xian1 ox 36 先 first, earlier; elder, ancestor, deceased**

See BC Chapter 1.

放 **fang4 square 317 放 place, put, lay; expel, let go, set free.**

This is a radical+phonetic character. The rules of the radicode system make *square* the radical, but etymologically *hit*, on the right, is the radical and *square* (fang) on the left is phonetic.

窗子 **chuang1zi window**

窗 **chuang1 cave 303** 窗 window

 This character is a pictogram of a house with a window, as seen in the *Shuowen* character on the right. The lines in the window presumably represent things seen inside the house. An LST character on the left may show curtains at the window. In the transition to the modern character, a detail of the roof has become the cave radical.

地图 **di4tu2 map**

地 **di4 earth 265** 地 **earth, ground; place; insight; mind; background. FR 21.**

See BC, Lesson 9. The high frequency is in part due to the use of 地 following an adjective to convert it to an adverb, much like what the suffix -ly does in English.

图（圖） **tu2 wall 354** 图圖 **picture, drawing, plan, design, chart, map. FR 476.**

See BC Lesson 3

挂 **gua4 hand 717** 挂 **hang, put up; think of; register, note. FR 1232.**

The hand radical fits something done with the hand. The phonetic, 圭 gui1, represents a stack of clay or jade tablets. Such jade tablets were held in the ruler's hands on ceremonial occasions. 圭 is also the name of an ancient Chinese device for measuring shadows cast by the sun.

墙（牆） **qiang2 wall**

The traditional character was of the radical+phonetic type with the phonetic qiang2 (a picture of a bed) on the left and a picture of grain (above) stored in a round silo (below) on the right. This is clear enough in the *Shuowen* version on the right. However, the sound – plus perhaps the flat surface of the bed – told the reader that it was neither the bed nor the grain nor the silo which was represented but the *partitions* inside the silo. And from those silo partitions came the word for the walls of modern houses. All that survived quite well into the modern traditional character, but the 1956 simplification was strange. The left side became 土 tu3 – earth – which could not possibly be thought of as a phonetic. Maybe we should think of walls of brick or rammed earth.

电脑 **dian4nao3 computer**

脑（腦） **nao3 moon 4176** 脑 **brain. FR 646.**

 Originally this character was just the right side of the traditional. On the left is an LST version from Wiktionary. It is an ideogram. It is thought that above it shows hair and below, the head of a child with fontanels still visible. The combination suggested "head". The "moon" radical was added later and is here, as usual, really the "flesh" radical. The right side was then borrowed to represent the "nao" sound in a few other characters.

The name "electric brain" unfortunately promotes the false notion that computers can think. As a long-time computer programmer, I can assure you that they cannot. Human programmers can make them *seem* to think, but they are just as mechanical as an automobile, which might seem to be alive.

世界 shi4jie4 world

世 shi4 aa 676 世 age, era, epoch; lifetime; generation; world. FR 181.

First a note on the stroke encoding. The 廿(which is 67) is read as starting above the big L (which is the final 6). There are numerous bronze versions such as the one on the left showing new leaves coming out on a tree branch, a nice way to depict a new generation, a new age. The DHZ calls 世 an ideogram. The *Shuowen* character is on the right. It is easy to see how the modern version evolved from it graphically, but apparently without any idea of what what was being represented.

界 jie4 field34 界 boundary, scope, extent; (in scientific classification) kingdom. FR 288.

This is a radical+phonetic character with the *field* radical and the 介 jie4 phonetic. If we want to ask someone what is the scope, extent and boundary of his work, we may well ask, "What **field** do you work in?" The Shuowen version (right) shows the field with the ancestor of the 介 character. This character goes back to shell-bone versions such as the one on the top left. By the time of the *Shuowen* it had evolved to the version on the lower left. Sears reports that it is thought to represent a man in armor defending a *boundary*. So we have another phonetic – this one exact – which also contributes nicely to the meaning. The current meaning of 介 (top 32) is *between, take seriously* – meanings that would surely please that old fellow in armor defending the border.

拿 na2 top 10 拿 to take, hold, fetch, seize, catch. FR 645.

The Shuowen ancestor of this character, shown on the right, is a radical+phonetic compound with 手, the hand, as the radical and 奴 nu2, – meaning *slave* and composed of a woman on the left and a hand on the right – as the phonetic. En route to the modern character, the 奴 was replaced by 合 he2 showing two mouths talking to one another. Ming dynasty scholars objected but to no avail. The substitution made no sense for either sound or meaning but produced a rather cute-looking character.

进(進) jin4 go 371 enter, come in; receive; buy; hand in, submit. FR 81.

This is a radical+phonetic character, and the *go* radical fits the sense. In the simplified character, the phonetic is 井 jing3, meaning and depicting a well. In the modern traditional, the Shuowen (right), and all earlier versions the "phonetic" is a bird (zhui1). It is so far from phonetic that there is some suspicion that it was never intended to be phonetic but followed a different reasoning. The character for *come* is 来(來) , showing crops coming in. and when the crops come in, well, the birds come too.

公里 gong1li3 kilometer

里 is a combination of 田 (field) and 土 (earth) and is a traditional, rather imprecise measure of distance in China. It is now standardized as one half kilometer, while a 公里 is a full kilometer.

长江 Chang2jiang1 Yangtze River

When we met 长 in BC Lesson 2, we noted "This common character has two different pronunciations with distinct meanings. Pronounced cháng, it means *long, length*. Pronounced zhǎng, it means *grow, increase; eldest, oldest; chief, head*." There we wanted the zhang3 pronunciation. Here we want the chang2 pronunciation. 江 Jiang1originally meant the Yangtze and 河 He2 originally meant the Yellow River. Both terms are now more broadly used, but it is not simple to know when to use one and when the other. Under 江 Wiktionary has an article on when which is used.

长城 Chang2cheng2 the Great Wall

景点 jing3dian3 scenic spot, tourist attraction

景 jing3 sun 41053 scenery, view; situation, scene; admire

This one can be left as an exercise. The *Shuowen* character is on the right. The *Shuowen* version of the *jing* of Beijing is on the left.

周围 zhou1wei2 surroundings

周 zhou1 aa 35710 周 circumference, circle, cycle; week. FR 490.

See BC Lesson 5.

围 wei2 wall 7115 围 Surroundings. FR 576.

See above in the discussion of 韩 Han2 = Korea.

224

太平洋 Tai4ping2yang2 the Pacific Ocean

太 is in BC Lesson 3.

平 ping2 aa1743 平 flat, level; impartial, fair; calm, peaceful; first tone. FR 215.

This is a phonetic loan character. It is a drawing of a single tiny floating duckweed plant. A bronze example is on the left, and the *Shuowen* is on the right. Duckweed makes a flat, green surface on water, so that the not only the sound but also the appearance make it the perfect picture to borrow for the senses of 平. The drawing has been returned to its original meaning by adding the grass and water radicals in 萍 ping2. Duckweed is one of smallest blossoming plants, and when it is in bloom it turns the surface of the pond it covers into a brilliant white.

The expression *Tai Ping* inevitably brings to mind the Tai Ping Rebellion in China, the longest and bloodiest war of the 19th century. If you don't know about it, learn about it; and whenever you eat General Tso's chicken recall that the dish was named by its New York creator in honor of the general who put down the rebellion and kept Qing dynasty in power a few more decades.

洋 yang2 water 4317 洋 ocean; vast; multitudinous; foreign; modern. FR 803.

A simple radical+phonetic character. We met 羊 yang2, the sheep, in several combinations and alone in BC.

大西洋 Da4xi1yang2 the Atlantic Oean

No new characters here.

附近 fu4jin4 vicinity, nearby.

附 fu4 place 32 附 add, get together, agree on. FR 923.

A radical+phonetic character. The phonetic is 付 fu4 meaning *hand over to, pay*. In it we see on the left the man who pays or hands over; and on the right, the hand that hands over.

近 jin4 go 3312 close, near (BC Lesson 9). FR 374.

房间 fang2jian1 room

房 fang2 doorB 41 房 house, room. FR 512.

This is a radical+phonetic character with the doorB radical and the 方 fang phonetic. This is our first encounter of the doorB radical, 户, which differs from the door radical, 尸, only by the addition of a 4 stroke on top.

间 **jian1 gate 01** 间 **between, among; space, room; gap. Classifier for rooms. FR 135.**

The sun *between* the gate posts is a nice ideogram.

公寓 **gong1yu4 apartment**

寓 **yu4 roof 07 reside, live; residence, home; imply. FR 2199.**

寓 is a radical+phonetic character. We say we have a "roof over our heads" when we have a place to live, so the roof radical fits the meaning. The phonetic is 禺 yú, a pictogram of a money; a bronze version is on the top left, and the *Shuowen* version below it. The monkey is given the face of a demon, looking like 田. Directly below the monkey's face is his curling tail. Left of the tail is one hand, and right of it is the other but with the hand closed. (This interpretation is from Wiktionnaire.) The bottom of 禺 is the same as that of 禹 Yu the Great, the legendary founder of the Xia dynasty. The current meaning of 禺 according to Wiktionary is "a kind of large monkey with a long tail and red eyes" and "an area or district" – the latter being presumably a phonetic loan. The usual character for monkey is 猴 hou2.

It was interesting to note that 寓言 "home talk" means folktale or fable and recall that the Brothers Grimm called their stories *Hausmärchen*, "house tales".

厨房 **chu2fang2 kitchen**

厨 (廚) **chu2 cliff 10** 厨 **kitchen. FR 2132.**

The Shuowen (right) and the traditional versions show that this character has nothing to do with *cliff* (as in the simplified) but rather with *shed* or some covered space, which is natural enough for a character meaning *kitchen*. On the right is the *Shuowen* character; in it we see,

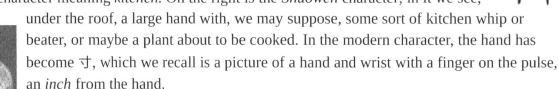

under the roof, a large hand with, we may suppose, some sort of kitchen whip or beater, or maybe a plant about to be cooked. In the modern character, the hand has become 寸, which we recall is a picture of a hand and wrist with a finger on the pulse, an *inch* from the hand.

In the lower left of 厨 there is a 豆 *dou4* container or bowl. The dou ranged from a simple kitchen bowl on a stem to elaborate bronze vessels such as that shown on the left.[2] The dou must have often contained beans, for the character now denotes all

---

2. Image from http://www.chinaknowledge.de/Art/Bronze/bronze.html.

sorts of beans and peas and appears especially in 豆腐 dou4 fu3, better known in America by the Japanese pronunciation, *tofu*.

客厅 ke4ting1 living room.

Literally, "guest room", but not in the sense of a bedroom for house guests.

客 ke4 roof 530 客 guest. See BC Lesson 2.

厅廳 ting1 cliff 15 厅 Hall, big meeting room, government office. FR 1217.

The traditional character showed a shelter and under it an ear 耳, a king 王, an eye looking straight ahead representing moral rectitude 直, and a heart 心. What more could you hope for in a government office? Note that all of this has to do with meaning, not sound, The character is of no great antiquity; it is not even in the *Shuowen* or among the other seal characters. However, a character with some of the same components, 德 de4, has many bronze examples, such as on the top left. It adds to the heart and eye-looking-straight the road or way and means virtue, morality, ethics and upright conduct. In the simplified character, all this is replaced by a nail, 丁! The nail, 丁 ding1 now represents the 4th Heavenly Stem and and has been phonetically borrowed to mean *man* or *member*, but has been restored to its original meaning of *nail* by adding the metal radical in 钉. It is a good phonetic in 厅.

饭厅 fan4ting1 dining room

饭 (飯) fan4 eat 3354 饭 cooked rice or other grain; a meal. FR 935.

See BC Lesson 3

卫生间 wei4sheng1jian1 bathroom

Literally, "sanitation room".

卫生 wei4sheng1 sanitation, hygenie

Literally, "guard (well) being".

卫（衛） wei4 aa 521 卫 defend, guard, protect.

There are numerous shell-bone examples of this character; a particularly clear one is shown on the upper left. In it we see an intersection of two roads, a man in the middle of it, and footprints leading away in all four directions. The man must be a *guard* who repels all attackers and *protects* the roads. In some other shell-bone examples such as the figure in the middle on the left, we still have the intersection of roads, but the figure in the middle appears to be related to the 韋 *wei* figure we met above on page 219 in connection with 韓 Han2. In the center, however, is not a 口-- which might be mistaken for a *mouth* – but a shell-bone version of 方, which – as you well know – is a *square*. On the bottom left is a shell-bone version of the 方 character for comparison. So in this figure the guard and the fleeing feet have been replaced by a phonetic for *wei*. A similar bronze version is in the middle on the right; and the *Shuowen* rendition is on the upper right. Below the 韋 *wei* figure in the *Shuowen* character is a piece of cloth, just to be sure we understand. If it does not look like a piece of cloth to you, compare it to the Shuowen version of 布 on the lower right, which we know is a hand holding a piece of cloth.

As for 卫, it is not easy to see what the simplifiers had in mind. I fantasize that the 5-stroke on top is a fist *defending* the 丄, What do you see?

楼上 lou2shang4 upstairs

楼（樓） lou2 tree 7436 楼 story (of a building), a building of two or more stories. FR 876.

This is a radical+phonetic character. The tree radical is appropriate for traditionally most buildings were made of wood. The phonetic, 婁 lou2, is common as a phonetic but very rare as a character. It seems to mean something like *to wear* and to show a woman (below) with a chain of objects such as beads or a rosary. The idea is that the woman *wears* the chain of objects.

楼下 lou2xia4 downstairs

No new characters here.

边（邊） bian1 go 35 边 side, edge, border, margin, boundary. FR 316.

This is mainly an ideogram composed of two pieces, 臱 and the *go* radical 辶, but 臱 mian2 also helps to indicate the sound. Its components are 自, 穴, and 方. The last is here just representing some unspecified object. The object is under the cover, 穴, and thus has *disappeared* from the sight of the eye, 自.

So, the whole 臱 character means "to disappear, vanish." And thus the whole 邊 character means "go where you may disappear". Wiktionnaire illustrates such a place with the photograph on the left. It is is certainly a border, a boundary, and edge.

While the simplified, 边, is not quite so dramatic, it could be read as "go where you need strength", and the same scene would surely qualify.

Text of the Last Conversation

(The first conversation makes sense only with the pictures.)

老师: 今天是新学期的第一天. 我们把教室重新布置一下儿, 好不好?
学生: 好老师, 请告诉我们怎么做.
老师: 先把这些新书防在书架上.
学生: 书架还放在老地方吗?
老师: 我们把书架换个地方, 把它放在两个窗子的中间, 你们觉得好不好?
学生: 我们觉得很好.
老师: 我买了一张中国地图. 请把它挂在教室后面的墙上.

学生: 我有一张世界地图. 我能不能把它挂在中国地图的旁边?
老师: 好主意.
学生: 老师, 电脑放在哪儿? 放在你的桌子上吗?
老师: 不, 学校给我们买了一张电脑桌子. 我们可以把电脑在电脑桌子上.
学生: 太好了! 电脑桌则在哪儿?
老师: 请把它放在教师的后面.

229

The conversation in traditional characters.

老師: 今天是新學期的第一天. 我們把教室重新布置一下兒, 好不好?

學生: 好老師, 請告訴我們怎麼做.

老師: 先把這些新書防在書架上.

學生: 書架還放在老地方嗎?

老師: 我們把書架換個地方, 把它放在兩個窗子的中間, 你們覺得好不好?

學生: 我們覺得很好.

老師: 我買了一張中國地圖. 請把它挂在教室後面的牆上.

學生: 我有一張世界地圖. 我能不能把它挂在中國地圖的旁邊?

老師:好主意.

學生: 老師, 電腦放在哪兒? 放在你的桌子上嗎?

老師: 不, 學校給我們買了一張電腦桌子. 我們可以把電腦在電腦桌子上.

學生: 太好了! 電腦桌則在哪兒?

老師: 請把它放在教師的後面.

And since there is still room on the page, here is the Shuowen font:

230

Lesson 5. School and School Life

初 **chu1 dress 53** 初 **beginning, primary, first, elementary. FR 667.**

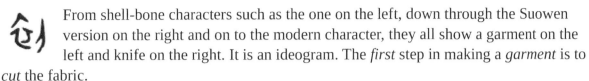

From shell-bone characters such as the one on the left, down through the Suowen version on the right and on to the modern character, they all show a garment on the left and knife on the right. It is an ideogram. The *first* step in making a *garment* is to *cut* the fabric.

高 **gao1 hat 025** 高 **high, tall. FR 134.**

See BC Lesson 1.

年级 **nian2 ji2 (of school) grade, year**

年 **nian2 aa 3172 year**

See BC Lesson 5.

级 **ji2 silk 534** 级 **grade, level, step, degree. FR 415.**

This is a radical+phonetic character. It has the silk radical because it originally referred to the *grade* of cloth. The phonetic is 及 ji2, meaning *to catch up with, to reach*. It is an ideogram showing a hand on the right grabbing a man on the left. The hand has *caught up with* the man. A shell-bone version is on the top left and a bold bronze version lower left. The *Shuowen* version of 及 is on the bottom right and of 级 on the top right.

数学 shu4xue2 mathematics

数（數） **hit 743 shu3: count, count as; blame; FR 234**

  shu4: number, numeral; quantity; few; fate, doom

  shuo4: frequently, repeatedly

This character has three slightly different pronunciations with three different meanings, one as a verb, one as a noun, and one as an adverb. There are several explanations of its origin of which the most plausible seems to me to be that of Wiktionnaire, which considers it an ideogram with a string of beads on the left and a hand using them to count on the right. This view fits well with the LST version shown on the left. In the *Shuowen* version, right, the top and bottom beads are evolving towards their forms in the modern traditional character.

外语 wai4yu3 foreign (outside) language.

No new characters here. A foreigner, a non-Chinese, is a 外国人.

体育 ti3yu4 physical education

体 ti3 man 7341 body, essence, form, style. FR 149.

本 ben3, meaning *base, foundation*, is an indicative character. It is a tree, 木, with a line added at the bottom to emphasize the base. 体 is an ideogram. The idea is that the base of man is the *body*.

育 yu4 hat 64251 育 to give birth to, to rear children, to educate. FR 609

  Shell-bone versions such as the one on the top left show a woman who has just birth to a child, who is shown upright. In all the known bronze examples, the child is upside down, as on the lower left. In the Shuowen version (right) – as in all the LST examples – the upside-down child has floated to the top and the mother has turned into a pork chop! And that is exactly what we have in the modern character that means to educate – an upside-down child and a pork chop!

自然科学 zi4ran2 ke1xue2 natural sciences

自然 zi4ran2 nature, natural, naturally

自 zi4 nose 自 self, personal; from, since; certainly, of course.

The character is a picture of a nose, and from *nose* to *self, personal* is a short step. To the other meanings is a longer step, but by now we are used to some long steps.

然 ran2 fireB 354 然 yes, right, -ly

This is an ideogram that has been phonetically borrowed. Its original meaning was *to cook*. The Shuowen character (on the right) shows a pork chop (left) and a dog (right) *cooking* over a fire (bottom). It was then phonetically borrowed for its current meaning and restored to its original meaning by adding a second fire on the left to get 燃 ran2 and meaning *to cook*.

As to the meanings of *natural, naturally* for 自然 you can try "of course right." Yet it remains surprising to me that the language of a people that so love and appreciate nature do not have a better word for it than 自然, but that seems to be the case. On the other hand, our word *nature* comes from Latin *natura*, originally meaning just *birth*. Perhaps the ancients were so surrounded by Nature that they had no word for it.

科学 ke1xue2 science

科 ke1 grain 447 科 branch, division, field of study; family (in scientific classification). FR 277.

This is an ideogram. On the left is grain and on the right is 斗 dou3, a picture of a grain scoop, a meaning which it retains, though it is now also a measure of grain standardized as a decaliter (10 liters). On the top left is a shell-bone example of 斗; the scoop has a grain in it, a grain on either side of the handle, and a handguard on the handle. A bronze version, lower left, leaves out the grains. Some of the LST seal characters, such as the one on the lower right, stay close to this image, but others, and in particular the Shuowen (upper right) miss the idea. The hollow scoop proper has turned into two parallel lines. In the modern version, these two lines – the erstwhile scoop – have fallen completely off the handle and reversed slope. On the right of 斗 is the old handle and handguard.

So what is the ideogram in the whole 科 character? Well, the scoop *divides* the grain.

With that mystery resolved, it still strikes me as strange that the main word for science derives from dividing rather than from knowing or unifying.

美术 mei3shu4 fine art

术（術）shu4 tree 4 (road 74311) 术 art, skill, technique; ways and means; tactics, strategy. FR 328.

The basic meaning of 术（術）is a way, road or path, much the basic meaning of the road radical. The middle of the character, 术 shu4, provides the sound. Sears, our usual source for ancient forms of characters, has nothing before the *Shuowen* for this character. The OECCD and Wang, however, provide the two shell-bone examples on the left with the comment that they show a hand with sticky food adhering to it – actually to the wrists! It was then combined as the phonetic with the road radical to produce the *Shuowen* form of 术（術）on the right. In Chinese as in English, the *way* idea includes both the way (road) by which to reach somewhere and the way to do something. So we find the character evolving to mean *skill* and *technique* and eventually *art*. Meanwhile, the sound and sticky connotations of 术 were employed to combine it with the grain radical to get 秫 shu2, a glutinous, sticky variety of foxtail millet. Note how here again the phonetic is especially appropriate also for the meaning. Now, of course, the character look not like "sticky grain" but "artistic grain"!

大多数 da4duo1shu4 majority, most of

We had 数 on page 231; the other two are familiar.

选（選）xuan2 go 3713 select, choose, elect; selections, anthology. FR 499.

This is a radical+phonetic character with a basic meaning of *to choose*, as to choose a path; hence the *go* radical. In the simplified, the phonetic is 先 xian1 (BC Lesson 1), which works well enough phonetically but is not related to the phonetic of the

traditional or earlier versions of the character. The phonetic of the traditional is 巽 or 巺 xun4, ☴, the fifth of the eight trigrams used in divination in the I Ching. As a character, it has the meaning of *modest, obedient* with a FR of 5255. Sears thinks it shows two people at a table with lots to eat. The Shuowen's 选 is on the right.

毕业 bi4ye4 to graduate (literally, to finish studies)

毕（畢） bi4 aa 6167 毕 finish, close, terminate. FR 1093.

Shell-bone versions (top left) show a hand holding a net on a stick, presumably a device for catching small animals in the field. In most of the dozen or so bronze versions, a field has appeared at the top of the character and the hand has merged with the stick and appears as just a horizontal line across the bottom of the stick (lower left). Wang says that the field, 田, is a symbol of hunting; and indeed it appears in a number of the characters in his section on characters related to hunting. An American magazine devoted to hunting and fishing is called *Field and Stream*. Initially, the character was clearly a

pictograph. The authorities do not use the words *phonetic loan* for it, so we should probably think of a gradual evolution in meaning. To 畢 an animal clearly meant to *close* in on it, *finish* it off, and *terminate* it. The *Shuowen* 畢 is top right.

业（業） ye4 aa 2243 industry, business, studies; do; already; karma. FR 130.

The simplified character is just the very top of the traditional character. Both the GHZ and the OECCD assure us that the bronze versions such as shown on the left are pictures of a wooden stand for hanging a musical instrument such as perhaps some sort of chimes. The tree at the bottom may be part of the stand or may indicate that it is made of wood, or both. (The function of the mouth in this example is unclear; it did not survive.) The resemblance of the top half of the character to 丵 zhuó, a now rare character meaning (and showing) thickly growing grass seems to be pure coincidence. The picture of the chime stand was then phonetically borrowed for the current meanings, but since the chime stand had gone out of use, the picture did not need to be returned to its original meaning by addition of a radical. Top right is the *Shuowen* version of 业. (Secretly, I see in the two vertical lines tall smokestacks of *industry*.)

研究生 yan2jiu1sheng1 graduate student

研究 yan2jiu1 research

研 **yan2 stone137** 研 **to grind; study thoroughly. FR 447.**

开 The stone radical, referring to the millstone, fits the *grind* sense. The phonetic is 开 jian1, a very rare character meaning *same, equal.* The *Shuowen* version of 开 is on the left; it is an clearly an ideogram with the meaning suggested by the sameness and equality of the two components. The Shuowen 研 is on the right. I was amused by this character because in my graduate- student days someone who studied all the time was called a *grind*.

究 **jiu1 cave 36** 究 **examine, study carefully; finally, at last. FR 429.**

The DHZ says quite simply that 究 is a radical+phonetic character with the cave radical and 九 jiu3 as the phonetic. End of discussion. But what does *cave* have to do with the meaning of this character? Wiktionnaire is bolder. If sees in 九 = 9 the *end* of the first cycle of numbers. Indeed, each cycle of ten ends with a 九. So read 九 as "go to the end." Then "go to the end of the cave" is a great way to express in picture language "study carefully, examine thoroughly" as well as "finally, at last". So once again, the phonetic does double duty. Whether or not this explanation is historically correct – something no one really knows – it is good way to remember the meaning of the character.

读 (讀 or 讀) **du2 speech 75** 读 **read, study, read aloud; attend school. FR 754.**

The *Shuowen*, the GHZ and OECCD all blithely assert that 读 is a radical+phonetic character with 卖 (買 or 賣) mai4 as the phonetic, as if there were nothing strange about a character pronounced mai4 being used to suggest the pronunciation of one pronounced du2! If so, pronunciations have certainly changed radically. Wiktionnaire takes the problem seriously and suggests rather that the character is an ideogram, that 賣 is an eye looking at a sales contract (represented by the cowrie shell), presumably reading it, and that 言 indicates that the *reading is aloud*. This explanation at least makes sense. The earliest examples of 賣 are a few bronze characters such as shown top left. From them, it is clear that what later became a net was originally an eye. What is above the eye is less clear. In connection with the 厅 character on page 227 we saw that a line coming out of an eye might mean just the sight itself. That may well be the case here also. If so, what is above the shell is just an eye looking at it, that is, reading the sales contract. And the speech radical indicates that the reading is aloud. The *Shuowen* version of 读 is on the top right. I have seen no ideas about what is in its top right corner, nor do I have any, save that it looks unrelated to 士.

硕士 shuo4 shi4 master's degree

硕（碩） shuo4 stone 132 硕 large, huge. FR 2304.

This is a radical+phonetic character, but the phonetic is 石 shi4 and the radical is *head* 页. In the radicode system, the radical is *stone*, for left is stronger than right. The traditional system has no rule, so one would not know under which radical to look for this two-radical character. By its meaning, however, 硕（碩） belongs under the *head* radical. It can be compared with our word *chief* and French *chef* which both come from Latin *caput*, head. These words, however, indicate great in importance rather than physical size. While 碩 can be used as just a synonym of 大, in 硕士 it is clearly not the size of the gentleman that is intended but his importance. We should think of 硕士 as meaning *great gentleman* or *great scholar* and try not to think of a stone-headed 士.

博士 bo2 shi4 doctoral degree

博 bo2 ab77 extensive, ample; to obtain, win. FR 965.

On the left we have 十 shi2, ten, and on the right 尃 fu1, to scatter widely. Wiktionary says it is a radical+phonetic character, but the DHZ says it is an ideogram. I tend to agree with the DHZ. Ten times *scattered widely* is surely *extensive*. Indeed, 十 as the end of a cycle of numbers – the upper limit of what we can count on our fingers – has a connotation of *utmost*. So the 博士 is the utmost gentleman, the max scholar. As for 尃 fu1, it is a very rare character that did not make it into Jun Da's frequency list, but is made up of two common components, the inch radical below – which here as usual is used just to mean hand, the hand that scatters widely – and the 甫 fu3 phonetic above. The radicode of 甫 is aa742 and its meaning is *just, just now* with frequency rank of 2152.

现...再 xian1 … zai4 first … then

现（現） xian4 jade 2536 现 to show, reveal; now, the present; in stock, on hand. FR 70.
See BC Lesson 5.

再 zài aa 127 再 again, more. FR 242.
See BC Lesson 2.

决定 jue2 ding4 decide, decision

決 **jue2 ice 351** 决 **(of a dike or dam) burst, be breached; break off, rupture; decide. FR 273.**

This is a radical+phonetic character with ice as the radical and 夬 guai4 as phonetic. There are no bronze or earlier characters, so the Shuowen version is as early as we have. It shows a water radical rather than an ice radical, though if we think of a burst water pipe instead of a dam, the ice radical fits fine. Sears sees in the *Shuowen* character a foot over a hand an advances the idea that the hand works with the foot to be *certain*, which may be the meaning of 夬, an image preserved an older traditional form of 夬. The Wiktionnaire authors see the hand as holding something and speculate on what it may be. Wiktionary shows 夬 appearing in 22 other characters, but as a character by itself it is extremely rare.

定 **ding4 roof 12** 定 **tranquil, fixed; to fix, to decide**

See BC Lesson 7.

出 **chu1 aa 26262** 出 **out, go out; exceed; issue; attend; leave; produce; happen. FR 28.**

See BC, Lesson 9.

容易 **rong2 yi4 easy, likely, liable to**

容 **rong2 cave 340** 容 **hold, contain; let, permit; appearance. FR 442.**

容 is placed under *cave* in the *Quick Guide*, and I believe that that is the natural place to look for it. But both the Wiktionnaire and the GHZ say that is wrong etymologically and that it should be under roof, for it is composed of a roof and the character 谷 gu3 meaning a narrow gorge with a stream flowing in it. Several shell-bone images such as shown on the top left make clear that this is no roofed structure as might appear from the modern version. The mouth at the bottom is really the spring from which the stream in the gorge flows. Some bronze examples, such as on the lower left make plain that the "mouth" is really no mouth. The *Shuowen*, upper right, is unconcerned with where the spring needs to be relative to the gorge. But wait! Sears thinks the mouth is a mouth after all and is babbling and chattering away, just like Tennyson's brook that says

> I chatter, chatter, as I flow
>   To join the brimming river,
> For men may come and men may go,
>   But I go on for ever.

But what does all of this have to do with the meaning of 容? Well, both the GHZ and Wiktionnaire maintain that 容 is an ideogram,

An American 谷: *Watkins Glen*

that on the top we have a roof, representing a house, a home, and below we have a beautiful mountain stream in a gorge. And what do they have in common? They are things we should enjoy, and *enjoy* is the basic, original meaning of 容, from which the modern meanings have evolved.

易 **yi4 sun 3533** 易 **easy; change, trade, exchange; amiable; clear land. FR 461.**

There are many shell-bone images mostly quite similar to the one shown top left. The most plausible interpretation that I have seen is that of Wiktionnaire, which suggests that the object on the right is a shallow cup or dish shown on edge throwing out whatever was in it, thus portraying the idea of *change*. There are also numerous bronze examples mostly similar to the one on the lower left. But the idea seems to have been lost, for the concavity goes in the wrong direction. In the *Shuowen*, (top right) the base of the plate seems to have turned into the sun and the discarded contents into rays of sunshine!

This is the *yi* of the 易經 (*Yi Jing*) commonly known in English by the Wade-Giles transcription of its name as the *I Ching* or *Book of Changes*. (Bear in mind that Thomas Wade would have pronounced *I Ching* just like we pronounce the pinyin *Yi Jing*.) 經 jing1 means *warp*, the vertical threads in a loom, and shows on the right a loom with the warp emphasized.

所以 **suo3 yi3 therefore**

所 **suo3 ax 33 place, building, office, institute; actually; what; classifier for houses. FR 54.**

There is no doubt about what is depicted: a door on the left and an ax on the right. (But the door is not enough like our door radical, 戶, to count as the radical.) The question is, How does door+ax = place? Both Wiktionary and the GHZ maintain that 所 is a radical+phonetic character with the ax as the radical, 戶 hu4 as the phonetic and originally representing the sound of the ax felling a tree, presumably for building a house. And, of course, the 戶 phonetic – with its meaning of *door* contributes to the meaning of 所 as *building* and a classifier for houses.

以 **yi3 ab 6434** 以 **to use; with, by means of; according to; so as to; by; because. FR 23.**
See BC Lesson 7.

As to how 所以 came to mean something like *therefore*, try "what because of" – not very good English but not unlike "there for".

一流 **yi1 liu2 first-rate, first-class**

流 **liu2 water 416 flow, spread, circulate; stream, current; class, grade; exile. FR 396**
See above, page 200.

那么 na4 me so, to such a degree

那 na4 that; see BC 7; 么 me – see BC 1.

通过 tong1 guo4: pass

通 **tong1 go 542 open, go through; pass on; connect; understand, know; open. FR 190.**

See BC Lesson 6. Remember 普通话. (Riding on the *go* radical is a bell going tong, tong, tong!)

过 (過) **guo4 go 514 过 to pass through. FR 46.**

See BC Lesson 8.

严格 **yan2 ge2: rigorous, strict, tough**

严 (嚴) **yan2 aa122431 ⺤ tight, serious, stern, strict, rigorous. FR 545.**

The earliest examples are bronze example, notably the one on the left. (Sears has no bronze examples; this one is from Wiktionary.)

The GHZ sees this as a radical+phonetic character with 吅 xuan1 as the radical and a character exactly like the lower part of 嚴 pronounced yin2 as the phonetic. The problems with this explanation are two. First, 吅 as a radical is a variant of three other, very different characters, one meaning *neighbor*, another meaning *noisy*, and the third meaning *to accuse* – none of them related in any way to the meaning of 嚴. Second, the alleged phonetic is so rare that it escaped Unicode, is not in any other character pronounced *yan* or *yin* (except when combined with 吅). Indeed, it is not in the DHZ itself. Despite my great respect for the DHZ, I am not satisfied with this explanation.

Wiktionnaire takes seriously the problem of the picture's meaning and notes that it occurs in bronze inscriptions only in passages infused with dignity and respect. The scene is in an underground grotto where an arm and hand rise out of a *mouth*, the arm supported by a second hand on the lower right. Above the grotto seem to be three mouths. One is reminded of the Greek mysteries at Eleusis, which involved underground initiations, but the discipline was so *strict, rigorous,* and *stern* that to this day we do not know precisely the content. In the *Book of Revelations* at the end of the *New Testament* we have the vision of a being of light from whose *mouth* comes a two-edged sword (Rev 1.16). Such a sword is a symbol of strength just as is the arm with hand in our image. In the initiation services, besides the hierophant from whose mouth go forth the words of power, there would be a helper (an acolyte) represented by the second hand, and doubtless also a choir, represented by the three mouths, which may have been outside the inner sanctum.

Of all this, only the grotto and some strange relics of the upper mouths remain in 严. The initiation scene has turn into just a big blank.

As to the relation of this scene to the modern meaning of the character, it comes, as already indicated, from the strict, rigorous, and stern discipline connected with the mysteries.

格 **ge2 tree 3540 格 frame, rule; division, check, standard, style. FR 325.**

This is a radical+phonetic character, and we need to first deal with the phonetic, 各 ge4, which means to come in or simply to come. A shell-bone example, top left, shows a foot entering an open house. The modern 各 also has two elements, but the house has turned into a mouth and the foot looks more like a hand; the bronze character on the lower left shows an intermediate step; the house has turned into a mouth and the foot is moving towards 夂 zhi3, the top of the modern character.

There are quite a number of bronze versions of 格 like the one on the left of this paragraph. They clearly show a tree – the radical – on the left and the foot going into a house, the phonetic, on the right. The original meaning was a frame or form made of wood, and the character with the tree radical represented it well. The Shuowen rendition is on the right, and the modern character follows from it. Just try to think "foot entering house", not "foot in mouth".

考试 kao3shi2 examination

考 kao3 old 1 give or take an examination; check; study

Under 烤 kao3 in BC Lesson 8, we read "The phonetic 考 kao3 shows an old man with long hair leaning on a cane. as seem in the bronze version on the left and the *Shuowen* version on the right. It formerly meant *deceased ancestor* and *to depend..* Currently, however, presumably by phonetic loan, it has come to mean a test or examination."

试 **shi4 speech 641 试 try (in the sense of test out), test. FR 643.**

See BC Lesson 7.

成绩 **cheng2 ji1; grade, result, achievement.**

成 **cheng2 spear 5 成 completed, successfully accomplished; become, fully developed. FR 59.**

绩(績) **ji1 silk 711 twist hempen thread; achievement, merit, accomplishment. FR 1547.**

This is a radical+phonetic character with 责 ze2 as phonetic. The *Shuowen* version is on the right. The silk radical fits the original meaning of 绩: to twist hempen thread.

The other meanings must be phonetic loan. The phonetic element 责 goes back to shell-bone examples, such as the one on the top left. It is a radical+phonetic character with the cowrie shell (money) as its radical and 朿 ci4 – 圭 much flattened into – as phonetic. It has the sense of *demand, extort, exact* – meanings that go well with the shell = money radical. The phonetic in 责, 朿 ci4, a rare character, is a pictogram of a tree with thorns. The thorns – at least one of which is visible in the shell-bone image on the upper left – contribute nicely to the meaning of 责. The picture of the tree survived fairly well up to the *Shuowen* (top right), but was seriously smashed in the modern characters.

或 **huo4 lance 01** 或 **or, probably, someone. FR 160.**

See BC Lesson 1 in connection with the characters 国(國) in the supplementary characters at the end of the lesson.

分 **fen1** **aa 3453** 分 **divide; allot; distinguish; branch;** *minute***; fraction. FR 79.**

See BC, Lesson 5.

又 **you4 aa 54** 又 **further; repeated, again, also, too. FR 126.**

 This phonetic loan character is simply a picture of a right hand. There are jillions of examples from shell-bone times (left) up through the *Shuowen*, right.

必须 **bi2 xu1 must**

必 See 蜜 page 190.

须 See 参 page 188

辛苦 **xin1 ku1 hard, toilsome**

辛 **xin1 club** 辛 **hard, laborious, hot (spicy), sad, bitter, suffering.**

This is our first encounter of the club radical, 辛, in a simplified character. It was discussed, however, in BC, Lesson 3, under 办 (辦). It seems to be a picture of some ancient instrument of punishment.

苦 **ku1 grass 70 bitter, hardship, suffer from; patiently; give someone a hard time. FR 634.**

This is a radical+phonetic character. The grass radical no doubt refers to the bitter taste of some herbs. The phonetic is 古 gu3, meaning old. We discussed it in BC Lesson 4 under the character 做. One could take 古 just as an indication of sound and nothing more, but is it not true that *old* people must often *suffer hardship patiently*?

很少 **hen3 shao3, seldom, rarely**

很 **hen3 road 56** 很 **very**

See BC Lesson 1.

少 shao aa 2343　　少　**shao3 – few, little, lack, lost, missing, a little while.**

See BC Lesson 4.

教育 **jiao4 yu4 educate, education**

教 **jiao1 and jiao4 hit 73** 教 **jiao1 to teach; jiao4 education, religion.**

See BC Lesson 3.

育 yu4 See above, page 232.

A: 你在哪儿上学?
B: 我在第五中学上学.
A: 你上初中还是高中?
B: 我上高中.
A: 你现在是几年级?
B: 我现在是高中一年级.
A: 你们班有多少学生?
B: 我们班有四是个学生.
A: 你们有些什么课?

B: 我们有中文,数学,外语,历史,体育.音乐,自然科学和美术等等.
A: 你们有什么外语课?
B: 我们有英语,法语和日语,但是大多数学生都选英语.
A: 你们有没有外国老师?
B: 有,我们有两个外国老师, 一个是英国人,一个是日本人.他们叫我们英语和日语.

* * *

A: 你在哪儿上学?
B: 我不上学了. 我毕业了.
A: 你已经毕业了? 真快. 你有没有找到工作?
B: 我没有到工作, 我想读研究生.
A: 你想读什么?
B: 我想读历史.
A: 读研究生要几年?
B: 读硕士要两年, 读博士一般要五年.

A: 你要读硕士还是博士?
B: 我现在还不知道. 我想先读硕士,以后再决定要不要读博士. 你呢?你还上学吗?
A: 不, 我也毕业了, 正在找工作.
B: 你想做什么?
A: 我学得是英语,我想当英语老师.
B: 听说很多学校现在要老师.你一定能找到老师的工作.
A: 那就太好了.

* * *

A. 小王,有人说在中国进大学难,出大学容易在美国进大学容易出大学难. 你觉得是怎每样吗?
B. 是这样. 中国每年有很多高中毕业生,他们都想进一流大学, 但是没有那么多一流的大学. 所以不是每个人都能进最好的的大学.

A.一般怎么进大学呢?
B. 你要通过很严格的考试.如果这成绩不好,就不能进大学或不能进很好的大学.
A. 在美国上大学不要通过考试, 但是要进好的大学也不容易.

A: 你在哪兒上學?
B: 我不上學了. 我畢業了.
A: 你已經畢業了? 真快. 你有沒有找到工作?
B: 我沒有到工作, 我想讀研究生.
A: 你想讀什麼?
B: 我想讀曆史.
A: 讀研究生要幾年?
B: 讀碩士要兩年, 讀博士一般要五年.

A: 你要讀碩士還是博士?
B: 我現在還不知道. 我想先讀碩士, 以後再決定要不要讀博士. 你呢? 你還上學嗎?
A: 不, 我也畢業了, 正在找工作.
B: 你想做什麼?
A: 我學得是英語, 我想當英語老師.
B: 聽說很多學校現在要老師. 你一定能找到老師的工作.
A: 那就太好了.

* * *

A. 小王, 有人說在中國進大學難, 出大學容易在美國進大學容易出大學難. 你覺得是怎每樣嗎?
B. 是這樣. 中國每年有很多高中畢業生, 他們都想進一流大學, 但是沒有那麼多一流的大學. 所以不是每個人都能進最好的的大學.

A. 一般怎麼進大學呢?
B. 你要通過很嚴格的考試. 如果這成績不好, 就不能進大學或不能進很好的大學.
A. 在美國上大學不要通過考試, 但是要進好的大學也不容易.

A：你在哪兒上學？
B：我在美國中學上學。
A：你上初中還是高中？
B：我上高中。
A：你現在是幾年級？
B：我現在是高中一年級。
A：你們班有多少學生？
B：我們班有四十個學生。
A：你們有些什麼課？

B：我們有中文、數學、外語、歷史、體育、音樂、自然科學和美術等等。
A：你們有什麼外語課？
B：我們有英語、法語和日語，但是大多數學生都選英語。
A：你們有沒有外國老師？
B：有，我們有兩個外國老師，一個是英國人，一個是日本人。他們教我們英語和日語。

* * *

A：你在哪兒上學？
B：我不上學了。我畢業了。
A：你已經畢業了？真棒。你有沒有找到工作？
B：我還沒有找到工作，我想讀研究生。
A：你想讀什麼？
B：我想讀歷史。
A：讀研究生要幾年？
B：讀碩士要兩年，讀博士一般要五年。

A：你要讀碩士還是博士？
B：我現在還不知道。我想先讀碩士，以後再決定要不要讀博士。你呢？你還上學嗎？
A：不，我也畢業了，正在找工作。
B：你想做什麼？
A：我最愛是英語，我想當英語老師。
B：聽說很多學校現在要老師。你一定能找到老師的工作。
A：那就太好了。

* * *

A. 小王，有人說在中國進大學難，也大學容易；在美國進大學容易，也大學難。你覺得是怎麼樣呢？
B. 是這樣。中國每年有很多高中畢業生，他們都想進一流大學，但是沒有那麼多一流的大學。所以不是每個人都能進最好的大學。

A.一般怎麼進大學呢？
B. 你要通過很嚴格的考試。如果考試成績不好，
A. 在美國上大學不要通過考試，但是要進好的大學也不容易。你不能進大學或不能進很好的大學。

245

Lesson 6: Health and Sickness

舒服 **shu1fu – feeling well, comfortable**

舒 **shu1 ab 341545** 舒 **spread out, stretch, relax; easy, leisurely. FR 1459.**

It seems that both sides of this character are phonetic elements, the left side representing the initial consonant and the right side the final vowel. The left side, 舍 she4, means an inn or residence and descends from shell-bone pictograms (such as shown top left) showing a thatched cottage. The square at the bottom of 舍 was added to make clearer that this was a space, a house, not some pointed object. The right side, 予 yu3, means "to give". The Shuowen form is shown on the middle left. Wiktionary says it shows two hands, one above and one below, passing an object from one orkto the other. Sears thinks – more plausibly I believe – that it is a picture of a shuttle going back and forth – or actually up and down in the picture. The thread trails behind the upward bound shuttle. The idea is that one hand "gives" the shuttle to the other, which "gives" it back. A bronze version of the whole 舒 character is shown bottom left. The whole right side is missing, but at the bottom is an object which could be a shuttle but not a hand. The Shuowen version of 舒 is on the top right. The GHZ strangely gives no etymological explanation.

服 **fu2 moon 52** 服 **serve, obey; clothes. FR 365.**

See BC Lesson 7. (Remember the boat and the galley slave.)

脸色 **lian3se4 – look(noun), complexion**

脸（臉） **lian3 moon 3414** 脸 **face, countenance, front. FR 615.**

This is a radical+phonetic character. The "moon" radical is, as usual, a graphical variant of the "meat" radical used for parts of the body – unless, of course, we prefer to think of the *face* of the man in the moon! This character is not in the *Shuowen* or earlier sources.

The phonetic is 佥(僉) qian1, meaning *unanimous, altogether*. It appears as a phonetic in five characters in the *Quick Guide* pronounced *lian* but in no other character there which is pronounced *qian*. From looking at the modern traditional or at the *Shuowen* version (top right) we might easily conclude that it shows two men whose mouths are speaking as one mouth – the one on the top of the character. The problem with this nice explanation is that there are also bronze versions such as on the top left which have some graphical resemblance to the *Shuowen* character but cannot possibly be so interpreted. What on earth do they depict?

色 **se4 aa 3556** 色 **color; look, facial expression; scenery; feminine charm; lust, sexual passion. FR 304.**

See BC Lesson 7.

感觉 **gan3jue2 – feeling**

感 **gan3 spear 104** 感 **to feel, move, affect, touch. FR 243.**

感 is a radical+phonetic character with the heart radical – which fits the meaning nicely – and the somewhat remote phonetic 咸 xián. In traditional characters 咸 means *all, whole.* (In simplified characters it also means *salt* or *salty,* which is 鹹 in traditional characters. But that meaning is recent and irrelevant to its origin.) On the upper left one of many shell-bone examples of the early versions of 咸. It clearly shows a mouth and an ax. It probably meant words (the mouth) which ended a meeting or ceremony. Hence the idea of completion, wholeness, cutting off of anything further. A typical bronze example is on the lower left; the Shuowen version is on the upper right. The cutting edge of the ax has become the whole left side. The lower side of ax head is the line above the mouth. The handle hand-guard and handle remain close to the bronze versions. The ax is still there – once you see it!

觉（覺）**jue2 see 44** 觉 **sense, feel, become aware. FR 327.**

We met this schizophrenic character pronounced jiao in BC Lesson 5 and pronounced jue2 in BC Lesson 7 with contrasting meanings.

头（頭）**tou2 aa 44314** 头 **head; beginning; end, top, first, near, edge. FR 147.**

Note the application of the "whisker rule" in making up the stroke code. It causes the the two 4 strokes in the top left corner to be coded before the long 3 stroke. The traditional character is a straight-forward radical+phonetic character with the head radical on the right and the bean-pot *dou* phonetic on the left.

This is the dou of dou-fu 豆腐 = tofu. The simplified character for *head,* 头, must be somehow derived from 頁, which is a picture of a human head or face, but 头 is surely a very strange head.

疼 **teng2 sick 3544 – hurt (verb), it hurts; ache, pain; love dearly. FR 1710.**

This is a radical+phonetic character. The *sick* radical fits, and our friend 冬 dong1 – meaning winter – is a pretty good phonetic.

The origin of the *sick* radical as in 病 or 痛 is fairly clear from the *Shuowen* form of 病 shown on the right. The left side is a bed stood on end. The line at the top indicates some sort of shelter. The rest is phonetic. Subsequent to the *Shuowen,* the bed – a pretty good picture for illness – merged with the shelter to form a shed with the remnants of bed legs on the left side. This radical is used in the names of most diseases like *cancer, jaundice,* or *smallpox* and other words associated with illness.

医生 **yi1sheng1 – physician**

This expression was covered in BC Lesson 1.

感冒 **gan3mao4 – have a cold**

感 was covered a few characters above here in this lesson.

冒 **mao4 eye 25 冒 to emit; to risk. FR 1222.**

See 慢 man4 in BC Lesson 6. It is a picture of a cap pulled down over the head.

发烧 **fa1shao1 – have a fever**

发（發）**fa1 aa 3645 send forth, fire, shoot, develop. FR 47.**

This is a radical+phonetic character, but only the traditional makes any sense at all. In it, the bow, 弓, in the lower left corner is the highly appropriate radical and the rest of the character is the phonetic 癶 ba2. The *Shuowen* version of 癶 is shown on the left. Sears says it means *to trample*; Wiktionary says it means to remove or level out grass with one's feet. The Shuowen version of 发 is on the right.

烧（燒）**shao1 烧 fire 613 burn; cook, bake, stew, roast; run a fever; fever. FR 1201.**

This is a radical+phonetic character with the very appropriate fire radical. The phonetic is 尧 (堯) Yao2, a legendary king of ancient China roughly dated in the century from 2356 to 2255 BC. Apparently King Yao has his very own character, but he lets it be used as a phonetic in other characters such as 挠, 铙, 蛲 – all pronounced nao or 浇 and 侥 pronounced jiao.

咳嗽 **ke2sou4 – cough (noun and verb)**

Both characters mean simply *cough*, so 咳嗽 is bisyllablism.

咳（欬）**ke2 mouth 4163 cough. FR 2373.**

Remember 次 – the picture of the sneeze – from BC Lesson 8? The right-hand side of the traditional form of the present character is exactly the same. The left side is twelfth terrestrial branch

亥 hai4. Sears interprets it as phonetic. I suspect the whole character has an origin similar to that of 次 as a picture of a sneeze or cough. When we want to make a sound like a sneeze but can't produce a real one, we say "ke-chew". And the sound of 欬 is *ke*. (I can make nothing of the little scrap of evidence found by Sears; *Wiktionnaire* offers nothing.)

嗽 sou4 mouth 703 嗽 cough. FR 2815.

Notice that we have the sneezer again on the right and a mouth on the left. They are presumably related to the meaning. The new element is 束 shu4 (meaning to tie or bind). It is probably a phonetic hint. An ideogram, it is a picture of a bag tied at both ends. A shell-bone example is on the top left, a bronze example below it, and the *Shuowen* version bottom right. There is no *Shuowen* or earlier version of 嗽.

检查 jian3cha2 – examine, inspect; examination, inspection

检（檢）jian3 tree 34144 检 inspect, examine; be circumspect.

This is a radical+phonetic character. The phonetic element, 佥（僉）qian1, was encountered above in this lesson on page 247in the character 脸 lian1. Here it indicates a rhyming pronunciation: jian3.

The mystery in this character is what the tree radical has to do with the meaning. Wiktionnaire suggests that the state inspector – to prove his identity to those he was inspecting – carried a *wooden* mold with which he could make an impression to be compared with an impression already possessed by the party being inspected.

The *Shuowen* version appears on the top right. There are no known earlier versions.

查 cha2 tree 011 查 a log raft; to examine, inquire, look into, look up. FR 459.

This is a phonetic loan character. Originally it represented a kind of tree, the hawthorn. There is an older traditional form, 查, which is the key to its origin. In this form, we see a tree over the character 且 qie3, which, as we mentioned in Lesson 2, shows a cabinet for holding devotional sacrifices. 查 is then readily seen to be a simple

山楂 *Crataegus pinnatifida*+

250

radical+phonetic character, with 木 as the radical and 且 as the phonetic. This character for the name of the tree was then phonetically borrowed for the meanings cited above. Then the 且 fell apart in 查 through the error of scribes. It was this form which was returned to its original meaning by adding yet another tree in 楂 zha – the hawthorn. The character is not in the *Shuowen* or earlier sources.

In China, be sure to enjoy the delicious products of the 山楂, the mountain hawthorn, *Crataegus pinnatifida*. The red juice is often available in bottles in restaurants. It is also boiled down to make candy-like wafers or flakes that make great snacks. Or you may chance upon a street vendor of hawthorn berries impaled on a stick and under a sweet glaze to be eaten as you walk along.

治 zhi4 water 640 – control, harness; manage, order; treat, cure. FR 274.

This is a radical+phonetic character with the water radical and the phonetic 台 tai2. In a nation that has long managed and controlled major rivers such as the Yellow and the Min, connecting water with managing and controlling is very natural.

In modern speech the phonetic is not especially close, but it is not hard to imagine that it was once closer. In simplified characters, 台 has a number of meanings, but in traditional characters only one – *your* when used with special respect. Thus, this is the only meaning we have to explain from its form. There are many bronze examples, all quite similar to the one on the top left. We see something over a mouth. The mouth, I believe, is that of the speaker addressing the respected person. Back in BC Lesson 5, we read "The *Shuowen* version of 厶 is on the right. It depicts not an object but an idea: being self-enclosed, private, shut off from the outside, complete in one's self." Here we find that same figure representing the respected person whose privacy and distance is to be honored.

不要紧 bu2 yao4 jin3 – doesn't matter; not important

不 bu2 (or bu4) aa 1324 不 no, not.
See BC Lesson 1.

要 yao4 woman 1220 要 want; important; should
See BC Lesson 7.

紧（緊）**jin3 silkB 225** 紧 **close, tight, urgent. FR 560.**

We may note first that the figure in the upper left corner of the traditional, 臣 chen2, is an eye looking downward, as is clearer in many surviving shell-bone examples such as that on the top left or the bronze example below it. By the time of the Shuowen, it had reached nearly its modern form, as shown on the lower right. As a character (FR 1138) it means a *vassal*, but also *minister, official, statesman*. As a whole character it survives among the simplified characters in its traditional form, but as a component it uniformly turns into the two vertical lines as in the case of 緊 → 紧.

紧 is a radical+phonetic character. The silk radical (at the bottom) refers to the string that pulls something *closed tight*. At the top is the phonetic element, 臤 qian1 (meaning firm. solid, rigid, stable) and itself composed of 臣 chen2 – the phonetic element – and 又 , a hand which, as the meaningful element, suggests the idea of a steadying hand.

开药 **kai1 yao4 – prescribe medicine**

开 **kai1 to open, start, begin, liberate, exploit, expand, develop. See BC Lesson 5.**

药（藥）**yao4 grass 6613** 药 **medicine, to cure with medicine; to poison.**

Another radical+phonetic character. Probably the medicine will be herbal – hence the grass radical. The phonetic, 约 yao4 (FR 424), means to weigh in a balance – and is hence a splendid phonetic since it gets the sound exactly right and contributes nicely to the meaning, since the pharmacist may weigh the herbal medicine. You may well wonder how a character with such an arcane meaning gets such a high frequency. The answer is that 约 has another pronunciation, yue1, with many more common meanings such as:

> restrict, restrain
> a pact or agreement
> make an appointment
> ask in advance
> economical, frugal
> simple, brief
> about, approximately
> reduction of a fraction (e.g. 5/10 to ½)

The silk radical may refer to a cord that *restricts* or to a silk ribbon that is part of the seal on an agreement. The right side is a spoon, 勺 shao2. It seems a possible phonetic for yao, but for remembering 药 we can perhaps better think of it as the *spoon* for taking the *medicine* while we are sick in a bed with *silk* sheets!

完 wan2 roof 1136 完 finish, pay; intact, whole, complete; used up, over. FR 301.

This is a radical+phonetic character. A house is *finished, whole* and *complete* when the *roof* is put on. 元 yuan2 is a pretty good phonetic. To quote from BC Lesson 4, "The *Shuowen* version of 元, 元 yuan2, is a picture of a man with the head emphasized by the line at the top. It can mean the head, the beginning, or various other things, but it is most common as the symbol for the Chinese currency, the yuan." The Shuowen version is on the right. There are no known earlier versions.

病 bing4 sick 1325 病 become sick; sickness, disease

Another radical+phonetic character. The sick radical clearly fits. The phonetic is 丙 bing3, the third heavenly stem.

全 quan2 top 171 全 completely, entirely. FR 124.

There are several authoritative but "completely" contradictory explanations of this elegant character. I will stick by that of the GHZ (which is also that of Wiktionary) that it is an ideogram combining 人 and 玉 (written as 王). But 人 is not to be thought of as representing "man" but as a picture of the idea of *unified, whole.* Thus 全 pictures the idea of a whole piece of jade, pure jade, *completely and entirely* jade.

休息 xiu1xi – rest, relax

休 xiu1 man 731 rest, stop, cease. FR 1082.

An ideogram: the man is resting under the tree.

息 xi1 nose 46 息 breathe; stop, cease; news, interest; reproduce. FR 428.

This is another ideogram. Above is a nose; below is a heart. Breathing requires the cooperation of the nose, the lungs and the heart (to get the blood to the lungs). So the character is a good way to express breathing. As for the use in the expression 休息, remember the English expressions "catch my breath" or "take a breather" or "a breathing spell." This idea may also explain the stop and cease meanings of the character.

身体 shen1ti3 – health, body

身 shen1 aa325113 body; life; pregnancy; main part; identity; status. FR 164.

We met exactly this figure in the character 谢 xie (thanks) in BC Lesson 2, but it turned out to have nothing to do with the independent character 身. This character is a pictograph showing a pregnant woman, as is clear from numerous bronze examples such as that shown on the left. The idea is still detectable in the Shuowen form on the right, and – once you know it – you can still see it in the modern version. 身 is a radical in the traditional system, but since it claimed only two characters in the *Quick Guide,* it was not counted as a radical in the radicode system and these two characters went into the AB section.

体 **ti3 man 7341** 体 **body, essence, form, style. FR 149.**

This is an ideogram. 本 ben3 – one of the few characters characterized as indicatives – means *base.*

Thus 体 means the base of man. The character and its meanings leaves open the question of whether that base is the physical *body* or a spiritual *essence* or *form.*

过敏 **guo4min3 – allergy**

过 (過) **guo4 go 514** 过 **to pass through. FR 46.**

See BC Lesson 8.

敏 **min3 hit31** 敏 **quick, nimble, clever; try harder. FR 1436.**

This is a radical+phonetic character. The hit radical on the right, the hand-with-a-stick, roughly fits the meaning. The phonetic 每 mei1 – meaning *all* – we discussed in connection with 海 in BC Lesson 3.

中医 **zhong1yi1 – Chinese medicine, doctor of Chinese medicine**

We know both characters.

西医 **xi1yi1 – Western medicine, doctor of Western medicine**

Again we know both characters.

锻炼 **duan4lian4 – physical exercise, workout**

锻 **duan4 metal 37136 forge, temper; to disciple. FR 2531.**

254

The metal radical of this radical+phonetic character fits it basic blacksmith-related meanings. 段 duan4 is an exact phonetic, but it is also more than a phonetic. Today it means a section or part of something. But there are three known bronze examples of 段, all very similar to the one shown on the top left. Sears suggests – quite plausibly I believe – that they show a hand with a hammer (lower right) striking chimes (the two horizontal lines) hung from a frame (top left). The *Shuowen* version 段 is on the lower left. Now from striking chimes with a hammer to forging is a relatively short step – the hand with the hammer is still totally appropriate. And thus 段 contributes nicely to the meaning of 锻.

炼 (煉) lian4 fire 61 炼 refine, purify, smelt. FR 1763.

This is another radical+phonetic character. The fire radical clearly fits. 柬 jian3 serves as the phonetic. It now means a letter, card or invitation. But this is a phonetic borrowing, and 柬 has been returned to its original meaning by adding a hand radical in 拣 (揀) which means to *choose, select*. The LST character on the left shows the idea clearly: things that have been bound up in a bundle are being selected and taken out. The hand in 揀 is, of course, the hand that selects and takes out. Now compare the "select, take out" original meaning of 柬 with the "refine, purify" meaning of 煉 and you see that we have another case of the meaning-appropriate phonetic. The Shuowen version of 炼 is on the top right.

特别 te4bie2 – especially, particularly; only, just; special agent, spy.

特 te4 ox 715 特 special, unusually. FR 173.

This is a radical+phonetic character. Its original meaning was a large breeding bull. It was then phonetically borrowed for the meanings given above. It seems that precise description of different types of bulls and oxen became no longer so important as to require separate characters, so the character was not returned to its original meaning. For the convoluted origins of the phonetic, the right side, see 等 in BC Lesson 7.

别 bie2 knife 035 don't; separation; distinguish; other, unique; fasten or pin. FR 222.

This appears to be a radical+radical character. The knife radical on the right certainly fits the idea of separation. 另 ling4 means *another, separate, besides*. It is of recent origin; Sears found no pre-modern examples. But no one seems to know how it is supposed to mean what it does. Notice that its pronunciation, *ling,* is totally remote from *bie,* but its meaning is similar to that of 别.

老年人 **lao3nian2ren2 – old people**

老　**lao3 old 63 老 old.**

See BC Lesson 1.

年　**nian2 aa 3172 年　year.**

See BC Lesson 5.

人　**ren2 top - man, person.**

See BC Lesson 1 under 你.

慢跑 **man4pao3 – jogging, to jog**

慢 **man4 heart 010 慢 unenthusiastic, slow, cold. FR 822.**

　　This is a radical+phonetic character. The heart radical relates to the *unenthusiastic* part of the meaning. *Slow* and *cold* can also refer to emotions, but in our particular case the meaning is only physical: 慢跑 = slow run = jog. The phonetic, 曼 man4, means *prolong, draw out, graceful*.

It is a radical+phonetic character. The hand at the bottom is the radical and presumably does the the prolonging and drawing out. The phonetic, the top two elements, is an abbreviated form of 冒 mao.

See 慢 man4 in BC Lesson 6. 冒 is a picture of a cap pulled down over the head but with an eye looking out.

跑 **pao3 leg 355 run, flee, escape; evaporate, leak away. FR 864.**

　　This is a radical+phonetic character. The *leg* radical fits the *run* meaning. Antecedents of the phonetic 包 bao1, such as shown on the top left, have now been found on bamboo slips dating back the Warring States period. What is depicted is clear in the Shuowen form, lower left, namely a fetus in the mother's womb. 包 appears as the phonetic in many characters pronounced *pao* such as 袍, 泡, 炮, 刨, 疱 and many more. There is no *Shuowen* nor earlier version of 跑.

方式 **fang1shi4 – method, form, way**

方 **fang1 square 方 square, upright, honest, <u>way, plan</u>, direction. FR 60.**

See BC Lesson 9, character 旅 lü3.

式 shi4 aa641121 type, style, pattern, form, formula, ceremony. FR 303

See BC Lesson 7, character 试 shi4.

各种各样 ge4zhong3ge4yang4 – various, all kinds of

各 ge4 mouth 354 各 each, every, various, different. FR 209.

See 格 on page 253.

种 zhong3 grain 20 种 seed, race, kind, sort. FR 57.

This is a radical+phonetic character. The grain radical is clearly appropriate for a character meaning *seed*. And 中 is the perfect phonetic except for tone. (It is usually first tone.)

样 (樣) yang4 tree 4317 shape, form, model, pattern, kind, type. FR 88.

This is a nice, simple, clear radical+phonetic character. The tree radical goes with the meaning because forms and patterns were usually made of wood. 羊 yang2 gets the sound right except for tone. The phonetic of the traditional, 羕, got the tone right also. (It means *long*, but is applied only to rivers.)

Supplemental Words and Expressions

太极拳 tai4ji2quan2 – taiji (taichi)

太 tai4 aa3144 太 too, most, greatest

See BC Lesson 3.

极 (極) ji2 tree 534 极 pole; extreme, extremely, utmost

See BC Lesson 8.

257

quan2 aa3433 fist, punch; Chinese boxing; curl, bend.

(aa 4333 is given as an alternate coding in the *Quick Guide* and now appears to me preferable.)

 This is a radical+phonetic character. The hand on the bottom is a clearly appropriate radical. The figure on the top is the phonetic. It usually indicates a pronunciation of *juan* as in 卷,眷,券, 桊, 帣, 絭 and some other characters. Our character's *quan* pronunciation is similar. When one of these characters appears in the *Shuowen,* the phonetic has the beautifully symmetric shape shown in our character's form (on the right) and in that of 卷 *juan3* (on the top left). This form shows rice and two hands. There is another character with only the rice and hands (lower left), but it is so rare that it is not in my computer's fonts, and I had to fetch this image from the Unicode site. Sears thinks the hands are sorting (uncooked) rice; the Wiktionary authors say they are rolling (cooked) rice into balls, which seems to me more plausible. Wiktionnaire refers to the phonetic as the rice-roller. I have not found any character with this phonetic going back before the *Shuowen*.

散步 **san4bu4 – take a walk**

 san4 hit 721 散 **break up, disperse, dispel; lay off (employees). FR 866.**

This character is all one ideogram. Its earliest meaning was to scutch, that is, to break up by beating the woody part of flax or hemp so that it can be removed leaving the fiber that can be made into cloth. The shell-bone character at the top left shows the character at this stage of its meaning. In the bronze characters (lower left), it was extended to cover the process of making dried stringed meat. (A pork chop has been added on the lower left.) The *Shuowen* (right) combined all this into a clear and complete character. The modern meanings clearly derive from these ancient processes. If the use in the expression 散步 – literally "break a step" – to mean "take a walk" seems surprising, remember our expression "take a *break*".

 bu4 foot 233 步 **step, pace, stage (in a process).**

 The numerous surviving shell-bone examples such as the one on the left make perfectly clear what is meant. In cases like this, I am often not sure whether the character should be called a pictograph – it shows a picture of the space between two footprints – or an ideogram. The GHZ calls this one an ideogram.

为了 **wei4le – for, for the sake of, in order to**

为（為） **wei4 force 44** 为 **do, act, act as, become, be, make, take. FR 18.**

See BC Lesson 10. Remember that it is a phonetic loan character. It shows a hand – the dot in the upper left corner – leading or feeding an elephant, but that has nothing to do with the present meaning. It often translates well as *is*.

把 ... 作为 **ba3 ... zuo4wei2 – treat ... as**

把 **ba3. (Direct object shifting preposition.)**

作 **zuo4 man 3211** 作 **to do, to work. FR 49.**

See BC Lesson 3.

为 **wei2** （為） **wei4 force 44** 为 **do, act, act as, become, be, make, take. FR 18.**

The elephant again.

交通工具 **jiao1tong1gong1ju4 – means of transportation**

交 **jiao1 hat 347** 交 **deliver, hand over, exchange; join, intersect. FR 320.**

We met this figure in BC Lesson 2 in the story of 校. We saw that it came from a picture of a man with crossed legs, as in the bronze example on the left and the Shuowen character on the right. Perhaps we should take the *intersect* meaning as primary, for the lines of the crossed legs certainly intersect. Somehow the crossing of the legs came to represent the "change of hands" of goods.

通 **tong1 go 542** 通 **open, through, connect, understand, clear, accessible. FR 190.**

Remember the 通 of 普通话 in BC Lesson 6.

工 **gong1 aa 121   work. FR 118.**

See BC Lesson 2.

具 **ju4 aa25134 tool, utensil; posses, provide. FR 391.**

This is an ideogram. Bronze examples such as on the left and the Shuowen (right) show a cowrie shell above two hands. The cowrie shell represents money, payment. The fundamental meaning, according to the GHZ, is to supply, provide. Wiktionnaire says, on the contrary, the fundamental meaning is to pay one's debts, a meaning which certainly fits the picture, but I find no other source

259

indicating this meaning, The "tool, utensil" meaning is common in compounds, but is so remote from the picture that it must be phonetic borrowing. It is, however, the meaning relevant for our phrase.

And so we have that a 交通工具 , an "exchange connection work tool" is a means of transportation.

不是 … 而是 bu2shi4 … er2shi4 – not … but rather

而 er2 aa1325 而 and, as well as, and yet, but

In its modern meanings, this is a phonetic loan character. It is a picture of a beard, as is easily seen in its shell-bone forms such as shown on the left. Bronze forms resembled the one on the lower left. The *Shuowen* form is on the right.

Like many characters that have been phonetically borrowed, 而 has been returned to it original meaning by adding another meaningful component. In this case, the feathers or hair radical was added to get the character 耏 nai4 which, however, is very seldom used. (须 xu1 is a more common character for *beard*.)

Some of the Supplementary Words and Expressions

炎症 yan2zheng4 – infection

炎 yan2 fire 3433 scorching, fiery hot, inflammation. FR 1324.

Fire over fire! Need more be said?

症 zheng4 sick 12211 症 disease, illness. FR 1258.

This is a radical+phonetic character. The sick radical certainly fits, and the phonetic, 正 zheng4, conveys the pronunciation exactly. It means *straight, honest, upright* and shows a foot "toeing the line." 止 zhi3, you will recall, is a picture of a foot but means *stop*.

嗓子 sang3zi – throat, voice

嗓 sang3 mouth 5454 throat, larynx; voice. FR 2496.

This is a radical+phonetic character with the very appropriate mouth radical. The

phonetic 桑 sang1 started off in shell-bone times as a picture of a mulberry tree, as shown top left. Now the mulberry is no ordinary tree in China. Its leaves are the food of silk worms. They are picked by hand and brought to the silkworms to feed upon. So by the time of the *Shuowen* character, right, the branches and leaves of the tree have been replaced by human hands. Actually, the base of the tree has become a whole tree with three leaf-picking hands above. The *Shuowen* form then turned into the modern form with only the usual modifications.

子, of course, means *child* or *small thing*. So we could interpret 嗓子 as "child of the throat" = voice. Here are some other examples of the use of 子. 筷子 must mean some *small thing* related to bamboo and pronounced something like 快 kuai4. We call those things chopsticks. 饺子 must be small things to eat called something like 交 jiao. We call them dumplings. So what is a 帽子? It is – or used to be – made of cloth and must be pronounced like 冒 which we had earlier in this lesson. The answer is in the upside-down footnote. [1]

牙 ya2 – tooth

See the discussion of the character 举 in Lesson 1 of IC. (It is a picture of upper and lower front teeth.)

肚子 du4zi – stomach

肚 du4 moon 71 肚 belly, abdomen, stomach. FR 1800

This is a radical+phonetic character. As usual, the moon radical is representing *meat* and in this case a part of the body. The earth radical 土 tu3 is serving as the phonetic in this character.

背 bei4 meat 2116 – back

This is another radical+phonetic character but this time the meat radical picturing a pork chop has not turned in a moon. The phonetic on top we recognize as the character 北 bei3 meaning *north* but picturing two men sitting *back-to-back*. Thus it is another "phonetic plus" which not only provides the pronunciation but also contributes to the meaning.

腿 tui3 moon 454 腿 leg, thigh. FR 1351.

This is another radical+phonetic, but this time the meat radical has again turned into a moon. The phonetic is the character 退 tui4 meaning to *retreat, withdraw, decline, return,* and *cancel*. 退 in turn is the go radical with 艮 gen3 as phonetic. You will recognize 艮 as the phonetic in your old friend 很 hen from BC Lesson 1: 我很好. 你呢?

---

1   Hat or cap.

针刺 zhen1 ci4 – acupuncture (from Latin *acus* needle)

针 zhen1 metal 7 针 needle, acupuncture. FR 1116.

 This is a relatively new character. It is not in the *Shuowen* or earlier sources. The GHZ notes that the original character with the same meaning and pronunciation is 箴. This older character is a radical+phonetic character with the bamboo radical and the phonetic 咸 *xian2* (meaning *all, whole*). It has a Shuowen version as shown on the top left. Perhaps acupuncturists objected to the implication that the needles used in acupuncture were made of bamboo and invented the modern character with the metal radical. But what is on the right side of the new character? Maybe it is the character 十 shi2 meaning *ten,* but that is not a very good phonetic, especially not for a character of recent origin. Right or wrong, I think of it as a picture of the acupuncture needle.

Both characters are in use, but 针 is six times more frequent than 箴.

刺 ci4 knife 725 thorn; sting, pierce, stab, murder. FR 1058.

In this radical+phonetic character, the knife radical on the right fits nicely the meanings – especially the last two. The *Shuowen* version of 刺 is on the right. The phonetic of 刺, 束, is said to be pronounced ci4, but it is so rarely used alone that its pronunciation is probably deduced from the characters in which it is the phonetic.

 There are two views about what it depicts. One view holds that it is a tree with thorns, the other that it is some kind of arrow with barbs. Sears has images that support both views. The tree view is supported by the Shuowen version of 束 on the right and by a shell-bone version below it. The arrow theory is supported by numerous shell-bone and bronze versions, such as on the left. Either way, it is a prickly character and certainly contributes to meaning as well as to pronunciation.

药房 yao4fang2 – pharmacy

药 (藥) yao4 grass 6613 药 medicine, to cure; certain chemicals; poison. FR 662.

This is a radical+phonetic character. The grass radical fits the herbal medicines originally meant. The phonetic of the traditional is 樂 yue4 meaning *music* and *make music*. It was simplified to 乐, but that simplification was not used in this character. Instead the character 约 yao1 was substituted. It is actually a closer phonetic than was the traditional. Moreover, its meaning – to weigh in a balance – supports the meaning of 药 very nicely – better than did 樂.

房 fang2 doorB 41 房 house, room. FR 512.

This is a radical+phonetic character. The door radical indicates a house, and 方 is the fang character we have met oft before.

The reason the 房 character looks a bit different is that it is in a different font to give it the same form it has the text book. In the FreeSerif font generally used in the present book, this character looks like this: 房. The same is true of doorB characters.

运动 yun4dong4 – exercise, sports

In both of these radical+phonetic characters, the phonetic is 云（雲）yun2, meaning *cloud*. It is a pictograph, originally a picture of a cloud as in the shell-bone example on the left. In the *Shuowen* (right), rain was added, and it was kept in the modern traditional character for cloud, 雲. It is interesting that the cloud picture shows the cloud having a flat top and a fluffy bottom. I think we would tend to draw a cloud the other way around. But when looking down on clouds, as from a mountain, one often sees a flat top.

运（運）yun4 go 116 motion, movement, exercise; to move, carry; luck, fate. FR 345.

This is a radical+phonetic character. The *go* radical fits its meaning, and the yun-cloud phonetic fits the sound. In the traditional, the phonetic is 軍 jun1, currently meaning *military, army, troops*, and composed of 車 "cart; chariot" + 勹 "to surround". The earliest know versions are bronze, and the upper component is not 勹 but a hand (see top left). Sometimes the arm of the hand was extended around the right side of the chariot, as in the image on the lower left. By the Shuowen (right), the wrap was complete and the hand idea was lost. But the hand is the essence of the whole thing. The 車 is a military chariot and the hand is that of the foot soldiers that surround it. That is why the character means *troops*. Every infantryman knows that tanks are most effective when accompanied by infantry, and the same must have been true for war chariots. But notice how the chariot in the phonetic subtly supports the idea of motion in the whole character. Even in the simplified – where the war chariot has become a cloud - maybe the cloud is drifting by. (The simplified version of 軍 is 军.)

动（動） dong4 force 11 to move, act, start, induce. FR 73.

The traditional is a typical radical+phonetic character. The force radical fits the meaning well enough, and the phonetic, 重 zhong4, is reasonably close. 重, an ideogram, means *heavy*; a bronze example, top left, shows a man above a bundle. The man is about to pick up the bundle, and he is no doubt thinking, "Heavy, heavy, heavy." The Shuowen version, lower left, has added

263

an earth radical at the bottom to stress the weightiness. The 云 yun2 – meaning *cloud* – of the simplified, by contrast, is a very poor phonetic. I can makes no sense of it unless 云 is supposed to graphically abbreviate 重.

健身房 jian4shen1fang2 – gymnasium

健 jian4 man 54251 健 strong, healthy. FR 979.

This is a radical+phonetic character. The radical is the man on the left who is strong and healthy. 建 jian4 is an exact phonetic. It means to *build, construct, erect, establish, propose* and is an ideogram. A bronze example (on the left) shows a carpenter's square and a hand holding a brush and drawing on paper – a fine way to show the combination of design and handwork in *construction*.

身 shen1 aa325113 body; life; pregnancy; main part; identity; status. FR 164.

See page 253

房 fang2 doorB 41 房 house, room. FR 512.

See above in this lesson.

游泳 you2yong3 – swim, swimming

游 you2 water 41331 to float about, swim, rove, stroll, travel. FR 695.

泳 yong3 water 4553 泳 to swim. FR 2607.

The right side of this character, 永, originally meant *to swim*. It is a pictograph showing a man in the middle of a stream presumably swimming. There are a number of shell-bone examples similar to the one on the left. But then it got phonetically borrowed to mean *long, forever* but was then returned to its original meaning by adding the water radical on the left. This process had occurred by the time of Shuowen, which therefore shows one stream on the left with no one in it and another stream on the right with swimmer in the middle. If we compare 永 with the character for water, 水, we see that main difference is the dot on top in the center. That dot is the swimmer!

球（毬） qiu2 jade 54 ball, sphere, the earth, or other heavenly body. FR 628.

This is a radical+phonetic character, but not a simple one. The Shuowen version on the right is the earliest example we posses. The thing on the left is thought to be a feather while that on the right to be a fur coat. The 毬 form is found back as far as the Tang dynasty; the 球 form goes back only as far back as the Qing dynasty. It was not, however, introduced in the simplifications of 1956, but was then confirmed as the standard form. The transition from feather to jade was probably mostly a matter of just leaving off the long "foot" of the feather, but it also involved a shift in the idea conveyed by the radical. The feather stressed the lightness of the ball; the jade implied that it was a beautiful plaything.

The phonetic on the right, 求 qiu2, is a picture of a fur coat. Sears has nothing back of the *Shuowen* version shown on the right of this paragraph. Wiktionary, however, has the shell-bone example shown on the top left and the bronze example below it. The coat seems to have been made from the whole skin of the animal including the legs and head – which are still detectable in 求. If it still does not look like a fur coat to you, then the best proof that it is indeed a coat and not just a hide is that when it was phonetically borrowed to mean *to request, seek, or beg,* it was restored to mean precisely *fur-coat* by adding the *clothing* radical at the bottom in 裘 qiu2. 求 has a frequency rank of 312; 裘 of 2868.

A: 你是不是舒服? 你的脸色不太好.
B: 我是有点儿不舒服.
A:你有什么感觉?
B:我头疼. 我想我今天不能去上班了.
A:你是不应该去上班. 你应该去看医生.

* * *

A: 你那儿不舒服?
B: 医生, 我有点儿头疼, 感觉很累.
A: 你是什么时候开始头疼的?
B: 昨天晚上.
A: 发布发烧?
B: 我想不发烧, 但是我咳嗽.
A: 我给你检查一下儿吧.

* * *

A: 医生怎么说?
B: 他说我感冒了.
A: 他有没有说怎么治?
B: 他给我做了检查, 说不要紧.
A: 他有没有给你开药?
B: 开了. 医生说我吃一个星期的要就会好的. 如果要吃完后并还不好, 他要我去看他.

* * *

A: 你昨天怎么没来上课?
B: 我病了.
A: 你怎么了?
B: 我一点儿发烧.
A: 你的病 现在有没有好?
B: 今天比昨天好多了, 但是还没有全好.
A: 你有没有去看医生?
B: 没有, 我想是小病,不要紧.
A: 你要多休息.
B: 我会的.

* * *

A: 听说你最近身体不好, 常常去看医生. 你怎么了?
B: 我过敏.
A: 你对什么过敏?
B: 我不知道, 医生们也不知道, 所以谁都治不好我的病.
A: 你可以试试中医.
B: 你觉得中医能治好西医治不好的病马?
A: 有可能.
B: 这是好主意. 你认识一个好中医吗?
A:我的中医林医生不错. 你可以去看他.

* * *

Here is the text in modern traditional characters.

A: 你是不是舒服? 你的臉色不太好.
B: 我是有點兒不舒服.
A: 你有什麼感覺?
B: 我頭疼. 我想我今天不能去上班了.
A: 你是不應該去上班. 你應該去看醫生.
* * *
A: 你那兒不舒服?
B: 醫生, 我有點兒頭疼, 感覺很累.
A: 你是什麼時候開始頭疼的?
B: 昨天晚上.
A: 發佈發燒?
B: 我想不發燒, 但是我咳嗽.
A: 我給你檢查一下兒吧.
* * *
A: 醫生怎麼說?
B: 他說我感冒了.
A: 他有沒有說怎麼治?
B: 他給我做了檢查, 說不要緊.
A: 他有沒有給你開葯?
B: 開了. 醫生說我吃一個星期的要就會好的. 如果要吃完後並還不好, 他要我去看他.
* * *
A: 你昨天怎麼沒來上課?

B: 我病了.
A: 你怎麼了?
B: 我一點兒發燒.
A: 你的病 現在有沒有好?
B: 今天比昨天好多了, 但是還沒有全好.
A: 你有沒有去看醫生?
B: 沒有, 我想是小病,不要緊.
A: 你要多休息.
B: 我會的.
* * *
A: 聽說你最近身體不好, 常常去看醫生. 你怎麼了?
B: 我過敏.
A: 你對什麼過敏?
B: 我不知道, 醫生們也不知道, 所以誰都治不好我的病.
A: 你可以試試中醫.
B: 你覺得中醫能治好西醫治不好的病馬?
A: 有可能.
B: 這是好主意. 你認識一個好中醫嗎?
A:我的中醫林醫生不錯. 你可以去看他.

267

And here, to remind you of what you have just learned, is the text in Shuowen characters.

A: 你是不是舒服？你的脸色不太好.
B: 我是有点儿不舒服.
A: 你有什么感觉？
B: 我头痛. 我想我今天不能去上班了.
A: 你是不能去上班. 你应该去看医生.

* * *

A: 你哪儿不舒服？
B: 医生，我有点儿头痛，感觉很累.
A: 你是什么时候开始头痛的？
B: 昨天晚上.
A: 发不发烧？
B: 我想不发烧，但是我咳嗽.
A: 我给你检查一下儿吧.

* * *

A: 医生怎么说？
B: 他说我感冒了.
A: 他有没有说怎么治？
B: 他给我做了检查，说不要紧.
A: 他有没有给你开药？
B: 开了. 医生说我吃一个星期的药就会好的. 如果我吃完后还不好，他要我去看他.

* * *

A: 你昨天怎么没来上课？
B: 我病了.
A: 你怎么了？
B: 我一点儿发烧.
A: 你的病现在有没有好？
B: 今天比昨天好多了，但是还没有全好.
A: 你有没有去看医生？
B: 没有，我想是小病，不要紧.
A: 你要多休息.
B: 我会的.

* * *

A: 听说你身体身体不好，常常去看医生. 你怎么了？
B: 我过敏.
A: 你对什么过敏？
B: 我不知道，医生们也不知道，所以很难帮治好我的病.
A: 你可以试试中医.
B: 你觉得中医能治好西医治不好的病吗？
A: 有可能.
B: 那是好主意. 你认识一个好中医吗？
A: 我的中医林医生不错. 你可以去看他.

268

Lesson 7: Holidays and Festivals

介绍 **jie4shao4 to present, say something about, introduce**

介 **jie4 top 32** 介 **situated between, upright, take seriously. FR 831.**

See 界 page 233.

绍（紹） **shao4 silk 530** 绍 **continue, carry on. FR 1234.**

This is a radical+phonetic character with shell-bone ancestors such as shown on the top left. (On the let of this drawing are silk cocoons; on the right, a knife.) The silk, of course, suggests thread; and the thread suggests following the thread, continuing, carrying on. The knife, now pronounced dao1, is phonetic. On the lower left, is the one and only known bronze example. The phonetic – a knife and a mouth, now the character 召 zhao4 (meaning *call together*) – is across the top. In the Shuowen version, right, the 召 has moved to the right, where it has stayed in the modern character.

节日 **jie2ri4 holiday, festival**

节（節） **jie2 grass 52** 节 **node, joint, section, period, festival, knot (speed of a ship)**

The basic meaning is a node on a bamboo cane. See BC Lesson 9.

日 **ri4 sun** 日 **sun, day, date. FR 101**

See BC Lesson 1.

重要 **zhong4yao4 important**

重 **zhong4 aa 370** 重 **weight, heavy. FR 140.**

See page 263. Pronounced chong2, this same character means *to repeat, duplicate.*

要 **yao4 woman 1220** 要 **want; important; should. FR 26.**

See BC Lesson 6.

元旦 **yuan2dan4 (Gregorian) New Year**

元 **yuan2 first, beginning, chief, coin, monetary unit.**

See 远 in BC Lesson 3.

旦 **dan4 sun 1 dawn, morning, day.**

This character is a picture of the sun rising above the horizon.

一样 **yi2yang4 the same**

样(樣) **yang4 tree 4317** 样 **shape, form, model, pattern, kind, type. FR 88.**

See page 257.

对 ... 来说 **dui4 ... lai2shuo1 as far as ... is concerned, for**

对(對) **dui4 inch 54** 对 **to set, adjust; right, correct; answer, respond; facing; mutual. FR 33.**

See BC Lesson 5.

来 (來) **lai2 aa74313 to come, arrive. FR 15.**

See BC Lesson 1.

说 **shuo1 speech 430** 说 **speak, say, discuss, explain. FR 24.**

See BC Lesson 6.

放假 **fang4jia4 have a vacation or day off**

放 **fang4 square 317** 放 **place, put, lay; expel, let go, set free. FR 291.**

See page 234.

假 **jia4 man 521** 假 **falsehood, fake, false, borrow, make use of; vacation. FR 636.**

See BC Lesson 10.

国庆节 **Guo2qing4jie3 National Day**

庆 (慶) **qing4 shed 314** 庆 **celebrate, congratulate, celebration.**

The simplified character was a totally new creation by the simplifiers of 1956. Maybe it suggests a pavilion *shelter* with a *big* celebration going on under it. 广 guang3 by itself also means *vast, wide*. Neither component gives any hint of the pronunciation. The only connection to the traditional is the frame around the top and left side. The traditional character goes back to bronze examples such as shown on the left. It is an ideogram composed of three traditional radicals (1) 鹿 lu4 deer, (2) 心 xin1 heart and (3) 夂 zhi3 foot. How how do they combine to mean *congratulate*? The GHZ gives the key: the deer is really a fine buckskin, given as a present to express *heart*-felt congratulations. The foot, to judge from the bronze examples,

270

may have originally been the foot of the deer. In the *Shuowen* version, right, the foot is a downward-pointing hobbled foot.

中秋节 **Zhong1qiu1jie2 Mid Autumn Festival**

秋 **qiu1 grain 343** 秋 **autumn**

See BC Lesson 10 or just remember the season when the grain fields look like they are afire.

月亮 **yue4liang moon**

亮 **liang4 hat 04536 bright, light, clear, enlightened; show, reveal. FR 848.**

This is an ideogram composed of a high building and a man. The building suggests that the man is of a high spiritual order, upright, and enlightened. Sears found two bronze versions; one is on the left and the other is similar. The character is not in the *Shuowen,* but there are several LST versions such as shown on the right. The upright man has crawled under the high building, and there he is to this day, though the building has been reduced to just the top three pieces of 亮. (In stroke code, the second number is a 4 rather than a 3 because the stroke is considered a dot, and all dots are coded 4.)

圆 **yuan2 wall 025** 圆 **round, circular; satisfactory; Chinese currency unit. FR 1145.**

This is a character which has been phonetically borrowed returned to its original meaning by the addition of a radical, in this case, the wall radical but representing a circle. See page 203.

月饼 **yue4bing3 moon cake**

饼 (餅) **bing3 eat 431** 饼 **cake, pancake, pastry. FR 2359.**

This is a radical+phonetic character. For the phonetic, see 普 pu3 in BC Lesson 6. If you are lucky, you can still find vendors of 煎饼 jian1bing in parks or on university campuses in Beijing. When you indicate that you want one, the vendor will scoop up a ladle full of pancake batter, pour it on a hot circular griddle, spread it thin out to the edge of the griddle, crack an egg onto it, spread the egg, sprinkle on chopped fresh green herbs, flip the whole thing over (so any germs are killed on the hot griddle), spread on hoisin sauce, lay on a large piece of fried pie crust, fold it all up, apply two small sheets of paper (so you can hold it without burning your fingers), and you walk off eating this healthy delight as if it were an ice-cream cone. I got a vendor to teach me how to make a 煎饼. Chinese who saw me making my own 煎饼 declared that they too wanted one made by the 美国人.

不同 **bu4tong2 difference, different**

同 **tóng aa 2510** 同 **same, equal, alike, together; agree. FR 69.**
See BC Lesson 2.

除夕 **chu2xi1 eve**

除 **chu2 place 3415 besides; eliminate, except; divide; steps. Frequency Rank 864.**
See page 201.

夕 **xi1 aa 354** 夕 **sunset, evening, night.**

A picture of a half moon. A shell-bone example – of which there are many – is on the far left. Next to it is a typical bronze example. The *Shuowen* character is on the right. We met the 夕 glyph previously in 外 wai4, meaning *outside*, in BC Lesson 4.

Recall that the basic meaning of 除 is *steps, stairs*. So the eve (除夕) of a holiday is like moon-lit steps leading up to it.

团聚 **tuan2ju4 get together, reunite, have a reunion.**

团 (團) **tuan2 wall 513** 团 **round (like a ball or roll). FR 405.**

This is a radical+phonetic character. The square *wall* radical is, in this case, a squared-off circle. In the Shuowen character, right, the corners are at least rounded.

In the simplified character the phonetic is 才 cai2 – not helpful as a phonetic. The interesting part of this character is the phonetic in the traditional. The standard traditional version is 專 zhuan1, but there is an older traditional 叀. (The simplified version of this character is 专.) It is a phonetic loan character with meanings unrelated to what it pictures. What it pictures is a drop spindle and a hand, and there are numerous shell-bone examples such as shown on the top left. Since the flywheel of the drop spindle spins round and round, this phonetic contributes also to the meaning of 團. The drop spindle itself is now 叀 zhuan1. Sears found 203 shell-bone examples, one of which is on the lower right; Jun Da found none in the Internet sample from which our frequency ranks are made. The OECCD thought it necessary to explain that a 叀 is a 纺锤 fǎngchuí, that is to say, a spindle, undoubtedly a drop spindle – a simple device to convert fiber (which has no tensile strength) into strong yarn from which cloth can be made. If you have never used a 叀, do so and feel a connection to the millions of women and men who over

A modern drop spindle

thousands of years spent countless hours patiently spinning, converting wool and flax into yarn from which cloth and clothes could be made.

聚 ju4 ear 543 assemble, gather together. FR 1306.

The *Shuowen* character, on the right, is almost self-explanatory: the three men on the bottom have *assembled, gathered together*, while the top is phonetic 取 qu3 is a common character (FR 323) meaning to take, get, choose, select. On the left is an ear, and on the right is a hand. I suspect that 取 refers to the practice, well documented among the Greeks, of stealing cattle by leading them away by the ear.

大人 da4ren2 adult, grown-up

No explanation necessary.

包 bao1 wrap 561 包 bag, package; wrap; bun; include; reserved; take responsibility. FR 454.

See 跑 page 256.

装 (裝) zhuang1 dressB 24 裝 hold, load, install; dress up, clothing, costume. FR 467.

This is a radical+phonetic character with the dressB radical on the bottom. The phonetic, the top, is 壮 (壯) zhuang4 meaning *strong, robust, magnificent*. It in turn is a radical+phonetic character with the sir radical on the right and on the left the phonetic 爿 or 丬 qiáng, meaning a bed.

着 (著) zhe eye 431 (aspect marker) FR 41.

Exactly the same character pronounced zhao1 expresses agreement or means *put in, add;* pronounced zhao2 it means *to touch, give off light, or go to sleep*. It is not in the *Shuowen* or earlier sources and has a complicated recent history. I cannot presume to explain it.

Note carefully the difference from 看 kan (look).

大家 da4jia1 everyone, people

家 jia1 roof 135 家 family, home. FR 56.

Surely you remember from BC Lesson3 the pig under the roof who represents the family and home.

交换 **jiao1huan4 exchange (noun and verb)**

交 **jiao1 hat 347** 交 **deliver, hand over, exchange; join, intersect. FR 320.**

See page 259

换 **huan4 hand 352** 换 **change, exchange**

See page 135.

礼物 **li2wu4 gift, present**

礼 (禮) **li2 altar 6** 礼 **ceremony, rite, courtesy, gift, present. FR 926.**

This is an ideogram. It shows an altar on the left and a drum on the right. (The drum plays an important role in Chinese temple ceremonies.) The drum itself (a rectangle) sits on a stand at the bottom of the character. We are looking at the side of the drum; the heads are perpendicular to the page. What is above the drum seems to be a picture of "boom! Boom! BOOM!" – the sound emerging from the drum. There are a number of shell-bone (top left) and bronze (bottom left) versions of the drum by itself. The drum always looks the same; the sound – as you would expect – has a great variety of fanciful representations. The *Shuowen* version of 礼 is on the right. The representation of the altar on the left is standard for the *Shuowen*; the boom-boom has become rather hum-drum.

物 **wu4 ox 35** 物 **things, objects. FR 142.**

See BC Lesson3 page 66.

习惯 **xi2guan4 habit, custom**

习 (習) **xi2 aa 541** 习習 **to practice. FR 676.**

See BC page 77.

惯 (慣) **guan4 heart 567** 惯 **to be in the habit of, indulge, spoil. FR 1226.**

Note that the figure in the upper right corner is not a rectangle but a trapezoid made with a 5 and a 6 stroke. The usual rule for deciding which stroke is coded first breaks down because they both begin at the same point and end at the same point. If however we left of that last point, the 5 would come first, so I have coded the character as heart 567. (In the Quick Guide, it is coded as heart 65, but I cannot defend that coding.)

This is a radical+phonetic character. "A habit," says *Wiktionary*, "is what one does by *heart*." The (exact)

phonetic, 贯 guan4 (FR 1478) means *to pierce, to string* presumably originally referring to making a string of cowrie shells.

饺子 jiao3zi dumplings

饺 (餃) jiao1 eat 41 饺 dumpling

This is a radical+phonetic character. The eat radical is fitting; the phonetic 交 jiao1 we last encountered earlier in this lesson.

猜 cai1 dog 711 猜 guess, speculate. FR 1598.

This is a radical+plus phonetic character with the dog radical and the 青 qing1 phonetic which we met in the character 请 qing3 in BC Lesson 3. The puzzle is What does dog have to do with speculate? Sears says it formerly meant *to hate*. That may be so, but I do not find it in other sources. I suspect that it is more like *to sniff out* which has an element of suspicion, guessing and speculating and is certainly a canine activity.

属(屬) shu3 door 32 属 class, category; born in the Chinese zodiac year of ___. FR 610.

There is a conflict of authorities on this one. All agree that it comes from the *Shuowen* character on the right. The GHZ and Wiktionary say the radical comes from 尾; Sears says explicitly that it does not come from 尾. He believes the *Shouwen* character shows a man defecating. The idea, then, is that the scat shows *what kind of* animal was there.

生 sheng1 give birth to, be born, produce. FR 34.

See BC Lesson 1.

因为 yin1wei2 because

因 yin1 wall 314 cause, reason; because, as, for. FR 96.

For an abstract idea like *cause* or *reason* we can expect a phonetic loan character, and that is indeed the case here. The character is a picture of a mat with the character 大 woven into it as a design. It is returned to something like its original meaning by adding the grass radical in the character 茵 yin1 meaning *mattress*. There has been little change from the shell-bone version (left) to the *Shuowen* (right) to the modern version. Note also the expression 因特网 yin1 te2 wang3 = Internet.

为 (為) wei4 force 44 为 do, act, act as, become, be, make, take.

See BC Lesson 10 page 185..

得到 **de2dao4 receive, obtain, acquire**

得 **de2 road 0115** 得 **obtain, get, result in; fit, prosper; satisfied; finish; permit. FR 39.**

(The high frequency of this character is due to its being also both a grammatical particle and having a second pronunciation dei1 with which it means *must, ought, have to*.) Numerous shell-bone versions, such as the one on the left, show just a hand picking up a cowrie shell, a perfect picture of *get, obtain*. Some of the bronze versions add a road: pick up along the road. The Shuowen version is on the right.

到 **dao4 knife 164** 到 **arrive, reach, go to, leave for. FR 22.**

First of all, recall that knife, 刀 dao1, turns into two vertical lines in compounds and always forces itself to the right side, as in this character. We thus suspect that it is the meaningful component of a radical-phonetic compound. But it isn't. It is the phonetic component and 至 is the meaningful component. 至 shows – as in the shell-bone version on the left – an arrow having *arrived* where it was going, in this case, to the ground. So our character is pronounced *dao* and means *arrived*. *The Shuowen* version is on the right.

树 **shu4 tree 5451** 树 **tree, plant; cultivate, establish. FR 697.**

摆(擺) **bai3 hand 0227** 摆 **to place, put, display; show swing, wave; pendulum. FR 1158.**

This is a radical+phonetic, and the hand radical clearly fits. The phonetic is 罢(罷) ba which is another form of the particle 吧 ba discussed in IC Chapter 1. The traditional form, shows a net over a bear. There are no known ancient forms of 摆; the *Shuowen* form of 罢 is shown on the left. Besides its function as a particle, 罢(罷) ba4 (FR 1305) has the meaning of *to give up, finish, cease.* Perhaps the bear caught in the net knows he is *finished* and may as well *give up*.

装饰品 **zhuang1shi4pin3 decorations**

装 **zhuang1**

See page 273.

饰 (飾) shi4 eat312 饰 adorn, dress up; decorations; play the role of. FR 1604.

This is a radical+phonetic but etymologically the radical is 布 bu4, meaning *cloth* and not a standard radical (which is just 巾) and the phonetic is 亇 (食) shi2 which is a standard radical. Moreover, 亇, the phonetic, is on the left where the radical usually is. So it looks like some kind of food pronounced bu but is really something made of cloth pronounced shi.

品 pin3 mouth 00 品 objects, products.

This pictogram appears in numerous examples from shell-bone times to the present day in virtually unchanged form. In is often seen on the street in China in the names of companies. The *Shuowen* version is on the right.

花 hua1 grass 326 花 flower; smallpox; mixed; to spend (time or money). FR 410.

传统 chuan2tong3 tradition, traditional.

传 (傳) chuan2 man 5114 传 pass on, transmit; traditions; popularize; spread. FR 332.

This is a radical+phonetic character with a *man* radical because the actions it represents are so typically human. The phonetic is the drop spindle, *zhuan1*, again. (See page 285.) The simplifiers were not consistent in the way they simplified the spindle. The character on the left is bronze; on the right is the *Shouwen*.

统 (統) tong3 silk 416 unite, all together, connected system. FR 264.

In this radical+phonetic character the silk radical calls to mind "the ties that bind". The phonetic is 充 chong1 meaning *to be full*. The *Shuowen* version of 充, on the left, is a fine picture of *full*. In the *Shuowen* version of 统 (on the right) the man is so full he has split open.

庆祝 qing4zhu4 celebrate, celebration

庆 (慶) qing4 shed 314 庆 celebrate, congratulate, celebration. FR 1269.

This ideogram is thought to show a deer (鹿 lu4) skin with head and antlers still attached being scraped by a hand (at the bottom) and prepared as a present for those who are celebrating and being congratulated. A bronze version is on the left and the Shuowen on the right. My problem with this explanation is Why then is the heart emphasized? The simplifiers gave up on the deer and just show something *big* (maybe a celebration?) going on under a *shed*.

祝　zhu4 altar 036 to express good wishes; an incantation, spell. Frequency rank 1651.

See page 195
Conversations

A：你能不能给我介绍一下儿中国的节日？

B：当然能。 可是中国的节日很多。我们只能说重要的。

A：好。 我想先问问中国人过来不过元旦。

B：过。但是对中国人来说，元旦不是最重要的节日。最总要的 节日是中国新年。

A：中国新年是几月几号？

B：每年不一样。有时在一月，有时在二月。

A：除了中国新年，还有什么重要的节日？

B：十月一号是国庆节。全国都放假。

A：中国有没有圣诞节？

B：没有。虽然圣诞节不是中国人的节日但是现在有的人也过　这个节　日。

A：我听说有一个找哦你中秋节。这是什么接？

B："中" 的意思是 *middle* "秋"的意思是 *autumn* "中秋节" 的意思　　就是 *Mid-Autumn Festival*。这一天月亮最圆。人们吃月饼全家团聚。

A：中秋节是什么时候？

B：中秋节和新年一样，每年不同但是一般在十月。

* * * * *

A：你知道明年的中国新年时哪一天吗？

B：明年的中国新年是二月十号。

A：中国人一般怎么过年？

B：除夕的晚上，全家人团聚，做很多菜，吃很多菜。新年的那　　天，大人还有给小孩子红包。

A：什么是红包？

B：红包里装着钱，是给小孩子的礼物。

A：新年的时候大家交换礼物吗？

B：中国人没有这个习惯。

A：中国人过年一般吃些什么？

B：各种各样的东西但是大多数人都要吃饺子。

* * * * *

A：明年是什么年？

B: 明年是鸡年。明年生的孩子都属鸡。
A: 我不知道我属什么。你能告诉我吗?
B: 可以。你今年多大?
A: 我今年二十岁，我是一九九七年生的。
B: 你比我小两岁,
A: 明年是什么年?
B: 明年是鸡年。明年生的孩子都属鸡。
A: 我不知道我属什么。你能告诉我吗?
B: 可以。你今年多大?
A: 我今年二十岁，我是一九九七年生的。
B: 你比我小两岁 我是猪。你是牛年生的，你是牛。
A: 我知道了，如果你知道一个人属什么你就能猜到他有多大。
B: 你说的不错。一般是这样。

In traditional characters:

A: 你能不能給我介紹一下兒中國的節日?
B: 當然能。可是中國的節日很多。我們只能說重要的。
A: 好。我想先問問中國人過來不過元旦。
B: 過。但是對中國人來說，元旦不是最重要的節日。最總要的 節日是中國
新年。
A: 中國新年是幾月幾號?
B: 每年不一樣。有時在一月，有時在二月。
A: 除了中國新年，還有什麼重要的節日?
B: 十月一號是國慶節。全國都放假。
A: 中國有沒有聖誕節?
B: 沒有。雖然聖誕節不是中國人的節日但是現在有的人也過　這個節　日。
A: 我聽說有一個找哦你中秋節。這是什麼接?
B: "中" 的意思是 middle "秋"的意思是 autumn "中秋節" 的意思　就是
Mid-Autumn Festival。這一天月亮最圓。人們吃月餅全家團聚。
A: 中秋節是什麼時候?
B: 中秋節和新年一樣，每年不同但是一般在十月。
* * * * *
A: 你知道明年的中國新年時哪一天嗎?
B: 明年的中國新年是二月十號。
A: 中國人一般怎麼過年?
B: 除夕的晚上，全家人團聚，做很多菜，吃很多菜。新年的那　天，大
人還有給小孩子紅包。
A: 什麼是紅包?
B: 紅包裏裝著錢，是給小孩子的禮物。

A: 新年的時候大家交換禮物嗎?
B: 中國人沒有這個習慣。
A: 中國人過年一般吃些什麼?
B: 各種各樣的東西但是大多數人都要吃餃子。
* * * * *
A: 明年是什麼年?
B: 明年是雞年。明年生的孩子都屬雞。
A: 我不知道我屬什麼。你能告訴我嗎?
B: 可以。你今年多大?
A: 我今年二十歲, 我是一九九七年生的。
B: 你比我小兩歲,
A: 明年是什麼年?
B: 明年是雞年。明年生的孩子都屬雞。
A: 我不知道我屬什麼。你能告訴我嗎?
B: 可以。你今年多大?
A: 我今年二十歲, 我是一九九七年生的。
B: 你比我小兩歲 我是豬。你是牛年生的, 你是牛。
A: 我知道了, 如果你知道一個人屬什麼你就能猜到他有多大。
B: 你說的不錯。一般是這樣。

And in the Shuowen-like font:

A: 你能不能給我介紹一下兒中國的節日?
B: 當然能。可是中國的節日很多。我們只能說重要的。
A: 好。我想先問問中國人過不過元旦。
B: 過。但是對中國人來說, 元旦不是最重要的節日。最重要的節日是中國新年。
A: 中國新年是幾月幾號?
B: 每年不一樣。有時候一月, 有時候二月。
A: 除了中國新年, 還有什麼重要的節日?
B: 十月一號是國慶節。全國都放假。
A: 中國有沒有聖誕節?
B: 沒有。雖然聖誕節不是中國人的節日但是現在有的人也過這個節日。
A: 我聽說有一個我喜歡你中秋節。這是什麼懷?
B: "中"的意思是 *middle* "秋"的意思是 *autumn* "中秋節"的意思就是 *Mid-Autumn Festival*。這一天月亮最圓。人們吃月餅全家團聚。
A: 中秋節是什麼時候?
B: 中秋節跟新年一樣, 每年不同但是一般在十月。

* * * * *

A：你知道即将到来的中国新年是哪一天吗？
B：即将到来的中国新年是二月几十号
A：中国人一般怎么过年？
B：除夕的晚上，全家人团聚，做很多菜，吃很多菜。新年的那几天，大人还要给小孩子红包。
A：什么是红包？
B：红包里装着钱，是给小孩子的礼物。
A：新年的时候大家交换礼物吗？
B：中国人没有这个习惯。
A：中国人过年一般吃些什么？
B：各种各样的东西但是大多数人都要吃饺子。

* * * * *

A：即将到来是什么年？
B：即将到来是鸡年。即将出生的孩子都属鸡。
A：我不知道我属什么。你能告诉我吗？
B：可以。你今年多大？
A：我今年二十岁，我是一九九七年出生的。
B：你比我小两岁，
A：即将到来是什么年？
B：即将到来是鸡年。即将出生的孩子都属鸡。
A：我不知道我属什么。你能告诉我吗？
B：可以。你今年多大？
A：我今年二十岁，我是一九九七年出生的。
B：你比我小两岁 我是猪。你是牛出生的，你是牛。
A：我知道了，如果你知道一个人属什么你就能猜出他有多大。
B：你说的不错。一般是这样。

Lesson 8 Job Hunting and Interviewing

New words

被 **bei4 dress 25** 被 **wear; by; blanket, quilt, cover; passive marker. FR 154.**

This is a radical+phonetic character. For the dress radical, 衣, see page 96. The phonetic is 皮 pi2. It is thought to show a hand pulling fur from an animal skin. Perhaps the clearest early example is the LST character shown on the top left. It shows a hand and an animal skin. The hand is thought to be pulling fur from the skin. In the *Shuowen* version, lower left, the animal is much simplified and a tool of some sort has appeared above the hand. Since the skin is being made wearable, the phonetic contributes to the meaning. The Shuowen version of 被 is on the right. The passive marker function is thought to have evolved from the *wear* meaning.

解雇 **jie3gu4 lay off**

解 **jie3 horn 5** 解 **cut up; understand; solve. FR 301.**

The knife, upper right, has *cut up* the stier, lower right, and removed the horn, left. Note the idea that to understand and solve a problem one must cut it up.

雇(僱) **gu4 doorB 3412** 雇 **hire, employ. FR 1817.**

The traditional radical+phonetic character makes good sense. It has the *man* radical because both employer and employee are *people*. The phonetic, 雇 gu4, is itself a radical+phonetic character meaning *migratory birds*; 隹 the radical, is a picture of a bird (though not the standard bird radical) and 户 hu4 (a picture of a door) is the phonetic. Dropping the man radical in the simplified seems to imply that employees are migratory birds. The simplified is also sometimes found as a traditional character meaning *hire, employ.*

生意 **sheng3yi4 business**

生 **sheng2 aa 3711** 生 **living being, life, to be born, to give birth. FR 34.**

See BC Lesson 1.

意 yi4 hat 431 意 **Idea, wish, desire. meaning. FR 104.**

The ancient Chinese knew that ideas, as well as wishes, desires and meaning, come from the heart, so the heart radical makes perfect sense. There are no versions before the *Shuowen*, shown on the right. No one seems to know for sure what is above the heart; it is certainly not a mouth nor a sun. Maybe it is a picture of a beautiful idea rising from the heart!

(Inexplicably, this frequent character escaped the *Quick Guide to Chinese Characters*. Please pencil it in where it belongs in you copy.)

什么样 shen2me'yang4 **what kinds of**

什么 shen2me **(interrogative expression)**

See BC Lesson 2 (page 46).

样(樣) yang4 tree 4317 样 **shape, form, model, pattern, kind, type. FR 88.**

See page 257.

秘书 mi4shu1 **secretary**

秘 mi4 grain 436 **secret, mysterious; hide. FR 896.**

This is a radical+phonetic character, but the grain radical makes little sense, so it is not surprising to learn that the character is an (erroneous) variant of 祕 with the altar radical and originally meaning secret, *arcane rituals*. The altar radical fits perfectly.

The phonetic is 必 bi4, a phonetic loan character now meaning *must, surely, most certainly* but depicting the handle of a weapon. A bronze version is shown on the left. Though now quite similar to 心, there is no historical connection between the two. There is no *Shuowen* character corresponding to the corrupted 秘; the *Shuowen* version of the sensible 祕 is on the right. The altar is quite explicit; the dots on either side of the weapon handle have been stretched to the full height of the character. In most computer fonts, by the way, 祕 appears as 祕, thus preserving the *Shuowen* form of the altar.

书 (書) shu1 aa 245 书書 **book. FR 282.**

See BC Lesson 2.

283

人事部 **ren2shi4bu4 personnel department**

人 **ren2 top** 人 **man, person, people, human being. FR 7.**

See the character 你 BC Lesson 1, page 19.

事 **shì aa 5105** 事 **matter, affair, business, work, event. FR 58.**

See BC Lesson 2.

部 **bu4 placeR 4140** 部 **part, section, unit, ministry. FR 84.**

This is a radical+phonetic character with the radical on the right. The original meaning was
"part of a city". In the Shuowen version, right, the city is the circle on the top right with its

citizen below it. The phonetic is 音 pou3 meaning "to spit out". The mouth is at the bottom and
what is spit out is at the top. In the Shuowen version, (on the right) what is spit out is fantastic;
some of the LST versions, such as the one on the left, are closer to the more modest modern
version.

一 . . . 就 **yi2 ... jiu4 as soon as**

就 **jiu4 ab 41034** 就 **approach, undertake; right away; only; with regard to, to go with. FR 27**.

See page 197.

消息 **xiao2 xi news, information; word.**

消 **xiao2 water 2432** 消 **disappear, fade away; eliminate, remove; while away; pastime. FR 439.**

The Shuowen version of this ideogram shows on the right the blossom of plant upside-down, *wilting, fading* for lack of the water that is on the right. There are no other known early versions.

息 **xi1 nose 46** 息 **breathe; sigh; rest, stop, cease; news; interest. FR 428.**

The modern version, like the Shuowen version, shows a nose over a heart. We breathe through our nose, but if our heart stops, so does our breathing. Thus this ideogram shows the organs that must work together for us to breathe. As for how it comes to mean *news*, well everybody knows a newspaper reporter needs a good nose for scandal.

问 (問) **wen4 gate 0** 问 **ask, inquire, send greetings; denounce. FR 137.**

This ideogram of a mouth at the gate asking, inquiring has come down from shell-bone times with little change, and the *Shuowen* version, right, is virtually identical with the modern version.

兴趣 **xing4qu interest** (in the sense of what interests one, not payment on borrowed money)

兴 （興） **xìng xing4 aa 44313 to rise, prosper, be popular, in fashion; to found, start, promote; to begin; to be excited. FR 531.**

See BC Lesson 1.

 趣 **qu4 run12 interest, bent, inclination; delightful interesting. FR 1065.**

 In this radical+phonetic character the radical is 走 showing a man running above a foot, as shown in the Shuowen form on the left. He is running to what *interests* him. The phonetic, 取 qu3 shows a hand and an ear. It means *to take*. Most interpretations see the hand as taking the ear. I always remember the Greek practice of taking cattle away – stealing them – by leading them away by the ear. The *Shuowen* version of 趣 is on the right.

全职 **quan2zhi2 full time**

全 **quan2 top 171 全 complete, all, overall ; make perfect. FR 124.**

There seems to be no agreement on the etymology of this character. One plausible one is that it is an ideogram showing a piece of jade below while the figure above indicates that it is all together, hence perfect, complete. The *Shuowen* character is on the right.

职 （職） **zhi2 ear 034 职 job, position, post, office, duty. FR 616.**

 The English Wiktionary says that this is a radical+phonetic character with the ear radical and 戠 zhi1 as phonetic. That is plausible enough until you ask What does ear have to do with the meanings of this character? Now 戠 is an interesting character. Sears found more than 50 shell bone examples of it, such as the one on the left. On the right it shows a weapon and on the left a mouth speaking. (Many examples leave off the mouth and show just the speech.) Sears calls the character "sentry", and that seems an appropriate name, for the sentry is armed and must call out if the enemy appears. Of the bronze versions, such as on the middle left, he found only 7. In the *Shuowen* version (bottom left) the sentry's tongue has become quite eloquent. Today this character has all but disappeared, its place taken, I suspect, by the one derived from it by adding an ear on the left, as shown in the *Shuowen* character shown on the top right. Now a sentry has to use his ears as well as his tongue and spear; indeed, he is his commander's ears, so I suspect the augmented character continued for a while to be used for sentry, though today totally different characters (哨兵) are used – but note the mouth. A sentry, however, almost more than anyone else, has *a post, a position, a job.* ("I will walk my *post* in a military manner ....") and gradually the character came to refer to these rather than to the sentry himself. The simplified kept only the sentry's ear and added a totally different phonetic 只 zhi3, which is itself a simplification of another character, 隻, showing a hand holding a bird and now meaning *only, just, merely, but* – just one bird, not two 雙 . (The nice connection between 隻 and 雙 got lost when the first was simplified to 只 and the second to 双.)

半职 **ban4zhi2 part time**

半 **ban4 aa7431 half, in the middle, very little. FR 513.**
See page 201.

工资 **gong1 zi salary**

工 **gong1 aa 121 工 work, skill, profession. FR 118.**
See BC Lesson 2.

资 (資) **zi1 shell 4135 money, expences, supply, resources, capital, support. FR 257.**

This is a radical+phonetic character with the cowrie shell radical as befits a character with this

meaning. On top is the phonetic, the picture of the sneeze 次 ci4, which we met in BC Lesson 8, where we saw that it is a phonetic loan character now meaning *inferior, second*. The *Shuowen* version of 资 is on the right. There are no known earlier versions.

福利 **fu2 li4 benefits**

福 **fu2 altar 10 福 blessed, happiness, good fortune. FR 683.**

This radical+phonetic character is richly represented in the shell-bone examples, such as the one on the far left, and in the bronze examples, such as the one on the near left. The radical is *altar* – perfect for the meaning – and the phonetic is a picture of a jug or vase, 畐 fu2, still an exact phonetic. In the *Shuowen* version, the neck of the vase got brocken, and it has not been repaired in the modern version.

利 **li4 grain 25 利 gain, profit, advantage, benefit; sharp. FR 155.**
See page 213.

学历 **xue2li4 academic credentials, resumé**

学 (學) **xue2 child 44** 学 school, study, learn. **FR 66.**

See BC Lesson 1, page 35.

历 (歷) **li4 cliff 35** 历 **go through, experience; calendar. FR 480.**

See BC Lesson 4, page 75.

经验 **jing1yan4 experience**

经 (經) **jīng silk 541** 经 **warp; meridian; main north-south road; to rule, manage. FR 62.**

See BC Lesson 2, page 50.

验 (驗) **yan4 horse 341** 验 **inspect, examine, test, check; effective. FR 534.**

In this radical+phonetic character, the horse radical refers to the importance of "looking the horse in the mouth" – that is, *inspecting* it, before buying it. The phonetic 佥(僉) qian1 is a ideogram meaning *unanimous, with one voice, all together* and showing two people with huge mouths under one roof presumably speaking with one voice.

提供 **ti2gong4 provide**

提 **ti2 hand 01123** 提 **carry (by a handle), lift, improve, take out, extract. FR 196.**

This is plainly a radical+phonetic character with the the hand that carries, lifts and takes out as the radical while our familiar friend 是 shi4 is phonetic. The Shuowen character is on the right; there are no known earlier examples.

供 **gong4 man 7210 offer (in worship), supply. FR 550.**

This is a radical+phonetic character with the man radical, for only man offers in worship, and the appropriate (and exact) phonetic 共 gong4 meaning *to share* and showing two hands sharing something. Examples of 共 go back to bronze characters, such as the one on the left. The *Shuowen* version of 供 is on the right; there are no known earlier examples. Note how the phonetic supports the meaning: when man offers in worship he *shares* with the gods.

退休金 **tui4xiu1jin1 pension**

退 **tui4 go 651** 退 **retreat, withdraw, decline; return, cancel. FR 723.**

The authorities differ on this character. To begin with, Sears shows a number of shell-bone examples such as the one on the upper left which clearly show a foot entering a house, presumably *returning*, perhaps *retreating*. Wiktionary does not show any of these and begins with the bronze on the lower left. It shows a road on the left and on the right, from top to bottom, the sun, a hobbled foot, a mouth and another foot. The Shuowen version, right, keeps these elements except for the mouth. Wiktionary reads it as showing a foot walking away from the sun, that is, *retreating*. How we are supposed to know that the foot is walking away from the sun instead of towards it or just in its light is not clear. Sears adds that the original meaning was *slow*. Maybe the idea is that when the weather is sunny and hot, we walk slowly. For me, this one remains in the unsolved category.

休 **xiu1 man 734** 休 **to rest, stop, cease; be finished, divorce. FR 1082.**

Clearly, the man is resting in the shade of the tree in this nice ideogram.

金 **jin1 metalB** 金 **see the character** 错 **on page 25. FR 260.**

广告 **guang3gao4 advertisement, commercial**

广（廣） **guang3 shed** 广 **vast, wide, numerous, spread, Guangzhou. FR 468.**

See BC Lesson 6, page 111.

告 **gao4 ox 0** 告 **to accuse; tell, seek, ask for; declare. FR 310.**

To accuse is to gore with the mouth, just as this ideogram combining ox and mouth shows.

申请 **shen1qing3 apply, application**

申 **shen1 aa 70** 申 **to state, rebuke, reprimand. FR 110.**

This character is a drawing of a bolt of lightning now serving as a phonetic loan. There are a number of known shell-bone examples, such as shown on the far left and elaborate bronze specimens, such as near left. The *Shuowen* character is on the right. On first sight, it looks very different from the bronze examples, but studied more closely the forked ends of the bronze-age lightning bolt are seen to have just moved to the side of the central streak. In the modern character, the top of the bolt has fused with the bottom, and the picture is no longer obvious, but it is there if you know to look for it.

请 (請) **qing3 speech 7112** 请 請 **please; request, ask; invite. FR 421**

See BC Lesson 3, page 57.

工程师 **gong1cheng2shi1 engineer**

工 **gong1 aa 121** 工 **work, skill, profession, trade; worker, labor. FR 118.**

See BC Lesson 3, page 40.

程 **cheng2 grain 017** 程 **schedule, agenda; rule, order; journey; procedure, process. FR 314.**

Originally this character meant all manner of measurements. Grain is subject to much measurement and hence served as the radical of this radical+phonetic character. The phonetic, 呈 cheng2, has the basic meaning of *to show*. Its *Shuowen* form, on the left, seems to be a man on the bottom showing some object at the top. Why there are the two horizontal lines across the man's legs is unclear, but they survive in the modern form.

师 (師) **shi1 ab 231** 师 **teacher, master, expert; an army, a (military) division. FR 333.**

The original meaning of this ideogram is the military unit; in the sense of "teacher" it appears to be virtually a phonetic loan. There are many bronze examples such as the one on the left. The *Shuowen* character is on the right. The left side has become the modern character 𠂤 dui1 – meaning *mound* or *mound up* - and the right side has become 匝 帀 za1 meaning to encircle. So a unit of troops big enough to *encircle* a *mound* is a division. That is the closest I can come to making sense of the available sources.

自己 **zi4ji3 oneself, one's own**

自 **zi4 nose** 自 **self, personal; from, since; certainly, of course. FR 43.**

See IC Lesson 5, page 245.

己 **ji3 aa 516** 己 **self, oneself, personal, private. FR 162.**

己 is a phonetic loan character; it is a picture of a rope, perhaps a silk rope. There are numerous examples dating back to shell-bone times but looking just like the modern character.

离开 **li2kai1 leave**

离 **li2 hat 761** 离 **from; leave, depart. FR 418.**

(The coding given above is that of the *Quick Guide*, but it now appears to me that it should be *hat 672* since the tops of the 6 and the 7 are at very nearly the same height but the 6 is well to the left.) In the sense of "leave, depart", the traditional is 離, which originally meant the black-naped oriole but was phonetically borrowed for this meaning, but returned to its original meaning in 離黃.

 The etymology is unclear. Sears believes it to be a picture of a basket with handles. Wiktionary and Wiktionnaire build on LST versions such as the one shown on the left and see an animal, perhaps a yak, with tail at the lower right, horns at the top, powerful shoulders, and curving body. The *Shuowen* version is on the right.

开 **kai1 aa137** 开 **to open, start, begin, liberate, exploit, expand, develop. FR 94.**

See BC Lesson 5.

和 ... 有关系 **he2 ... you3guan1xi have to do with**

All characters already known.

更 **geng4 aa 1301** 更 **again, more, even more, once more, further. FR 221.**

 Historically, this character meant to improve a situation. An LST version (lower left) shows a house in flames and a hand coming to help. A bronze example, (upper left) shows the same situation save that it is harder to recognize the house in flames. In the *Shuowen* version, right, the flames have gone through the roof of the house.

The same character pronounced with the first tone means to change, to replace, to take turns.

列 **lie4 bad 25** 列 **list (verb), arrange; row, rank; kind; various; each and every. FR 300.**

This is a radical+phonetic character. The knife radical (on the right) is used because things must be separated, cut apart, before they can be arranged, put in rows and ranks. The *Shuowen* version is on the left. The phonetic on its left side evolved into something pronounced lie4 that looked like 罗 except that instead of the net at the top there was something like <<<. This then evolved into 歹 without, however, any suggestion that the result should be pronounced anything like *dai,* the pronunciation of 歹.

考慮 **kao3lü4 consider**

 kao3 old 1 考 **study, check, give or take and examination. FR 495.**

The character is a picture of an old man with long hair leaning on a cane. There are many bronze examples such as shown on the left. The original meaning was *elderly, long-lived,* or *deceased father.* The character has gone out of use in these senses and is used instead to mean 慮 *to examine, study, test, investigate, assess.* The *Shuowen* character is on the right.

慮 (慮) **lü4 tiger 46** 慮 **anxiety, concern; be anxious; ponder, consider. FR 901.**

A heart under a tiger – what better way to express anxiety! But wait. In the traditional, what is under the tiger is 思, which is a head above and a heart below and means *to think.* The structure of the character may therefore relate to its meaning of to *ponder* or *consider.* And the tiger, 虎 hu3, may be just an innocent phonetic in a semantic-phonetic combination. Note that this character is one of the rare cases in which the semantic element, 思, is *not* one of hundred or so standard meaningful radicals.

答复 **da2fu4 reply (noun and verb)**

答 **da2 bamboo 3410** 答 **answer, respond; return, repay. FR 559.**

See BC Lesson 6.

复 (復) **fu4 aa3101 come back, repeat; reply; review; duplicate. FR 426.**

 From left to right are shown here a shell-bone version, a bronze version, and the *Shuowen* version. The bronze one seems the clearest; it shows the road radical on the left, a house on the top right and a foot on the bottom right. Given its current meaning of *come back*, I see a foot *coming back* home.

要求 **yao1qiu require, requirement**

要 **yao4 woman 1220** 要 **want; demand, ask, request; important; should. FR 26.**

See BC Lesson 7.

求 **qiu2 aa 54143 beg, request; seek, strive for; try to get. FR 312.**

A phonetic loan character. It is a picture of a fur coat. See 球 on page 265.

291

房租 **fang2zu1 rent**

房 **fang2 doorB 41** 房 **house, room. FR 512.**

See IC Lesson 4.

租 **zu1 grain 251** 租 **to rent, hire, charter, rent out. FR 1397.**

See 姐 in BC Lesson 1. Originally, 租 represents a rent paid in grain.

生活 **sheng1huo livelihood, life**

生 **sheng1 aa 3711** 生 **living being, life, to be born, to give birth. FR 34.**

See BC Lesson 1.

活 **huo2 water 370** 活 **to live, exist, to enliven; livelihood. FR 219.**

The modern character looks like a wet tongue (舌), but etymologically it has nothing to do with 舌. Its *Shuowen* version is on the right and – according to Sears – originally meant the sound of moving water, a meaning the character retains in Korean, The water on the left is clear. The right side seems to be an ear listening to the gurgling water. (The standard *Shuowen* ear is shown on the left for comparison.) The right side of the modern character is just a graphical simplification of this ear. Alas, it turned into a tongue instead of a standard ear. (The GHZ explanation is different; in it the right side is phonetic.)

了解 **liao2jie3 gain understanding**

了 **liao2**

See BC Lesson 8.

解 **jie3 horn 5** 解 **cut up; understand; solve. FR 301.**

See page 282,

文化 **wen2hua4 culture**

文 **wen2 hat 7** 文 **writing, literature, language, culture, learning, science. FR 148.**

See BC Lesson 2.

化 **hua4 man 63** 化 **change, transform, make into. FR 178.**

See 货 in BC Lesson 7.

文凭 **wen2ping2 diploma, degree**

凭 (憑) **ping2 man 37136** 凭 **lean against, depend on, confide in; proof; based on. FR 1410.**

This character is both an alternative traditional form of 憑 and its simplified form. An ideogram, the *Shuowen* form, right, shows a man (left) leaning his weight or weighty burden on a stool or table. In the simplified character, both the man and the weight are on top of the table. The modern standard traditional is a radical+phonetic character with the heart radical plus the phonetic

馮 féng – to gallop. As to why the heart radical, one can speculate that it relates to the "confide in" meaning or to a heart pounding from struggling with the weighty burden.

阅读 **yue4du2 reading**

阅 (閱) **yue4 gate 4303** 阅 **read, go over, go through, experience. FR 1489**

In this radical+phonetic character, the gate radical relates to the "go through" meaning. 兑 dui4, the phonetic, is the simplified and a variant traditional form of 兌 meaning "to speak". Its *Shuowen* form is shown on the right and a shell-bone example on the left. They show a man at the bottom, his mouth in the middle, and presumably his voice rising up from his mouth. Note that this phonetic contributes to the "to read" meaning, for traditionally reading seems to have been done aloud, as illustrated by Augustine's surprise that Ambrose read without moving his lips.

读 (讀) **du2 speech 75** 读 **read, attend school. FR 752.**

The speech radical in this radical+phonetic character meaning *to read* is further evidence of the traditionally close connection between speaking and reading.

The phonetic 賣 mai4 (meaning *to sell*) in the traditional has a small mistake by scribes. It should be the very similar looking 賣 yu4 also meaning *to sell* but providing a plausible phonetic for

讀 du2. Both 賣 and 賣 simplify to 卖 mai4, so the the simplified character 读 **du2** appears to have – crazily – 卖 **mai4** as a phonetic. But of course the traditional character already had the same problem. The Shuowen version of 讀 is on the right; there are no known earlier versions.

Supplementary words

需要 **xu1yao4 need**

293

xu1 rain 132 需 **need, want; necessities, requirements. FR 408.**

Sears gives the figure on the left as a bronze form of this character with the meaning *bath,* an ideogram that is so clear it is almost a pictogram. It then came to mean – presumably by phonetic borrowing – *need, want.* In the *Shuowen* version, on the right, the man at the

bottom has become identical with with *Shuowen* version of 而 er2, meaning *and* and derived from a picture of a beard. Thus a perfectly sensible character has evolved into *rain over beard = need,* which makes no sense.

要 **yao4 woman 1220** 要 **want; demand, ask, request; important; should. FR 26.**

See BC Lesson 7

雇主 **gu4zhu3 employer**

雇 (僱) **gu4 doorB 3412** 雇 **hire, employ. FR 1817.**

See above in this chapter.

住 **zhu4 man 4171** 住 **dwell, live, reside; stop, cease; firmly; withstand. FR 309.**

See BC Lesson 3.

雇员 **gu4yuan2 employee**

雇 (僱) **gu4 doorB 3412** 雇 **hire, employ. FR 1817.**

See above in this chapter.

员 (員) **yuan2 mouth 2534** 员 **a person engaged in some work; member. FR 200.**

Surprisingly this character has nothing to do with shells. Rather it derives from shell-bone drawings (upper left) of a round pot, a *ding,* with three legs. Above the pot is a circle to draw attention to the *round* rim of the pot, and the meaning of the character was *round.* This picture survived in the bronze versions, such as the one on the lower left. In the *Shuowen* version, shown on the right, however, the shell appears – clearly just a visual confusion. It was then phonetically borrowed for its current meanings which include the conductor on a train, inspectors and controllers. It was then returned to its original meaning by adding the wall radical in

圆 (圓) yuan2 meaning *circle, round.* (The wall radical represents a circle in several characters.)

雇(僱) **gu4 doorB 3412** 雇 **hire, employ. FR 1817.**

See above in this chapter.

职员 **zhi2yuan2 staff, clerk**

职 (職) **zhi2 ear 034** 职 **duty, office, job, position, post. FR 616.**

The character represents the sentry, the quintessential office holder. The right half, 戠 zhi2, is an exact phonetic and by itself means *sentry*. It shows on the right the sentry's defensive weapon and on left his mouth with tongue protruding to give a warning cry if the enemy approaches. This character adds an ear on the left; again the sentry's ear is his most important sense.

员(員) see just above.

失业 **shi1ye2 lose one's job**

失 **shi1 to loose, to miss, to fail. FR 375.**

See BC Lesson 9.

业 (業) **ye4 aa 2243 industry, business, studies; do; already; karma. FR 130.**

See IC Lesson 5.

辞职 **ci2zhi2 resign, resignation**

辞 **ci2 tongue 41 bid farewell, say goodbye; decline**

职 (職) **zhi2 ear 034** 职 **duty, office, job, position, post. FR 616.**

See above in this chapter.

老板 **lao3ban3 boss**

老 **lao3 old 63** 老 **old, (but also a title of respect). FR 179.**

See BC Lesson 1.

板 **ban3 tree 335** 板 **board, plank, slab, shutter; accented beat; hard, stiff, unnatural. FR 930.**

板(闆) **ban3 tree 355 boss**

It would seem that the expression for *boss* is *old plank*. But that is true only in simplified characters. In fact, both 板 and 闆 are phonetic loan characters in this usage replacing 辦 ban4, meaning "to deal

295

with; to handle; to manage; to take care of." 老辦 lao3ban4 is at once a respectful and affectionate way to refer to one's boss. But this 辦 is not in the simplified characters at all. Only in the simplified characters, however, is the character for *boss* the same as that for *plank*.

空缺 **kong4que1 vacancy**

空 **kong1 cave 121 空 leave empty; vacant; air; run a deficit; opportunity. FR 272.**

See BC Lesson 10. We met this character in the expression 空调 kong1 tiao2, air conditioning.

缺 **que1 ab 3173 缺 lack, be short of; incomplete; absent; vacancy. FR 875.**

This character is of the sense-sound type, which usually we have called the radical-phonetic type, but here the sense element is not one of the usual radicals. It is the left side, a picture of a pot with a lid. A shell-bone version of this pot is on the far left, and the *Shuowen* version is on the near left. Sears suggests that we should think of the pot as *empty* to make sense of the character. On the right is the phonetic, which as a character by itself is now pronounced *guai4* and means *resolute, determined, certain*. It shows a foot over a hand. Perhaps the idea is that hand and foot work together when one is resolute, determined, and certain. But no one seems to know for sure.

面试 **mian4shi4 (job) interview**

面 **miàn aa 1302 面 face; surface, flat, plane; fade. FR 74.**

See BC Lesson 2.

试 **shi4 speech 6411 试 test, examination; try, attempt. FR 643.**

See BC Lesson 7.

特长 **te4chang2 specialty, expertise**

特 **te4 ox 715 special, unusual. FR 173.**

See page 255.

长（長）**chang2 aa631 长 length; long; strong point, good at. FR 109.**

Note that this character looks exactly like the 长 we met in Lesson 2 with the following pronunciation and meaning: 长（長）zhang3, chief, head; grow; eldest. The frequency is for the two characters combined.

经济 **jing1 ji4 economy, economic, economical**

经（經）jīng silk 541 经 **warp; meridian; main north-south road; to rule, manage. FR 62.**

See BC Lesson 2.

济（濟）ji4 water 417 **to ferry across a river; to help, aid, be useful. FR 360.**

 This radical+phonetic character shows the river to be crossed on the left and, as the phonetic element, 齊 qi2, a pictogram meaning *even-growing grain*. The *Shuowen* version is on the right, but the evenness of the grain is clearer in the LST character on the left.

条件 **tiao2jian4 terms, conditions, prerequisite, factor**

条 **tiao2 aa3545 twig, strip, bar, strip; stripe, streak; item. FR 214.**

条 is also a classifier for long, thin things. See BC Lesson 2.

件 **jian man371 piece, item, classifier for things that can be counted.**

See BC Lesson 7.

行业 **hang2ye4 profession, trade**

行 **háng road 115 行 line, row; occupation, line of business; seniority among siblings. FR 53.**

See BC Lesson 2. The frequency rank includes this character when pronounced *xing2*.

业（業）**ye4 aa 2243 industry, business, studies; do; already; karma. FR 130.**

See IC Lesson 5.

退休 **tui4xiu1 retire**

退 **tui4 go 651 退 retreat, withdraw, decline; return, cancel. FR 723.**

See page 288

休 **xiu1 man 734 休 to rest, stop, cease; be finished, divorce. FR 1082.**

See page 288

Conversations without pinyin.

A. 你今天怎么没有去上班？

B. 上个月我被解雇了。我没有工作了。

A. 你被解雇了？这怎么可能？

B. 我们公司的生意不好，所以解雇了很多人。

A. 这怎么可能?

B. 我们公司的生意不好，所以解雇了很多人。

A. 你有没有找到新的工作?

B. 我找了一个月，但是还没有找到。你知道哪儿要人吗?

A. 你想找什么样的工作?

B. 我做的是秘书。我还想找秘书的工作。你能帮我的忙吗?

A. 我试试看。我去问问我们公司的人事部。我们公司可能要人。

B. 谢谢你的帮助。

A. 不客气。我一有消息就给你打电话。

* * * * *

A. 小王，我们学校在找一位中文老师。你有兴趣吗?

B. 你们要全职老师还是半职老师?

A. 我们要全职老师。

B. 我对教书很有兴趣，可是我只能做半职工作。

A. 你知道不知道别人有没有兴趣教中文?

B. 我可以问问我的朋友们。你能不能告诉我你们学校的工资和福利?

A. 工资要看学历和经验。我们提供医疗保险和退休金。每年有三十天的假。

B. 好，我一有消息就给你打电话。你也可以在中文报纸上做一个广告，一定会有很多人来申请。(bottom of 171)

A. 好主意。

* * * * *

A. 我是来申请贵公司电脑 工程师的 工作的。

B. 你是怎么知道我们要电脑工程师的?

A. 我是在报纸上看到你们的广告淂。

B. 谢谢你对我们公司的兴趣。你能介绍一下儿你自己吗?

A. 当然. 这是我的学历。 我是去年从大学毕业的。毕业后在美国电话公司工作。

B. 美国电话公司是个大公司。你为什么要离开?

A. 不错，美国电话公司是个大公司，但是我做的工作和电脑没有关系。我想在贵公司能有更多的机会。

B. 你在大学学的的是什么专业?

A. 我学的是电脑。我的学历上写着我做过的工作。

B. 你什么时候能开始工作?

A. 三个星期以后。

B. 好。我们会考录你的申请，在一个星期里给你答复的。

A. 谢谢。

B. 你有没有问题问我?

A. 现在没有。

Here again in traditional characters.

A. 你今天怎麼沒有去上班?

B. 上個月我被解雇了。我沒有工作了。

A. 你被解雇了? 這怎麼可能?

B. 我們公司的生意不好，所以解雇了很多人。

A. 這怎麼可能?

B. 我們公司的生意不好，所以解雇了很多人。

A. 你有沒有找到新的工作?

B. 我找了一個月，但是還沒有找到。你知道哪兒要人嗎?

A. 你想找什麼樣的工作?

B. 我做的是秘書。我還想找秘書的工作。你能幫我的忙嗎?

A. 我試試看。我去問問我們公司的人事部。我們公司可能要人。

B. 謝謝你的幫助。

A. 不客氣。我一有消息就給你打電話。

* * *

A. 小王，我們學校在找一位中文老師。你有興趣嗎?

B. 你們要全職老師還是半職老師?

A. 我們要全職老師。

B. 我對教書很有興趣，可是我只能做半職工作。

A. 你知道不知道別人有沒有興趣教中文?

B. 我可以問問我的朋友們。你能不能告訴我你們學校的工資和 福利?

A. 工資要看學歷和經驗。我們提供醫療保險和退休金。每年有 三十天的假。

B. 好，我一有消息就給你打電話。你也可以在中文報紙上做一個廣告，一定會有很多人來申請。

A. 好主意。

* * * * *

A. 我是來申請貴公司電腦 工程師的 工作的。

B. 你是怎麼知道我們要電腦工程師的?

A. 我是在報紙上看到你們的廣告淂。

B. 謝謝你對我們公司的興趣。你能介紹一下兒你自己嗎?

A. 當然. 這是我的學曆。 我是去年從大學畢業的。畢業後在美國電話公司工作。

B. 美國電話公司是個大公司。你為什麼要離開?

A. 不錯，美國電話公司是個大公司，但是我做的工作和電腦沒 有關系。我想在貴公司能有更多的機會。

B. 你在大學學的的是什麼專業?

A. 我學的是電腦。我的學曆上寫著我做過的工作。

B. 你什麼時候能開始工作?

A. 三個星期以後。

B. 好。我們會考錄你的申請，在一個星期裏給你答複的。

A. 謝謝。

B. 你有沒有問題問我?

A. 現在沒有。

And in the *Shuowen*-like font:

A. 你今天是麼還可去上班?

B. 上個月我被解雇了。我沒有工作了。

A. 你被解雇了? 這怎麼可能?

B. 我們公司的生意不好，所以解雇了很多人。

A. 這怎麼可能?

B. 我們公司的生意不好，所以解雇了很多人。

A. 你有沒有找到新的工作?

B. 我找了一個了，但是還得再找新。你知道哪兒要人嗎？

A. 你想找什麼樣的工作？

B. 我做的是祕書。我還想找祕書的工作。你能幫我的忙嗎？

A. 我試試看。我去問問我們公司的人事部。我們公司可能要人。

B. 謝謝你的幫助。

A. 不客氣。我一有消息就給你打電話。

　　　　　　　*　　*　　*　　*　　*

A. 小王，我們學校在找一位中文老師。你有興趣嗎？

B. 你們要全職老師還是半職老師？

A. 我們要全職老師。

B. 我對教書很有興趣，可是我只能做半職工作。

A. 你知道不知道別人有沒有興趣教中文？

B. 我可以問問我的朋友們。你能不能告訴我你們學校的工資和福利？

A. 工资与有学历咪经验。我们提供医惯保险咪退休金。差不多有三十天的假。

B. 好，我一有消息就给你打电话。你也可以在中文报纸上做一个广告，一定会有很多人来申请。

A. 好主意。

* * * * *

A. 我是来申请贵公司电脑工程师的工作的。

B. 你是怎么知道我们要电脑工程师的？

A. 我是在报纸上看到你们的广告得。

B. 谢谢你对我们公司的兴趣。你能介绍一下儿你自己吗？

A. 当然。这是我的学历。我是在……大学毕业的。毕业后在美国电话公司工作。

B. 美国电话公司是个大公司。你为什么要离开？

A. 不错，美国电话公司是个大公司，但是我做的工作咪电脑得……有关系。我想在贵公司能有更多的机会。

B. 你在大学学的的是什么专业？

A. 我學的是電腦。我的學歷上寫著我做過的工作。

B. 你什麼時候能開始工作？

A. 三個星期以后。

B. 好。我們會考慮你的申請，在一個星期裏給你答復的。

A. 謝謝。

B. 你還有問題問我？

A. 現在沒有。

Lesson 9. Newspaper and Internet

华尔街 **Hua2er3jie1 Wall Street**

华(華) **hua1 man 637** 华 **flower, flower-shaped; small pox; multi-colored; mixed; hypocritical; blurred, dim; to spend. FR 412**

华(華) **hua2 man 637** 华 **China, Chinese; splendid, grand; glory.**

华(華) **hua4 man 637** 华 **Mount Hua in Shaanxi Province, the westernmost of the five sacred mountains.**

 We have met 华 several times, once as a man's surname and several times for sound, as here. We have skipped its etymology and waited for it to be used with its basic meaning, namely *flower*. I now see that that is not going to happen in the textbook we are following, so let's deal with it here. The traditional character descends from bronze versions, such as the one shown on the left, via the *Shuowen* version shown on the right. The simplified version kept only the bottom cross from the traditional character but added as a phonetic element the character 化 hua4, meaning *change, transform*. It shows two men. One is right-side up; the other is upside-down. The second is the first after having been *changed, transformed*.

尔(爾) **er3 aa35534 you; thus; so; like that; so that. FR 220.**

This phonetic loan character is a picture of a spindle. On the left is a Bronze version; the *Shuowen* character is on the right.

街 jie1road 717 街 **street, country fair, market. FR 1101.**
See BC Lesson 9.

时报 **Shi2bao4 Times (name of a newspaper)**

时(時) **shi2 sun 514** 时 **time; o'clock; era; epoch; season; period; hour; sometimes. FR 25.**
See BC Lesson 5.

报 (報) **bao4 hand 52** 报 **inform, report; announce; newspaper; repay. FR 234.**
See BC Lesson 6.

内容 nei4rong2 content

What is "inside held" is *content* in the literal etymological sense of con-tent.

内 **nei4 aa3254 inside, inner; one's wife and her family. FR 175.**

In the numerous, all very similar shell-bone examples, such as the one on the top left, whatever is inside looks like some structure and is always entirely *inside*. In all of the known bronze versions, what is inside floats inside, as in the example on the lower left. In the *Shuowen* character, shown on the right, what is inside has risen back to the top and in fact poked through the roof. If something specific is depicted, it has eluded modern commentators.

容 **rong2 cave340 容 hold, contain; let, permit; looks, appearance. FR 442.**

See IC Lesson 5

金融 jin1rong2 finance

金 **jin1 see discussion of metal radical in BC Chapter 1.**

融 **rong2 worm102 融 melt, blend; circulation (of money), finance. FR 1225.**

The character depicts its basic meaning: smelting of metals. The *Shuowen* version (on the right) – the earliest version we have – shows a tripod on the lower left and on it a pot (the loop) holding ore to be smelted or metal to be melted – the horizontal line. We have to supply the fire under the tripod. On the right molten metal is poured out of a ladle. It all fits perfectly with the basic meaning of melting metal. Money – metal – flowing about is a fine picture for finance.

The subsequent conversion of the molten metal into a worm is, of course, just a mistake of scribes who didn't get the picture. Sears and Wiktionary both interpret the corrupted right side as a phonetic element. Perhaps it was because, for a summer job in college, I worked with molten metal that I recognized it.

连(連) lian2 go 61 連 even; link, connect, join; in succession; a battalion. FR 399.

There is one and only one known example (left) before the *Shuowen* version (on the right). This bronze version shows a cart on the left, half of a road on the right, and a hand (not a foot) on the bottom. It seems to have been originally a hand-drawn cart and a road. Sears says that it originally meant *continue* as to continue on a road, and one can sense that meaning behind some modern meanings such as *connect, join*. In the Shuowen version the hand has turned into a foot, which has become the radical of the modern versions.

标题 biao1ti2 headline

标 (標) biao1 tree115 标 **topmost branches of a tree; mark, sign. FR 473.**

This is a radical+phonetic character, with the obviously appropriate tree radical. The phonetic 票 piao4 now means a ticket or slip of paper. Its original meaning has been lost, so it is impossible to say what it depicts. The *Shuowen* version is on the right; there are no known earlier versions.

题 (題) ti2 head011 题 **forehead; topic, subject; sign, inscribe. FR 218.**

This is a radical+phonetic character, but the phonetic is 是 shì and the meaning element is 頁, a picture of the human forehead.

新闻 xin1wen2 news

This expression appeared in BC Lesson 6.

股票 gu3piao4 stocks

股 gu3 moon 3654 **share, portion, section, part; thigh. FR 644.**

 The "moon" radical is, as usual, really *meat* in this radical+phonetic character whose original meaning was *rump* and thus a section of the carcass. The phonetic is 殳 shū, a picture of a hand holding a tool, shown on the left in a shell-bone form. Here the phonetic contributes to the meaning: the hand with the knife will cut up the meat into *shares, portions, parts.*

票 piao4 altarB 1 票 **banknote, bill, ticket, certificate. FR 910.**

See BC Lesson 7.

跌 die1 leg 3311 **to drop, fall (verb), stumble. FR 1590.**

Both sides relate to the meaning. The leg and foot on the left clearly relate to stumbling. The figure on the right is a hand 手 with something *falling* away on the bottom right. 失 shī can hardly be a phonetic. The Shuowen character is on the right.

厉害 li4hai terrible, formidable

厉 (厲) li4 cliff135 厉 **fierce, severe; strict, rigorous, stern; to sharpen. FR 1339.**

 The character is a picture of a scorpion hiding under a rock, as is fairly clear in the bronze example on the left. Those are the scorpion's claws raised above its head.

The stinging scorpion is a pretty good picture for the meaning of the character. In the *Shuowen* version, right, the claws have come to look like hands, the head is a loop with an x in it, and the legs project below. In the modern traditional character, the claws have come to look like the grass radical, and rest looks like the character 禺 yu2, a type of monkey not known to be in the least fierce. In the simplified, the rock is still there but everything else has turned into 万 wan = 10,000 and the character no longer makes any sense at all.

害 **hai4 roof7110** 害 **harm, kill, evil, suffer from. FR 579.**

 There are several bronze versions such as shown on the left and the somewhat similar *Shuowen* version shown on the right. It appears to be a tally stick in a case, and would seem to be a phonetic loan in its present senses.

担心 **dan1xin1 worry**

担 **dan1 hand011** 担 **shoulder pole or its load, a weight of about 133 pounds. FR 720.**

There is no *Shuowen* or earlier character.

心 **xin1 heart** 心 **heart, mind. FR 90.**

See 怎 in BC Lesson 1.

其实 **qi2shi2 actually**

其 See 期 in BC Lesson 5.

实 (實) **shi2 roof 44** 实 **full, compact, solid, real; true, sincere; seed, fruit. FR 100.**

 A cowrie shell – meaning *money* – under a roof had the original meaning of *prosperous*. A bronze example is on the left; the *Shuowen* version is on the right. The simplified character, a head under a roof, might also be a good way to write *prosperous*, but that seems not to be among its meanings any more.

平常 **ping2chang2 ordinarily, generally**

平 **ping2 aa1743** 平 **flat, level; impartial, fair; calm, peaceful; first tone. FR 215.**
See IC Lesson 4.

常 chang2 roof3 constant, often, always, ever; common, general. FR 187.

See 当 in BC Lesson 7.

国际 guo2ji4 international

国 (國) guo2 wall1741 国 country. FR 20.

See BC Lesson 1.

际 (際) ji4 place115 border, boundary, lot; among; when; on the occasion of. FR 423.

This is a radical-phonetic character with the place radical, appropriate for is basic meaning, and in the traditional the exact phonetic 祭 ji4. The phonetic means "to offer sacrifice", and in it we see an altar on the bottom, the sacrificial piece of meat on the top left and the hand offering the sacrifice on the top right. In the simplified, we have only the altar 示 shi4, so the character no longer makes sense – unless, of course, you remember the traditional behind it.

国内 guo2nei4 domestic, national

国 guo2 wall 1741 国 country, nation, state. FR 20.

See BC Lesson 1.

内 nei4 aa3254 inside, inner

See above in this lesson.

扔掉 reng1 diao4 throw away

扔 reng1 hand53 扔 throw, throw away. FR 1905.

In the one and only known shell-bone version (shown on the left) this pictogram shows a hand throwing something, perhaps a sort of boomerang. There are no bronze examples. By the *Shuowen* version on the right, the object thrown has moved to the right side and become 乃 nai3, meaning *breast*, which makes no sense anymore.

掉 diao4 hand2101 掉 drop, fall; lose; exchange; turn. FR 849.

See IC Lesson 3.

开 kai1 open, start, liberate, offer (goods or services), expand; Kelvin. FR 94.

See BC Lesson 10.

熟悉 shu2xi familiar

熟 shu2 fireB41 熟 ripe, cooked, processed; familiar, skilled.

This is a radical+phonetic character with the fire radical and the phonetic 孰 shu2. The fire radical fits the basic meaning of *cooked*. The phonetic 孰 is currently an interrogative pronoun meaning *who, which, what,* but in these meanings it is a phonetic loan character. Its original meaning, according to *Wiktionaire*, was to offer cooked food. In the bronze version on the left, we see on the lower right the hands making the offering, and above the container of the food. In the *Shuowen* version on the right, the person and the hand doing the offering are on the right while the covered dish with the food is on the left. If we assume that the food being offered is cooked – which looks likely – then we have another case of the phonetic contributing to the meaning.

悉 xi1 heartB374 know, learn; all, entire. FR 1428.

The ancient Chinese considered that we think and know with our hearts and do we not have the expression "I know in my heart"? The heart radical on the bottom is therefore not surprising. The character on top, 釆 bian4, is obviously not a phonetic but rather contributes further to the meaning. Wiktionary gives its meaning as *to distinguish; to discriminate*. It goes back to shell-bone characters such as the one on the left which is interpreted as animal scat and a track which are important to be able to recognize and *distinguish*.

查 cha2 check, consult. FR 459.

See above in Lesson 6

网站 wang3zhan4 website

网 wang3 aa2577 net, network; to catch with a net. FR 605

  A fish net between two poles is almost still recognizable in this pictogram character. A shell-bone example is on the far left followed by a typical bronze version on the near left and the *Shuowen* character on the right.

站 zhan4 stand21 stand, stop, halt; a station or stop. FR

This is a radical+phonetic character with the radical 立 li4, a picture of a person standing. We discussed 占 zhan4, under the character 店 dian1 in BC Lesson 3.

发 (發) **fa1 aa3645** 发 **send forth, fire, shoot, develop; send (email). FR 47.**

The modern traditional version of this radical+phonetic character is element-for-element the same as the Shuowen version on the right. The radical is the bow in the lower left corner, the perfect radical for a character with the basic meaning of *shoot, send forth.* The rest of the

character is 癶 ba2, which serves as the phonetic. It means to remove or level out grass with one's feet. Needless to say, it is very rarely used by itself.

电子信 **dian4zi3xin4 email** (literally, electric little letter)

信 **xin4 man411** 信 **believe; honesty; reliable, true; letter; information. FR 176.**

A man standing by his word: what better picture could there be of honesty and reliability than this ideogram?

爷爷 **ye2ye (paternal) grandfather**

爷(爺) **ye2 aa347 father, uncle, (paternal) grandfather. FR**

This is also a form of respectful address for an older man. It is a radical-phonetic character, though its radical – the top part – is not one of the radicals of the radicode system. This radical derives from a picture of a hand holding a stone ax as shown in the shell-bone and bronze examples on the far left and near left respectively. Work with the stone ax is definitely the job of the *father.* In the Shuowen version, right, the ax is less pronounced. In the modern characters, a second ax has been added at the end of the little finger of the hand. The phonetic, 耶 ye1, seems to have been originally a place name with a left side which was corrupted into the ear. The character is now used mainly just for sound in phonetic spelling, as of the English slang, *yeah.*

奶奶 **nai3nai (paternal) grandmother**

奶(嬭) **nai3 woman 53** 奶 **lady; breasts, milk, suckle, feed. FR 1278**

The traditional version shows a woman next to a warping wheel, a device for holding the warp while it is fed into a loom. This identification is by Richard Sears. In the simplified character, the phonetic is 乃 nai3 meaning *you, your, just, only, then, even, therefore.* There are numerous known shell-bone examples of 乃 such as shown on the top left. The *Shuowen* version of 乃 is on the bottom left. There is no Shuowen version of 奶, but there are several LST versions such as shown on the lower right. They are very similar to the modern traditiona0ol.

311

得 **dei3 road0115** 得 **ought, must, have to, certainly will. FR 39.**

In IC Lesson 7, see 得 de2 road 0115: obtain, get, result in; fit, prosper; satisfied; finish; permit.

互联网 **hu4lian2wang3 the Internet**

互 **mutual FR 819.**

 The *Shuowen* character, identical to the modern character, is on the right. Sears says it is a picture of interlocking roof tiles and adduces the LST character on the left as evidence. Wiktioary says it is "A spool to wind up rope (like a modern garden hose spool)." Wiktionnaire says it is a device for twisting threads together. Take your choice.

联 (聯) **lian2 ear431 to connect, join, unite; couplet. FR 592.**

This is a radical+phonetic but with the radical (silk) on the right; silk relates to thread and thread relates to connecting, joining, uniting. The character goes back to shell-bone forms (far left) and bronze (near left) forms. In these, the silk radical looks like a figure 8 and the ear takes various forms barely recognizable as ears. The modern pronunciation of 耳 is er3, which is pretty far from lian2, so we may assume that one or both characters have undergone substantial phonetic change.

网 **wang3 aa2577 net, network; to catch with a net. FR 605**

See above in this lesson.

资料 **zi1 liao4 information, data, material**

资(資) **zi1 shell4135** 资 **money, expenses, support, talent, supply. FR 257.**

The shell radical is natural for a character meaning *money, expenses*. On the top is our old friend the sneeze from "次 ci4 second, inferior; time" in BC Lesson 8. In the Shuowen version, right, the same elements are present but with the whole body of the sneezer included. There are no known earlier versions.

料 **liao4 rice447** 料 **feed; markings; material. FR 557.**

 Rice is a natural meaning element in this radical+phonetic character. The phonetic, 斗 dou4, means "dipper" and is a picture of a dipper somewhat the worse for 4000 years of wear.

A shell-bone example of 斗 is on the far left; it shows a cup held by a hand or maybe a cup with a handle, that is, a dipper . A similar bronze version is in the middle, and the *Shuowen* character for 斗 is on the right of this triplet. The character 斗 appears, by the way, in the Chinese names of the dipper constellations. The *Shuowen* version of 料 is on the right.

聊天 **liao2tian1 chat**

聊 **liao2 ear 36 chat, kill time; merely, just a little, rely on. FR 1932.**
See IC Lesson 3

天 **tian1 aa1314 天 sky, heaven; natural; day; climate; season; over; most. FR 78.**
See BC Lesson 5.

国外 **guo2wai4 overseas, abroad**

国 **guo2 wall 1741 国 country, nation, state. FR 20.**
See BC Lesson 1.

外 **wai4 ab 35424 外 outside, foreign. FR 131.**
See BC Lesson 6.

网吧 **wang3ba1 Internet cafe**

网 See above in this lesson.

吧 **ba mouth 56** *sentence final particle.* **FR 470.**
See IC Lesson 1.

Supplementary words

订 **ding4 subscribe to**

日报 **ri4bao4 daily (newspaper title)**

日 **ri4 sun (the whole character is the sun radical) sun**
See BC Lesson 1. Here the sun represents *day*.

报（報） **bao4 hand 52 报 inform, report; newspaper; repay. FR 234.**
See BC Lesson 6.

电子报 **dian4zi3bao4 e-paper**

电（電） **dian4 aa 601** 电 **lightning, electricity. FR 230.**

See BC Lesson 3.

子 **zi3 child** 子 **child, son, person; a title of respect; seeds, eggs, small things. FR 37.**

See BC Lesson 1.

报摊 **bao4tan1 newspaper stand**

报（報） **bao4 hand 52** 报 **inform, report; newspaper; repay. FR 234.**

See BC Lesson 6.

摊(攤) **tan1 hand5434** 摊 **spread out, display; vendor's stand; take a share in. FR 2154.**

This is a radical+phonetic character. The hand does the spreading out, the displaying. The rest, 難 nan2, is phonetic. For the origins of 难 (難), see 滩 in BC Lesson 10.

记者 **ji4zhe3 reporter**

记 **ji4 speech 516** 记 **memorize, remember, record, mark. FR 306.**

This is a radical+phonetic character with the speech radical on the left. There is obviously a strong connection between making a speech and memorizing and remembering. The phonetic on the right, 己 ji3, is a picture of a piece of silk rope, but by phonetic loan it is used to mean *self, oneself.* In this character, however, it is purely phonetic. A shell-bone example of 己 is shown on the left.

者 **zhe3 old01** 者 **one who (does the action of the preceding verb), -er, -ist. FR 103.**

As is to be expected for a character with a grammatical function such as this one has, it is a phonetic loan. It is a picture of a growing plant; Wicktionary says the plant is sugar cane. On the left is one of a large number of known bronze examples. There are no known shell-bone examples. The *Shuowen* version is on the right. 者 appears unrelated to 老 *old* and to the modern character for sugar cane 蔗.

社论 she4lun4 editorial

社 she4 altar71 altars and ceremonies for the god of the soil; society, organization. FR 270.

This is an ideogram combining "altar" on the left and "earth" on the right. The first meaning, the altars for the god of the soil, fits naturally the structure of the character. The problem is how to get from that to "society" Sears suggests something like "the local (土) god (示) + the people under his influence = society", A bronze version is on the left and the *Shuowen* on the right.

论(論) lun4 speech 3463 discuss; opinion; essay; theory; mention by. FR 205.

The speech radical fits well the meaning. The phonetic, 侖 lun2, means to bring together (亼) texts (冊) to compare them, meditate on them, and develop them. (*Wiktionaire*).

商业 shang1ye4 business, commerce

商 shang1 hat 432 商 trade, business; merchant; consult, discuss. FR 402.

See BC Lesson 3.

业 ye4 aa2243 业 industry, business, property; studies;do; already; karma. FR 130.

See IC Lesson 5.

杂志 za2zhi4 magazine

See BC Lesson 6 for this word.

文章 wen2zhang1 article

文 wen2 hat 7 文 writing, literature, language, culture, learning, science. FR 148.

See BC Lesson 2.

章 zhang1 stand017 章 chapter (of a book); movement (of a symphony). FR 539.

According to *Wiktionaire,* the character originally pictured a jade tablet, an insignia of dignity or authority. Current meanings such as *regulations, rules, charter* derive from the tablet as an emblem of authority.

报道 **bao4dao4 report (noun)**

报（報） **bao4 hand 52** 报 **inform, report; newspaper; repay. FR 234.**

See BC Lesson 6.

道 **dao4 go 43130** 道 **way, road, truth; Taoism; say; think; doctrine. FR 52.**

See BC Lesson 2.

篇 **bamboo 453 pian1 sheet, piece of writing; *classifier for articles and reports*. FR 1008.**

The character is a picture of a bound set of bamboo slips for keeping records. The Shuowen character is on the right; there are no known earlier versions.

无线 **wu2xian4 wireless**

无（無） **wu2 aa1316** 无 **nothing, no, none, not, without, -less. FR 105.**

 As may be expected of a character with abstract meanings such as these, this is a phonetic loan character. It shows a man dancing with ornaments hanging from both arms as shown in the bronze character on the far left. And, as often happens when a character has been phonetically borrowed, it has been returned to its original meaning by adding a radical, in this case, two feet below the dancer in the character second from left. In the *Shuowen* character on the right, the ornaments have outgrown the man, and in the modern traditional the picture has been totally lost. It looks more like a four-footed animal than a dancing man.

线（綫） **xian4 silk64113** 线 **thread, line, filament,wire; slim, very little. FR 430.**

This is a radical+phonetic character. The silk radical fits because it is used for any kind of thread, rope or wire. The phonetic 戋 (戔) jian1 in the traditional shows two small daggers and means small. The simplified 戋 is fairly rare with a frequency rank of 6653.

上网 **shang4wang3 get on the Internet, go on line.**

上 **shang4 on, above. FR 16.**

See BC Lesson 3.

网 **wang3 aa2577 net, network; to catch with a net. FR 605**

See above in this lesson.

网址 wang3zhi3 web address

网 wang3 aa2577 net, network; to catch with a net. FR 605.

See above in this lesson.

址(阯) zhi3 earth2211 址 place, site, location, address. FR 1848.

There could hardly be a better, more emphatic, way to draw the idea of *place* than the "earth and a foot" – a foot that has been put down. In the traditional character, we have "place and a foot". As for "web address", think "web place". The traditional character derives from the *Shuowen* character (right) in the standard way, There are no known examples prior to the *Shuowen*.

搜索 sou1suo3 search

搜 sou1 hand732 搜 look for, search. FR 1564.

This is a radical+phonetic character. We need to think of the searching as being done by a hand groping around, perhaps in the dark. The phonetic in the modern character is 叟 sou3 whichmeans *old man, old gentleman*. The *Shuowen* version of 搜, however, shows that it should have been the synonymous 窔 sou3, but that character is now so rare that that it is not even in the list we are using to find the frequency ranks. At my age, I like the idea that 窔 means an old man still going like a house afire.

索 suo3 silkb74 索 large rope; search, look for; demand; all alone; dull. FR 882.

As noted above, the silk radical appears in characters meaning wire, thread, string, rope and the like quite independently of what the object is made of. The *Shuowen* version is on the right. A number of LST examples, such as the one on the left, unite the plant-like trident on top with the sides. Sears suggests that this whole exterior represents vines, which would contribute to the meaning *rope*. The other meanings would seem to be phonetic loans and to have quite separate linguistic origins, as spelled out in the Wiktionary.org entry.

* * *

317

The following words which were in the first edition were removed from the second.

网址 wang3zhi3 web address; 退 tui4 reject, return; retreat; 垃圾 la1ji1 garbage;

邮件 you2jian4 mail; 必须 bi4xu1 must; 软件 ruan3jian4 software;

本地 ben3di4 local; 书评 shu1ping2 book review;

经济 jing1ji4 economy, economic; economical; 头版 tou2ban3 front page;

传真 chuan2zhen1 fax; 关于;guan1yu2 about, regarding, concerning.

Conversations

A：你每天都看报吗？

B：差不多每天都看。

A. 你一般看什么报？

B. 我一般看"华尔街时报"。报上的内容跟我的工作有大的关系。
   你呢？你看不看 "华尔街时报"？

A. 我很少看。我对金融没有兴趣。我一般看"纽约时报"。你看吧看
   "纽约时报"？

B. 我有时也看。

A. 你有没有看今天的"纽约时报"？

B. 没有。我今天很忙，连标题都没有时间看。今天有什么重要的新闻？

A.你担心不担心？

B. 我很担心。我有很都股票。

＊　＊　＊

A. 看星期天的报纸吗？

B. 喜欢。其实我只看星期天的报纸。平常太忙，没有时间看报。

A. 星期天的报纸内容太多你都看吗？

B. 我不都看。除了国际国内新闻，我大多看体育消息。你呢，你喜欢看
.   星期天的报纸吗？

A. 我不太喜欢。我只看标题。我觉得里面的歌广告太多。

B. 是这样。我买了星期天的报纸后做的第一件事就是把关广告扔掉。

The third and fourth conversations of this lesson are not reproduced here.

In traditional characters:

A：你每天都看報嗎？

B：差不多每天都看。

A: 你一般看什麼報？

B: 我一般看"華爾街時報"。報上的內容跟我的工作有大的關係。你呢？
你看不看 "華爾街時報"？

A: 我很少看。我對金融沒有興趣。我一般看"紐約時報"。
　　你看吧看 "紐約時報"？

B: 我有時也看。

A: 你有沒有看今天的"紐約時報"？

B: 沒有。我今天很忙，連標題都沒有時間看。今天有什麼重要的新聞？

A: 你擔心不擔心？

B: 我很擔心。我有很都股票。

＊＊＊

A: 看星期天的報紙嗎？

B: 喜歡。其實我只看星期天的報紙。平常太忙，沒有時間看報。

A: 星期天的報紙內容太多你都看嗎？

B: 我不都看。除了國際國內新聞, 我大多看體育消息。你呢, 你喜歡看
星期天的報紙嗎？

A: 我不太喜歡。我只看標題。我覺得里面的歌廣告太多。

B: 是這樣。我買了星期天的報紙後做的第一件事就是把關廣告扔掉。

319

In the Shuowen-like HYCuZhuanF font:

A：你每天都看報嗎？

B：差不多每天都看。

A. 你一般看什麼報？

B. 我一般看"参考消息報"。報上的內容跟我的工作有大的關係。你呢？你看不看"参考消息報"？

A. 我很少看。我對金融很有興趣。我一般看"經濟時報"。你看呢看"經濟時報"？

B. 我有時也看。

A. 你有沒有看今天的"經濟時報"？

B. 看了。我今天很忙，連標題都沒有時間看。今天有什麼重要的新聞？

A. 你忙也不忙也？

B. 我很忙。我有很多應酬興。

         *   *   *

A. 看星期天的報紙嗎？

B. 喜歡。其實我只看星期天的報紙。平常太忙，沒有時間看報。

A. 星期天的報紙內容那麼多你都看嗎？

B. 我不都看。除了國際國內新聞，我大多看體育消息。你呢，你喜歡看星期天的報紙嗎？

A. 我不太喜歡。我只看標題。我覺得裏面的歌廣告太多。

B. 是這樣。我買了星期天的報紙后做的第一件事就是把關廣告扔掉。

Lesson 10. China and America

久 **jiu3 aa354** 久 **for a longtime, of specified duration. FR 637.**

The Shuowen character, right, is the earliest version we have that can be dated. It corresponds, stroke for stroke, to the modern version, and there is clearly no "man" in it. Rather it is foot with a hobble attached. A hobbled foot implies slow movement and taking a *longtime* to get anywhere.

变化 **bian4hua4 change (verb and noun)**

变(變) **bian4 hat22354** 变 **change (verb), transform. FR 225.**

This one puzzles the experts. The modern traditional form, faithfully preserving the *Shuowen* form shown on the right, shows a hand holding a tool below and a mouth with projecting tongue in the center above and with silk on either side. How does this come to mean *change, transform*?

The hand with the tool may represent "change" and be the semantic element, while the top, 絲 luan2 is phonetic. Wiktionary gives as meanings of this rare character, 絲, "chaotic, orderly".

An alternative explanation comes from Sears. He suggests that the hand is that of a carriage driver who is using the reins (silk) and his voice (speech radical) to control – and *change* – the behavior of the horse, who is not shown. There are a few known bronze examples all very similar to the one shown on the left. The silk and speech are not there, but there is something that might be a horse on the left. What the hand is holding is unclear.

化 **hua4 man63** 化 **to convert, change, transform. FR 178.**

The character shows one man rightside up and another upside down, a radical conversion, change, or transformation. In the shell-bone versions, such as on the far left, the man on the left is upside down. In the bronze versions, he is right side up and the one on the right is upside down, and so they have remained in the *Shuowen* (right) and modern versions.

完全 **wan2quan2 completely, entirely**

完 **wan2 roof1136 intact, whole, complete; used up; over; finish; pay. FR 301.**

We met 完 as the phonetic in 院 yuan4 in BC Lesson 3.

全 **quan2 top 171** 全 **completely, entirely. FR 124.**

See IC Lesson 6.

特点 **te4dian3 characteristic, trait, feature.**

特 **te4 ox 715** 特 **special, unusually. FR 173.**

See IC Lesson 6.

点 (點) **dian3 fireB 2** 点 **spot, dot, drop; point; item, part; drip; some; o'clock. FR 128**

See BC Lesson 5.

印象 **yin4xiang4 impression**

印 **yin4 ab36152** 印 **seal, stamp, chop; trace, mark; tally with, fit.   FR 640.**

The object named by this character is the chop, ubiquitous in China, often made of stone, with the owner's name carved on the bottom. It is pressed onto an ink pad and then onto a picture or document to show ownership. Curiously, the character shows the owner (on the right or bottom) and his hand (left or top) but not the chop itself. A bronze version is shown on the left and the *Shuowen* on the right. The modern version has been rotated 90 degrees counter-clockwise from the *Shuowen* position (and thus back to the bronze position) and the man's arms and legs amputated.

象 **xiang4 aa5035** 象 **elephant; shape, form, image, symbol. FR 300.**

This is a picture of an elephant; see the character 像 in BC Lesson 8. In the other senses, it is a phonetic loan.

伟大 **wei3da4 great.**

伟(偉) **wei3 man715 great. FR 1107.**

This is a radical+phonetic character with the *man* radical and the phonetic 韦 (韋) wei2. By itself, this phonetic means the shuttle of a loom; the circle in the center is the shuttle itself, the vertical line is the thread, and the feet going left and right represent the back-and-forth motion of the shuttle.

大 **da4 aa314 big, huge, great, wide, deep, oldest. FR 17.**

This is a picture of a man with his arms and legs spread to look as *big* as possible. On the left is one of many shell-bone characters. There are scores of similar bronze examples, and the *Shuowen* form, right, retains the same form. The modern form turns the two arms into one straight line and curves the legs outward in a most alarming manner

深 shen1 water35 深 **deep, profound. FR 401.**

This is a radical+phonetic character with the water radical, which goes reasonably well with the "deep" idea. The phonetic is 罙 shen1 meaning *cave*. But why should there be a tree in the character for *cave* when there are certainly no trees in caves? So let's have a look at the *Shuowen* form of 罙 which is on the left. Sears, in a stroke genius, recognized in the center *a hand holding a torch to explore the cave*, which looks like a croquet wicket. Strangely, the hand is above the torch. Perhaps the torch is being held down to see the floor of the cave. Scribal error turned the hand holding a torch into a tree.

奇迹 **qi2ji1 miracle**

奇 qi2 aa31415 奇 **special, rare; strange; surprise, odd, weird, wonderful, fantastic. FR 563.**

This character was discussed under 椅 in IC Lesson 6.

迹(跡) ji4 and ji1 go 4135 迹 **footprint, trace, clue; site. FR1098.**

This radical+phonetic character with the basic meaning of *footprint* is a relatively recent creation. There is no *Shuowen* or earlier version, only some LST versions such as the one on the right. The elongated foot *go* radical fits the meaning. The phonetic, 亦 yi4, is a phonetic loan character meaning *also*. It pictures a man with something below his arms as in the shell-bone example on the left. There is no agreement about what is under his arms. My dictionaries give only the 4th tone pronunciation for 迹 but Google Translate gives the first tone in the expression 奇迹 and Wiktionary shows both first and fourth tone.

故宫 **gu4gong1 Palace Museum / Forbidden City**

故 gu4 hit70 故 **incident, on purpose, cause, hence, old friend, die. FR 572.**

See "做 zuo4 man 703 做 **do, make, produce, act, cook**" in BC Lesson 4.

宫 gong1 gong1 roof 00 宫 **palace. FR 277.**

See BC Lesson 8.

发展 **fa1zhang3 develop, development**

发(發) fa1 aa 3645 **send forth, fire, shoot, develop. FR 47.**

See IC Lesson 6.

展 **zhang3 door7216 to open up, spread out; use well; postpone, extend. FR 1637.**

The Shuowen version is on the right. Sears says that the original meaning was to turn over in bed, which indeed fits with the *Shuowen* definition as well as I and Google Translate can read it. In the *Shuowen* version of the character (on the right) – the earliest we have – we see the sleeper on the top and left side, the bed in the middle, and a garment – perhaps a nightgown – at the bottom.

建 **jian4 ab542** 建 **build, construct, erect. FR 386.**

This character is a picture of a hand drawing a plan with a brush. The hand with the brush has remained clear from numerous bronze example such as the one on the left through the *Shuowen* (on the right) down to modern version. Curiously, the paper or parchment on which the plan is drawn – simple and smooth in the bronze example – has been crumpled up over time.

座 **zuo4 shed 347 seat, (classifier for bridges, buildings, monuments, and the like). FR 753.**

There is no *Shuowen* or earlier example. It would seem to be two fellows seated under a shed, but Sears tells us there is more to it. It is a radical+phonetic character. The inside is phonetic, 坐 zuo4, which means to take a seat or to take a busk, train or airplane, and is a good example of a phonetic that contributes to meaning. The outside of 座, 广 guang3 is a picture of a shed attached to one side of a barn or house to *enlarge* it. Hence it now means *wide, to spread out* but can represent buildings in general, as in this character.

桥(橋) **qiao2 tree3313** 桥 **bridge.**

This is a radical + phonetic characgter. Historically, many if not most bridges were made of wood, so the tree radical fits. 乔(喬) qiáo

高速公路 **gao1su4 gong1lu4 highway, expressway**

高 **gao1 hat025 high, tall. FR 159.**

See BC Lesson1. If you are thinking that a road is not tall, remember English *high*way.

速 **su4 go703 quick, fast, rapid; speed, velocity. FR 617.**

The go radical clearly fits this radical+phonetic character. The phonetic, 束 shu4, is a picture of a sheaf of grain bound together around the middle.

公 **gōng aa 3464** 公 public, common. **FR 60.**

See BC Lesson 2.

路 **lu4 leg 354** 路 road, way, path; region, district; class. **FR 221.**

See BC Lesson 9.

至少 **zhi4shao3 at least**

至 **shi4 earth164** 室 room. **FR 267.**

See BC Lesson 3.

少 **shao3 aa2343** few, little; lack; lost, missing; a little while. **FR 233.**

See BC Lesson 4.

鸟 **niao3 bird. FR 1263.**

We met this character in the character for duck, 鸭 ya1 , in BC Lesson 8.

起重机 **qi3zhong4ji1 crane (construction machine)**

起 **qi3 run 526** 起 happen, occur; stand up, get up; begin; raise, build, set up. **FR 75.**

See BC Lesson 5.

重 **zhong4 aa370 zhong4** weight, heavy. **FR 140.**

We met in 重 in 懂 in BC Lesson 6.

机 **ji1 tree36** 机 machine; flexible, intelligent; crucial, key. **FR 111.**

百分之 **bai3 fen1 zhi1 percent**

百 **bai3 white 1** 百 hundred. **FR 407**

See BC Lesson 4.

分 **fen1 aa3453** divide; allot; distinguish; branch; minute; fraction. **FR 79.**

The character represents the concept of separation by 八 ba1 to which a knife, 刀 dao1, has been added. Thus, both elements of 分 relate to meaning and neither to sound.

之 zhi1 aa454 (a grammatical particle) FR 54.

One use of 之 – the one relevant here – is like the English -th suffix in ten*th* or hundred*th*. Another use – to which the character owes its origin – is to mean *to go*. Countless shell-bone versions similar to the one on the left supposedly show a foot setting out *to go* somewhere. There are also many known very similar bronze versions, and the Shuowen version, right has changed very little. The modern version has then changed drastically, but perhaps we can see in the top 4 stroke a remnant of the left side of the Shuowen character, then in the 5 stroke the remains of the right side, followed by the 1 stroke on the bottom. The very fact that the character was used so much led to its virtual destruction.

一直 yi4zhi2 all along, straight, always

直 zhi2 aa251 straight, straighten; vertical; perpendicular; frank; continuously. FR 255.

See the character 德 in BC Lesson 6.

海岸 hai3an4 coast

海 hai3 water3165 海 sea, ocean, very large. FR 189.

This is a radical+phonetic character with the clearly appropriate water radical and the no-longer-so appropriate phonetic 每 mei3, meaning a woman's hair. A bronze version is on the left and the *Shuowen* character is on the right.

岸 an4 mount131 shore, beach; lofty. FR 971.

This is a radical+phonetic character with the mountain and cliff as the meaning component and the item under the cliff, gan4 a pestle, as the phonetic. The *Shuowen* form of the pestle is on the left.

搬 ban4 hand33536 搬 move, remove, transport, change residence. FR 1766.

This is a radical+phonetic character with the appropriate hand radical. The phonetic, 般 chuan2, means a ship or boat. Since boats are used for transport, we see another phonetic contributing to the meaning. There is no *Shuowen* or earlier example of 搬.

著名 **zhu4ming2 famous**

著 **zhu4 grass7310** 著 **marked, outstanding; books, works; write books. FR 777.**

Presumably this is a radical+phonetic character, but there is no *Shuowen* or earlier version, no LST examples nor any meaning that I have found to explain the grass radical. The phonetic, 者 zhe3, is thought to be a much evolved version of a pictogram of sugar cane, left, now used as a phonetic loan character meaning a person who does something, like the -er or -ist in English worker or typist.

名 **ming2 mouth354** 名 **name; fame; express, describe; classifier for people. FR 203.**

See BC Lesson 2.

首都 **shou3du1 capital (of a country)**

首 **shou3 nose43** 首 **head, first, leader, chief. FR 481.**

This is a schematic picture of a human head reduced to an eye and hair. On the left is a bronze version – of which there are many – and on the right, the Shuowen character.

都 **dou1 and du1 placeR 7310 (du1) capital, major city; (dou1) all, even, already. FR 68.**

The structure of the character with the placeR radical relates to the "major city" meaning; the high frequency comes from its "all, even, already" meaning, a phonetic loan meaning. For the phonetic, see 著 above in this lesson.

更 **geng4 even more FR 221**

人口 **ren2kou3 population**

人 **ren2 man FR 7**

口 **kou3 mouth FR 212.**

人口, man-mouths, is surely a great way to express *population*, especially in a country where food is as good and important as in China.

you4 aa54 again, repeated; also, too, in addition. FR 126.

 This is a phonetic loan character. It is a picture of a hand, as is fairly clear in early forms such as the shell-bone version on the far left and the bronze form on the near left. The *Shuowen* character is on the right. We have seen that when a character is phonetically borrowed it is usually returned to its original meaning by

addition of a radical. That did not happen in this case. Instead, a different character, 手 shou3, took over the representation of the hand concept.

 can1guan1 visit

参(參) **can1 aa643143** 參 **join, take part in. FR 507**

 This character is traditionally interpreted as the three stars of the belt of the constellation Orion with the three lines on the lower left representing rays shining down. This explanation does not account well for the lower part of the character. The current meanings are phonetic loan.

观 (觀) **guan1 see5** 观 **look, see. FR 334.**

 Obviously, the *see* radical fits perfectly the meaning of this radical+phonetic character, and the guan4 phonetic – picturing an owl, famous for its ability to *see* at night – strongly supports the meaning as well as giving the sound exactly except for tone. (The character for the bird is not used in modern bird nomenclature, but the way the two eyes look out straight ahead make it look like an owl to me.)

先 ... 然后 **xian1 ... ran2hou4 first ... then**

先 **xian1 ox36 first. FR 188**

See BC Lesson 1.

然 **ran2 fireB 354** 然 **yes, right, so. FR 56**

See BC Lesson 7.

后 (後) **hou4 a3310 behind, future; ruler, king, queen. FR 48.**

See IC Lesson 1.

产品 **chan3pin3 product**

产 (産) **chan3 hat4313 产 produce, products, property; give birth to. FR 159**

The simplified character is the phonetic of the radical+phonetic traditional character. 生 – with its basic meaning of *to bear, to bring forth* – is the meaning-related component. The image on the left is a bronze example, and the *Shuowen* character is on the right.

品 **pin3 mouth00 品 product, grade, character, taste. FR 308.**

There are several known examples of shell-bone and bronze characters, all very alike except for an alternation between two on top and one on bottom and vice-versa. Though the character gets classified under *mouth,* the squares are not mouths but generic *things.* I imagine them as boxes of products ready to be shipped. It is one of the most common characters seen on the streets in China.

Supplementary words and expressions

省 **sheng3 eye234 province OR xing3 be conscious, aware. FR 666.**

On the left are shell-bone and bronze examples; on the right, the *Shuowen.* The original meaning was *to inspect,* and the character shows the eye of the farmer inspecting the plants (Sears).

市 **shi4 hat 225 市 market, trade, buy, sell; city. FR 254.**

See BC Lesson 2.

州 **zhou1 aa 3224 州 (in China) a former administrative division which survives in place names; (in USA) state. FR 721.**

See BC Lesson 6.

区 **qu1 district, borough, region, zone. FR 265.**

长 (長) **zhǎng aa 631 长   chief, head; grow; eldest. FR 109.**

See BC Lesson 2.

都市 **du1shi4 metropolis, large city**

都 **dou1 placeR 741** 都 **both, all, even, already. FR 68.**

See BC Lesson 2.

总统 **zong3tong3 president (of a country)**

总 (總) **zong3 heartB430** 总 **always; total; chief, head, commander. FR 228.**

As is to be expected with a character meaning *always*, this is a phonetic loan. The original meaning was *rope*, whence the silk radical. The right side, 悤 cong1, is the phonetic and means *hastily, hurriedly* and is itself again a radical+phonetic character with the quite appropriate heart radical at the bottom and the phonetic 囱 cong1 above. The Shuowen version of 囱 is on the left. It is thought to be a picture of a shuttered window or something similar.

统 (統) **tong3 silk 416 unite, all together, connected system. FR 264.**

See IC Lesson 8.

总理 **zong3gli3 prime minister, premier**

理 **li3 jade07 texture or grain (in wood or jade); reason, logic, science; manage. FR 89.**

This is a radical+phonetic character with the jade radical and the 里 li3 phonetic.

主席 **zhu3xi2 chairman**

主 **zhu3 jade4** 主 **host, owner, master; manage; signify; advocate; God. FR 87.**

See 住 in BC Lesson 3.

席 **xi2 shed6722 mat, seat, place, feast. FR 894.**

The shell-bone example on the left is a fair picture of a mat, the original meaning of this pictograph. There are no known bronze examples, and by the time of the *Shuowen*, right, the character has lost any resemblance to a mat or seat.

党 **dang3 roof3-036 (political) party; gang; kin; be partial to. FR 411.**

游 **you2 water4133** 游 **swim, float about, tour (verb). FR 695**

This is a radical+phonetic character with the water radical and phonetic 斿 you2. As a character, 斿 is extremely rare.

筑 (築)

建筑 **jian4zhu4 architecture**

建 **See 健 in IC Lesson 6.**

筑 (築) **zhu4 bamboo12136 build, construct. FR 1130.**

The simplified character, 筑, seems to have originally meant a musical instrument variously said to have been a similar to a lute or a zither. It was the phonetic element in the traditional character to which the tree was added at the bottom, representing lumber, to create a character meaning *to build*. The instrument having gone out of user, the simplifiers could drop the tree without confusion.

家乡 **jia1xiang1 hometown**

家 **jia1 roof 135** 家 **family. FR 56.**

See BC Lesson 3.

乡 (鄉) **xiang1 aa663** 乡 **countryside, native place, township. FR 922.**

We see the appropriate placeR radical on the right of the traditional character. Sears and Wiktionary show nothing before the *Shuowen* version on the right which shows two people on either side of something. *Wiktionaire* has found the shell-bone version on the left and a very similar bronze example showing a similar scene with the addition that the people are kneeling. The *Wiktionaire* authors discuss the possible meaning at some length and believe that this is some ceremonial meal with representatives of two neighboring towns who are discussing the management of the *countryside* between the two towns. That they representatives of the towns is supported by the circles – representing the towns – above their heads in the *Shuowen* character.

景色 **jing3se4 scenery**

景 **jing3 sun 41053 bright; scenery, view, situation, scene; admire. FR 814.**

See IC Lesson 1

色 **se4 aa 3556** 色 **color; facial expression; scenery; feminine charm; sexual passion. FR 304.**

See BC Lesson 8.

移民 **yi2min2 immigrant**

民 **min2 aa 5616** 民 **people, folk, residents, inhabitants. FR 113.**

See BC Lesson 7

移 **yi2 grain354** 移 **move, remove, change, alter. FR 880.**

The original meaning of this radical+phonetic character was *to replant*, hence the grain radical. The phonetic, 多 duo1 – meaning *many, much* – no longer helps remember the pronunciation nor the meaning. Perhaps, however, as the last character in this book, 移 serves as useful reminder of how much the Chinese language has changed over the last 3500 years. Indeed, note that 移 means *change*.

Conversations

A. 麦克，好久每见。你最近有没有什么新闻？

B. 有，我们全家去了中国。

A. 真的吗？你们玩儿的怎么样？

B. 我们玩儿的非常高兴。

A. 这是你们第一次去中国马？

B. 这是我和我太太第二次去中国，但是对孩子们来说这是第一次。

A. 你和你太太上次是什么时候去中国的？

B. 我们是十年前去的。

A. 你觉得中国在这十年里有没有变化？

332

B. 变化太大了。很多我以前去过的地方变 得完全不一样了。

A. 你们这次去了找哦你中国的什么地方？

B. 我们去了香港西安北京上海

A. 这些地方你最喜欢哪儿？

B. 我都喜欢。每一个地方都有自己的特点。

A. 你能不能说说他们的特点？

B. 当然。香港跟纽约一样，是一个国际城市，你能看到各个国家的人。西安有很久的历史，我虽喜欢那儿的博物馆。

A. 北京给我留下了很深 的印象？

B. 这是一个伟大的城市。长城是个奇迹， 故宫也是一个非常有意思的 地方。

A. 你觉得上海怎么样？

B. 在我们去过 的城市中，上海是我最喜欢的城市。我觉得上海比中国 别的 发展的都快。

A. 您恩更不能说说上海有什么变化？

B. 上海在过去几年里建了很多高楼建了十条地铁，三座大桥一条高速公 路，一个新机场。建这么多的东西在美国至少也要二十年。

A. 你知道上海的 city bird 是什么吗？

B. 不知道，是什么？

A. 是 "crane".

B. 我怎么没听说过？ 为什么是 "crane"？

A, 这个 crane 不是鸟， 是起重机。你知道吗？ 几年前,全世界百分之三十的 起重机 都在上海。

B. 我们打算明年再去一次上海。

The second conversation is not given here.

In traditional characters:

A. 麥克，好久每見。你最近有沒有什麼新聞?

B. 有，我們全家去了中國。

A. 真的嗎? 你們玩兒的怎麼樣?

B. 我們玩兒的非常高興。

A. 這是你們第一次去中國馬?

B. 這是我和我太太第二次去中國，但是對孩子們來說這是第一次。

A. 你和你太太上次是什麼時候去中國的?

B. 我們是十年前去的。

A. 你覺得中國在這十年裡有沒有變化?

B. 變化太大了。很多我以前去過的地方變 得完全不一樣了。

A. 你們這次去了找哦你中國的什麼地方?

B. 我們去了香港西安北京上海

A. 這些地方你最喜歡哪兒?

B. 我都喜歡。每一個地方都有自己的特點。

A. 你能不能說說他們的特點?

B. 當然。香港跟紐約一樣，是一個國際城市，你能看到各個國家的人。西安有很久的歷史，我雖喜歡那兒的博物館。

A. 北京給我留下了很深 的印象?

B. 這是一個偉大的城市。長城是個奇蹟， 故宮也是一個非常有意思的地方。

A. 你覺得上海怎麼樣?

B. 在我們去過 的城市中，上海是我最喜歡的城市。我覺得上海比中國別的 發展的都快。

A. 您恩更不能説説上海有什麼變化?

B. 上海在過去幾年裡建了很多高樓建了十條地鐵，三座大橋一條高速公路，一個新機場。建這麼多的東西在美國至少也要二十年。

A. 你知道上海的 city bird 是什麼嗎?

B. 不知道，是什麼?

A. 是 "crane".

B. 我怎麼沒聽説過? 為什麼是 "crane"?

A. 這個 crane 不是鳥， 是起重機。你知道嗎? 幾年前,全世界百分之三十的 起重機 都在上海。

B. 我們打算明年再去一次上海。

In the Shuowen-like font:

A. 哀亭，郎ㄟ老見。 休屌氖氜得氜什麼新貨?

B. 氜，我們全家在了中國。

A. 真的嗎? 休們玩見的怎麼樣?

B. 我們玩見的米棠高興。

A. 這是休們第一次在中國嗎?

B. 這是我婦我愈愈第二次在中國, 但是對阿兒們來説這是第一次。

A. 休婦休愈愈上次是什麼時候在中國的?

B. 我們是十秊前在的。

A. 休覺得中國在這十秊裏氜得氜變化?

B. 變化愈大了。很多我自前在過的地方變 得完全不一樣了。

A. 休們這次在了我哪休中國的什麼地方?

B. 我們在了喬檣氞宓水京上樣

A. 這些地方休屌喜歡哪見?

B. 我齡喜歡。每一個地方齡氜自己的情點。

335

A. 你能不能说说他们的特点?

B. 当然。香港跟纽约一样,是一个国际城市,你能看到各个国家的人。 有很多的历史,我最喜欢那儿的博物馆。

A. 北京给你留下了很深的印象?

B. 这是一个伟大的城市。长城是个奇迹, 故宫更是一个非常有意思的地方。

A. 你觉得上海怎么样?

B. 在我们去过的城市中,上海是我最喜欢的城市。我觉得上海像中国形的发展的缩影。

A. 德恩雪不能说说上海有什么变化?

B. 上海在过去几年里建了很多高楼建了十条地铁,三座大桥一条高速公路,一个新机场。建这么多的东西在美国也要二十年。

A. 你知道上海的 city bird 是什么吗?

B. 不知道,是什么?

A. 是 "crane".

B. 我怎么得听说过? 为什么是 "crane"?

A, 这个 crane 不是鸟, 是起重机。你知道吗? 几乎是,全世界百分之三十的 起重机都在上海。

B. 我们打算明年再去一次上海。

Vocabulary for Reading Dictionaries

As you continue in Chinese, you will of course meet several thousand more characters not covered here. Many of them will have radicals and phonetics you already know and will immediately make sense. But of course there are many others that are in whole or in part new. I hope you will want to investigate their origins. When you use the Chinese sources that have etymologies – such as the 古代汉语字典 (Gudai Hanyu Zidian) and the 汉字原流字典 — you will find that they nearly always tell you what kind of character it is. Here are the Chinese names for the types of characters.

象形 xiang2 xing2 "similar form", pictograph, ex. 山

指事 zhi4 shi4 "finger thing" indicative, ex. 本

会意 hui4 yi4 "repeat meaning" ideogram, ex. 好

形声 xing2 sheng1 "form sound" phonetic compound, radical+phonetic, ex. 妈

假借 jia3 jie4 "borrow lend" phonetic loan; ex. 能

转注 zhuan3 zhu4 "turn pour" mutual explanatories (a dubious and useless category)

Some other useful expressions for reading dictionaries are:

本义 ben yi4 basic meaning

指 zhi4 literally "finger", but it usually translates as *means*

意 yi4 meaning

而 er2 and

同 tong2 equals, same as

为 wei4 (translate as) is

部首 bu4 shou3 radical

部分 bu4 fen4 part

组成 zu3 cheng2 component part

Chinese Input with Google Docs

Google Docs offers a way to type in Chinese characters wherever you have Internet access. How to use it, however, is far from obvious. Here is how to get started.

1. Open Google Docs and create a new document (or open up an existing one)
2. Go to *File > Language* and select the language you want to start typing in. For instance, to choose the traditional Chinese characters used in Taiwan, I would select 中文（台灣）(literally: "Chinese, Taiwan")
3. The input tool will appear on the right side of your toolbar (it may be hard to see, but on my browser, it was to the right of the "clear formatting" button.)
4. Click on the tiny triangle next to the language symbol to choose your input method, which might be phonetic, romanization, or some other keyboard method.
5. As you enter characters, Google Docs automatically saves them.
6. Select and copy to the clipboard, then paste into a document on your computer.
7. Once you are finished, close out of the document or use *File > Language* to switch back to English.

Chinese zodiac

Here are the names (in order) of the animals of the "Chinese zodiac." Where there are several animals with the same character, the name generally used in English for the animal of the zodiac is underlined.

鼠 shu1 aa3256 鼠 <u>rat</u>, mouse. FR 1693.

牛 niu2 ox 牛 bull, <u>ox</u>, cow, bovine. FR 1018.

虎 hu3 tiger 虎 tiger. FR 1083.

兔 tu4 aa 350364 兔 hare, <u>rabbit</u>. FR 2364.

龙（龍）long2 aa 34163 龙 dragon. FR 696.

蛇 she2 worm 435 蛇 *snake*, serpent. FR 1689.

马（馬）ma3 horse 马 horse. FR 276.

羊 yang2 aa2317 羊 sheep. 山羊 shan1 yang2 <u>goat</u>. FR 1337.

猴 hou2 dog 32 猴 monkey. FR 2187.

鸡（雞）ji1 bird 35 鸡 chicken, <u>rooster</u>. FR 1391.

狗 gou3 dog 350 狗 dog. FR 1281.

猪（豬）zhu1 dog73 猪 pig. FR 1762.

Made in the USA
Monee, IL
23 January 2021